Realistic Drawing
for Beginners

How to Create Stunning, Lifelike Drawings of Any Subject

MATHEUS MACEDO

Realistic Drawing for Beginners

How to Create Stunning, Lifelike Drawings of Any Subject

MATHEUS MACEDO

Editor: Kelly Reed
Project manager: Lisa Brazieal
Marketing coordinator: Katie Walker
Copyeditor: Linda Laflamme
Cover design: John Calmeyer
Interior design: Aren Straiger
Composition: Danielle Foster
Cover Illustration: Matheus Macedo

ISBN: 979-8-88814-213-4

1st Edition (1st printing, November 2024)
© 2024 Matheus Macedo
All images © Matheus Macedo unless otherwise noted.
Cover image based on photo by Lipik Stock Media/Shutterstock.com

Rocky Nook Inc.
1010 B Street, Suite 350
San Rafael, CA 94901
USA

www.rockynook.com

Distributed in the UK and Europe by Publishers Group UK
Distributed in the U.S. and all other territories by Publishers Group West

Library of Congress Control Number: 2024936719

Realistic Drawing
for Beginners

How to Create Stunning, Lifelike Drawings of Any Subject

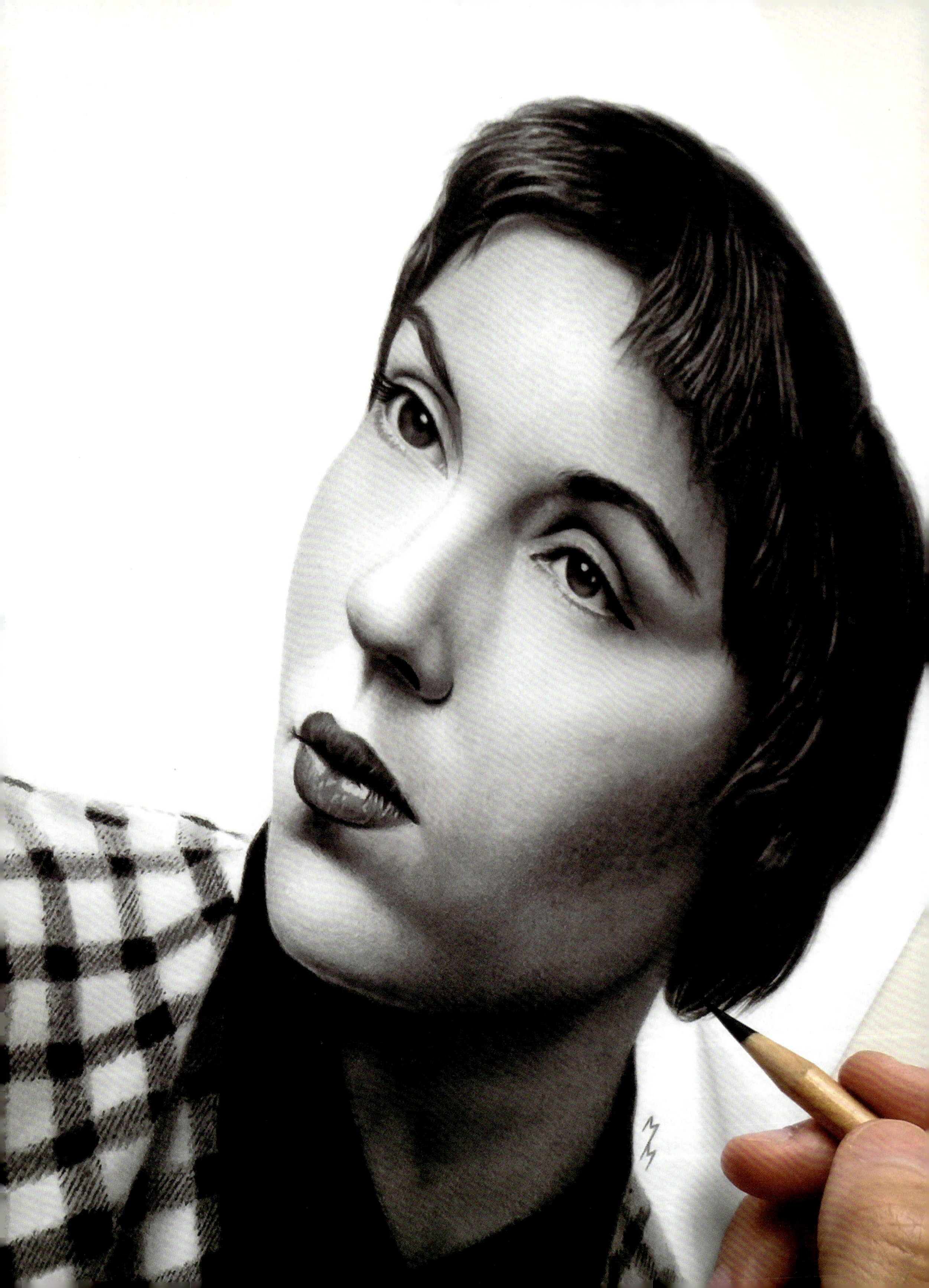

Table of Contents

Chapter 2: **Materials**   **23**

Chapter 3: **Sketching**   **35**

Chapter 4: **Shading**   **47**

Chapter 5: **Blending**   **61**

Chapter 6: **Texture**   **71**

Chapter 7: **Practicing**   **97**

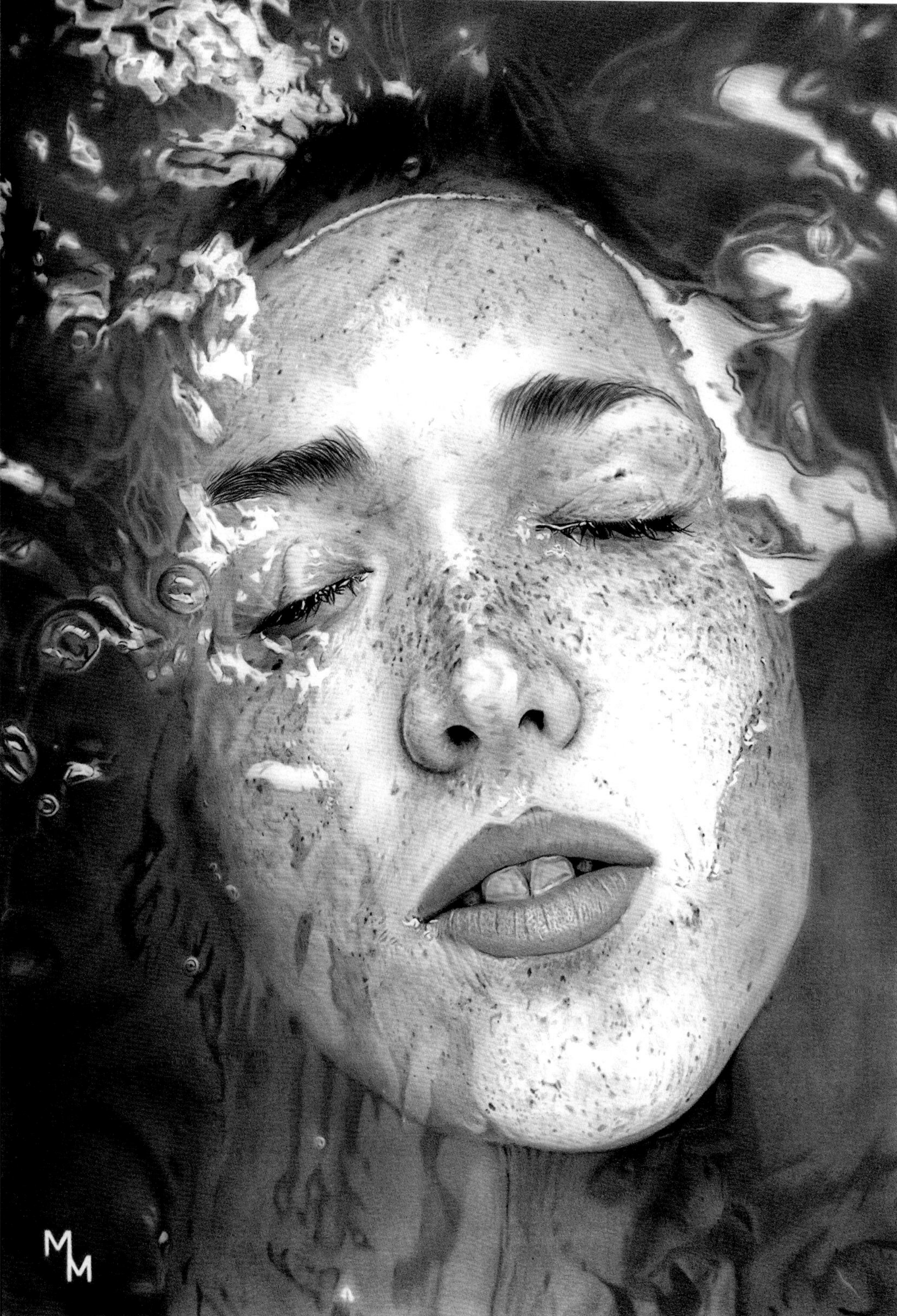

M
M

Introduction

The phenomenon of realistic art has never seemed to be more in evidence than it is today, especially given its popularity on social media. If you're a social media user, you've no doubt come across posts by artists from all over the world showing richly detailed drawings, often in generous dimensions.

But what is Realism? Art historians generally identify artistic movements, such as Realism in the 19th century and Photorealism and Hyperrealism in the 20th century, as eras when artists sought a faithful representation of reality in their works, whether drawings, paintings, or sculptures. However, if we extend the concept of realism from this point of view, we can even include older artists, such as Leonardo da Vinci and Johannes Vermeer, who took nature (or the "real" world) as a fundamental reference for the representation of their figures.

The technological advance of photography in the 20th century enabled this type of art to reach a new level, and artists can now produce works with a level of detail even greater than that of a high-resolution photograph. Without delving into conceptual definitions, I would say that this book's realistic drawing style lies here, because we will work with photographs as a reference for our drawings, seeking to reproduce them with the highest level of fidelity we can.

The realistic style is fascinating to the public, and many artists find meaning in it, striving to improve themselves more and more technically in order to raise the quality of their work. *Realistic Drawing for Beginners* was written in response to this desire.

Am I capable of making a realistic drawing?

Yes, dear reader, you are, and helping you do so is my ultimate goal.

Drawing realistically is less difficult than it looks. If you get to know your materials a little better and know how to handle them, your drawings will make an instant leap in quality, as you will have more resources for reproducing shadows and detailing textures. This doesn't mean that you'll become a master of realistic art overnight. As with any more complex activity, your evolution will depend on how much you dedicate yourself to it. Dedication is not simply about drawing a certain number of hours a day (although, the more you draw, the better, of course). Your evolution will also depend on *practicing consciously and deliberately*, trying to challenge yourself a little more with each new achievement. We'll talk more about this mindset in Chapter 1.

What you will (and won't) see in this book

Realistic Drawing for Beginners will introduce you to realistic drawing through practical exercises with a bit of theory mixed in. In my opinion, you can learn to draw only by drawing, so you'll do a lot of it throughout the book.

The aim of the chapters is to analyze the process of producing a realistic drawing from start to finish. I'll break the process down into smaller steps, which when viewed in isolation are all very simple. Linked together in a logical and organic way, these steps form a continuum because one step serves the other; you add texture, for example, only after you finish shading and blending. By separating them and looking deeply at each individually, however, you can better understand how a realistic drawing is made.

- **Chapter 1** deals with the fundamental issue of your **mindset**, addressing such questions as: What should my attitude be towards drawing? Do I need to draw every day? How long should I practice? What should I draw? Are there any rules to follow?

- **Chapter 2** discusses in detail the **materials** you'll use throughout the book. I will not only present the materials I normally use, but also give you suggestions of brands to keep an eye on. You may want to refer back to this chapter later during your reading.

- **Chapter 3** covers the production of your base **sketch**. The alternatives presented will enable you to produce perfect sketches from photographs—even if you don't know how to draw.

- **Chapter 4** is all about **shading**. Adding shading to a sketch establishes the foundation and general values of the drawing. Many beginning artists neglect this stage, which is a serious mistake. A bad foundation can ruin everything that follows.

- **Chapter 5** offers advice on **blending**, which is a way of spreading the graphite (or any other material you use) over the drawing's surface without leaving visible pencil or brush marks. In short, this step "disguises" the material used, eliminating the unwanted grainy appearance and covering the surface evenly.

- **Chapter 6** deals with **textures**, which seem like the most important thing in realistic art but are more like the icing on the cake. Through very accessible exercises, I'll show you examples of various textures to help you better understand how to create them, as well as to give you the confidence to venture into the most varied themes.

- **Chapter 7** gives you a chance to **practice** all you've learned. I'll walk you through three drawing studies that combine multiple textures and techniques. Remember, you can learn to draw only by drawing, so take advantage of this opportunity to flex your new skills.

If you're looking for an in-depth book to learn all the intricacies of *freehand* drawing, however, this book isn't it. That said, the lessons in this book, and the exercises in Chapter 3 in particular, *will* help you strengthen and develop your skills and gain confidence in your ability to draw freehand as well.

Why not just trace reference images, you ask. By drawing freehand, you also develop your ability to perceive. You learn how to observe the reference you use and to have a critical eye on the drawing you make. These principles will help you not only when sketching, but all throughout the creation of a realistic image. While creating new layers of light, shadow, and textures, you need to observe not only the parts you are working on, but also the context in which they are inserted. Think about drawing freckles on a nose. To draw them realistically, you need to observe the volume of the nose and how that affects the shape and tone of freckles in different positions.

So, even if freehand drawing is not the focus of this book, carrying out the exercises presented here will help you improve your perception of the shapes, proportions, and tones that make up any drawing. This awareness of the fundamentals of drawing is a key skill that every visual artist must possess.

Now, let's get started!

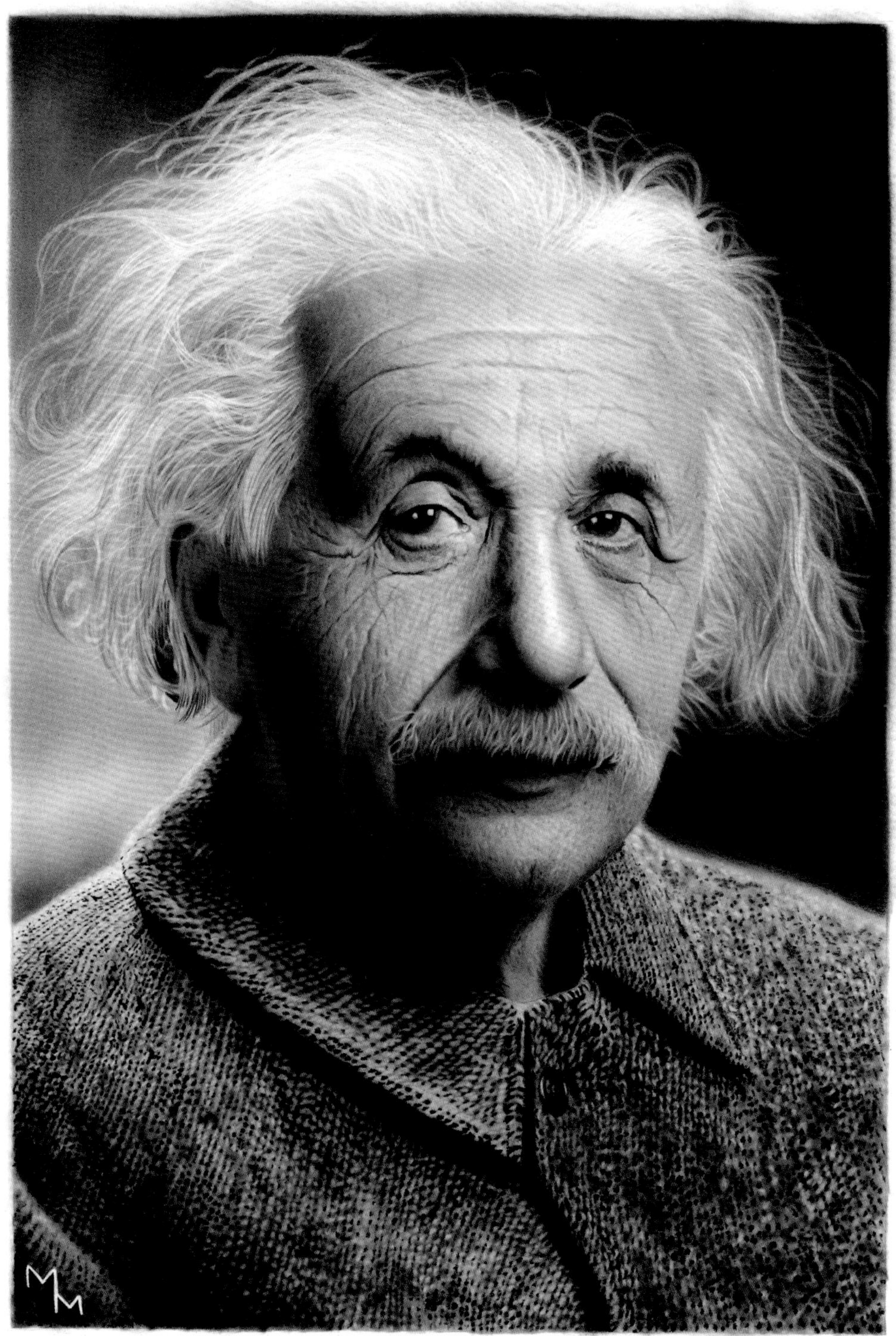

My drawing of Albert Einstein I completed in 2019 based on an iconic image of him from 1947.

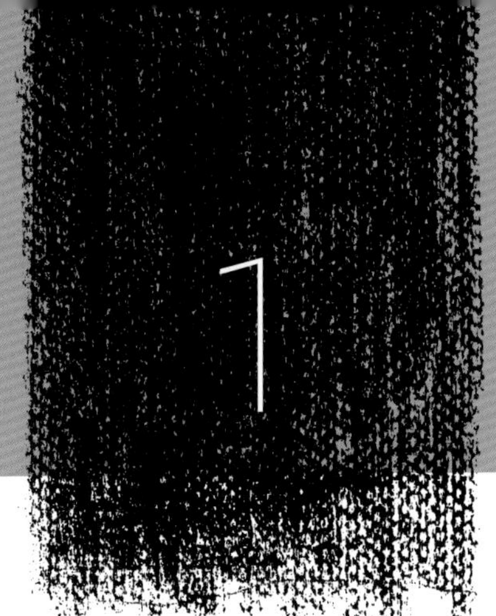

Mindset

Before you dive into the exercises, we need to talk about mindset, because your attitude towards the act of drawing will determine whether or not your journey will be successful. By "successful" I don't simply mean that you learn to "draw better," but that you find pleasure in your practice, want to maintain the habit of drawing, and enjoy the process with its successes and mistakes.

The sections that follow suggest some actions and attitudes you *should* follow. Emphasis on the word "should;" I don't intend to be dogmatic about anything presented in this book, because in art there are no rules and each person has their own personality, carrying with them a series of preferences, if not idiosyncrasies. In short, this chapter aims to help you do what makes you draw more and avoid what makes you draw less.

If you already stick to your practice, drawing for long hours at a time every day, perhaps this chapter has little to add and you can skip to the next one. If that's not your case, however, resist the urge to jump ahead. I think there's at least one tip or two here that might be useful to you.

No profit grows
where is no pleasure ta'en:
In brief, sir,
study what you most affect.

—WILLIAM SHAKESPEARE

Enjoy it

This may sound obvious, but drawing should be a pleasurable activity before anything else. Children draw for pleasure; for them drawing is a game like any other. As we grow up, however, we are taught to take an increasingly utilitarian view of things, and activities (including drawing) cease to be an end in themselves. We go to school because we need to get into college; we need to get into college to get a good job; we need a good job because we need a lot of money; we need a lot of money to be able to buy more things; and so on.

In addition to questioning what end drawing will help us achieve, we begin to question whether we are drawing well or not. We are swept away by a series of notions of right and wrong, caught up in the "rules" that a drawing needs to be balanced and proportional with a sense of depth, textures, and colors.

At this point you're probably saying, "But what's wrong with that? I'm reading this book precisely *because* I want to draw better!" Calm down, dear reader. Wanting to draw better is not a sin. My point is that drawing shouldn't be a source of stress and suffering.

Keep a positive mindset

Having a positive mindset is less about being upbeat than it is about understanding and accepting that we evolve only with a certain amount of discomfort. As the 17th century scholar Thomas Fuller wrote, "All things are difficult before they are easy." Will your early attempts at realistic drawing effortlessly flow from your pencil to look exactly like the book's examples? Probably not, and that's okay!

> **Whether you believe you can or you believe you can't, you're right.**
>
> —HENRY FORD

Get rid of the idea that you "don't have the talent" or that you "aren't cut out to draw." If you practice in the right way, you will *inevitably* become a better artist. Drawing shouldn't be a competition, so don't compare yourself with others. Instead, compare your current work with drawings you did previously. I'll bet you'll find areas of improvement and evidence that your practice sessions—even the monumentally frustrating ones—are paying off.

In her book *Mindset: The New Psychology of Success*, American psychologist Carol Dweck introduced the concepts of a *fixed mindset* and a *growth mindset*, two psychological attitudes that people can adopt from an early age when performing a certain task. For example, people who believe that only those with an innate talent for drawing can draw well have a fixed mindset. They believe that their aptitude for art was determined at birth and that, no matter how hard they try, they will never be able to evolve in drawing. Conversely, people with a growth mindset believe that they can draw better through practice and effort.

So, adopt a positive, growth mindset with regard to what you want to do well, because this belief will keep you firm in your purpose when you eventually come across frustrations.

Adapt your environment for drawing

To enjoy drawing more and practice consistently, prepare an environment that helps you to do so. Having a fixed place to draw will help you get into the habit of drawing and create the best possible conditions for that. Try to create a comfortable environment that doesn't make you fall asleep. Here are some aspects to consider:

- **Chair.** Choose a chair that you can sit in for long periods without feeling pain. If it has an adjustable height, all the better; you can fine-tune it in relation to your desk and preferred drawing position.

- **Table.** Choose a table spacious enough to accommodate your drawing, your materials, and room to rest your arms, if you like to lean on the table as much as I do. If you have back pain problems, consider using a tilted drawing board. This way you won't have to draw with your spine curved, which may lessen or even banish your pain. A tilted board also enables you to look at the drawing with less distortion due to the viewing angle.

- **Reference placement.** Decide where you will position your reference image for drawing. I like to look at it on a monitor at a height just above my eyes. I prefer a digital reference, because I can easily zoom in and out, as well as switch the brightness. Plus, printing my image is an extra step, one which doesn't always give a satisfactory result. I use a monitor specifically because it's larger than a tablet or cell phone, relies on wall power rather than a battery, and doesn't get too hot in situations of prolonged use. Tablets and phones, however, do have the advantage of portability and smaller footprints.

- **Lighting.** Draw in an environment that allows you to see all the details of your drawing, but without the light dazzling you or tiring your eyes. I love natural light, but not for drawing, as it varies throughout the day, even in a short space of time. The sun can be blocked out by a cloud precisely when you want to do detail work, which is why I recommend getting a lamp. I prefer LED luminaires that emit diffused light at a temperature between 4500 and 5500 K. The temperature issue is especially important if you intend to work with colors, as the lighting can distort them significantly.

- **Body position.** Position yourself so that the source of your light comes from your opposite side compared to your drawing hand. If you're right-handed, for example, place your lamp to your left, so that your hand doesn't cast a shadow on the drawing and the light doesn't reflect towards your eyes.

- **Climate.** Work in an environment with a pleasant temperature and ventilation. Avoid strong winds in the direction of your drawing, so that the sheet doesn't take off, you accidentally scratch it, or you drop it on the floor and get it dirty.

> **Pleasure and action make the hours seem short.**
>
> —WILLIAM SHAKESPEARE

- **Mood.** Set the mood and avoid distractions. Allow yourself to enter a *state of flow*. Leave a bottle of water nearby but be careful not to get your drawing wet. Prepare a playlist with the music or podcasts you want to listen to while you draw so that you don't interrupt your session to choose what to play next. If you live with other people, ask them not to interrupt you when you draw, if possible. Prepare your environment beforehand, leaving your drawing materials in sight and easily accessible. If you like, take breaks from time to time to stretch and stand up for a few minutes.

With all these tips, drawing won't just be an artistic activity, it will even be a meditative practice, and that's a very good thing.

Practice

We've all heard "practice makes perfect," and you now know that finding pleasure in drawing is a determining factor in whether you continue to practice. But what kind of practice, how often, and for how long? I often get asked these questions. There are no rules, but my thoughts on the subject follow.

> We are what we repeatedly do. Excellence, then, is not an act, but a habit.
>
> —WILL DURANT

How often and long to practice

It would be easy for me to say that you should practice as many hours a day as you can, but we all have other obligations to fulfill. Besides, even if you had all the free time in the world, filling it with only drawing could get exhausting in the long run, unless you're really obsessed with drawing and never tire of it.

I advocate making drawing a habit. After all, a drawing artist is someone who draws, right? Try to draw every day, or almost every day. The more, the better. If you're so busy that this sounds unfeasible, consider when and how you could carve out a part of your day for practice. If you can't give up anything to draw, then drawing isn't a priority and you're doomed not to progress.

Be sure to allow yourself enough time to really concentrate on drawing—at least one hour each day. Considering that realistic drawings are laborious in general, it's difficult to draw in sessions that are too short.

A strategy I like is to break down the drawing process into smaller stages. If I'm doing a portrait, for example, I set out to do one part of the face a day. So, let's say I draw the left eye on Monday, the right eye on Tuesday, the nose on Wednesday, the mouth on Thursday, finish the rest of the face on Friday, and so on. If I have more time to draw each day, I could do both eyes on Monday, the nose and mouth on Tuesday, the rest of the face and start the neck on Wednesday, and so on. I think a task-based goal is better than simply counting the hours, because looking at the clock makes me more anxious and impairs my ability to focus and get into the flow (more on this soon).

What if you can't draw at all during the week but are free for long drawing sessions on weekends? If it works for you, go for it. For me, it's not the ideal scenario. Long breaks between sessions tend to cause me to drift away from drawing and lose momentum. As I've said before, there's no formula to follow. Focus on what works for you.

What to practice

According to psychologist Anders Ericsson, you need 10,000 hours of practice in any field in order to achieve excellence in it. This magic number, however, can mean nothing if the practice is not *deliberate* and *intentional*. Imagine a boy who dreams of becoming a professional basketball star. If he simply bounces a basketball until he eventually reaches 10,000 hours, do you think he'll be a good player at the end of that time? Of course not—he should have practiced all the fundamentals of the sport instead of bouncing repeatedly.

So, accumulate hours of drawing practice, give priority to what you like to draw, but don't forget to challenge yourself by raising the level of difficulty and varying the subjects you practice with. If you've identified something you are having trouble with but would like to do better, focus on it until it becomes easy and natural for you. Exploring a variety of subjects will make you a more versatile artist and open up new possibilities, including improving on what you like best. Suppose for example, you love drawing animals but aren't so interested in landscapes. Neglecting landscapes during your practice could limit your ability to create an interesting background for an animal portrait you're drawing.

Enjoy challenging yourself

The *state of flow* is the ability of individuals to immerse themselves completely in an activity, so much so that they lose all sense of space and time. According to psychologist Mihaly Csikszentmihalyi, who studied and popularized this state of consciousness, a very important component for someone to enter this state is the relationship between the level of difficulty of an activity and the individual's ability to carry it out (**Figure 1.1**).

> You are in danger of living a life so comfortable and soft that you will die without ever realizing your true potential.
>
> —DAVID GOGGINS

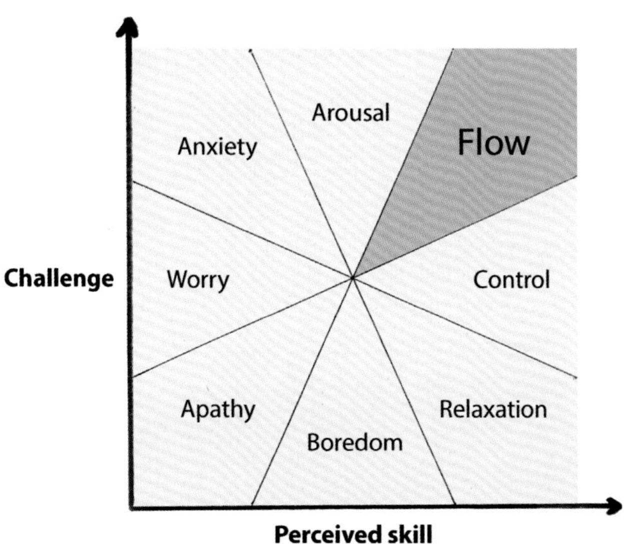

1.1 The relation of skill level to challenge level according to Mihaly Csikszentmihalyi

If you set out to draw something that seems too complex, for example, and that demands a level of mastery that you don't yet have, the drawing may leave you feeling frustrated, anxious, or worried. You may question yourself, lose self-confidence, and not find pleasure in drawing. On the other hand, if the drawing seems too easy, not challenging enough, or uninteresting, you may feel bored and that you're wasting your time on something that doesn't make you grow.

The state of flow happens when the level of challenge and the perceived skill are both at high levels, when you feel both challenged and capable of overcoming the challenge. Electronic game programmers, for example, know very well how to manipulate these factors to keep you interested in (aka addicted to) a game. They won't make you face super-challenging enemies or scenarios when you're still learning which button does what. The level of difficulty progresses as you become more skilled at playing the game.

I believe we should learn to enjoy doing difficult things, because ultimately those are the things that take us out of our comfort zones and make us move forward. It's the ability to do something different that will make you special; after all, everyone is capable of doing what's easy and that's why no one values it. Value is intrinsically linked to scarcity, and we are all capable of doing rare things.

So don't shy away from challenges. They will help keep you producing and evolving. Just make sure that the challenge is difficult enough—but not too hard—for your current level as an artist. If you're able to make this assessment yourself, that's great, and we can all develop this feeling as we gain experience. Alternatively, you could ask for help from a tutor— someone who has more experience than you—to guide you through the next steps.

Seek out a guide

Having a tutor makes a big difference. They can help you decide what you're going to draw and identify what you can improve. In an ideal world, you would hire a tutor to work directly with you, someone who knows what you need, understands your strengths and weaknesses, and can show you the way to overcome your obstacles. In the real world, geographical or financial limitations can make this difficult, but alternatives are available.

If you can't find good teachers where you live, look for them on the internet. As you consider the thousands of options around the world, prioritize tutors who offer the possibility of evaluating your drawings. Even if they are not available for video calls, which limits the interaction, text feedback can still be of great value. On the other hand, tutors who do not provide feedback on your drawings often charge less for their courses. This is not ideal, but if it's what you can afford, it's a possibility.

You can also find plenty of high-quality content for free on the internet. Most content creators publish tips and insights on their social media to attract students to their paid courses, and you can take advantage of this. The disadvantage is that, by the very logic of how social media works, these tips will be shared in an unsystematic, scattered way without the structure you would find in a course. Free content also tends to be more superficial. After all, the creator's goal is to get you to buy their paid course, which is not wrong in itself, because producing courses requires a high investment of time and effort.

> You can practice shooting eight hours a day, but if your technique is wrong, then all you become is very good at shooting the wrong way. Get the fundamentals down and the level of everything you do will rise.
>
> —MICHAEL JORDAN

Finally, consult books, like the one you have in your hands. Books are certainly cheaper options than face-to-face or online courses, but lack a personal feedback component.

Good guidance will give you a lot of shortcuts and help you progress. For example, I'd already been drawing for many years when I attended a realism course in 2016, at the age of 26. If you compare my earlier work (Figures 1.2 to 1.9) to drawings I did after the class (Figures 1.10 to 1.12), you'll notice a big change from then on. Having guidance helped me brush up on my skills very quickly in a short period of time.

I hope, dear reader, this book helps you make a similar leap forward.

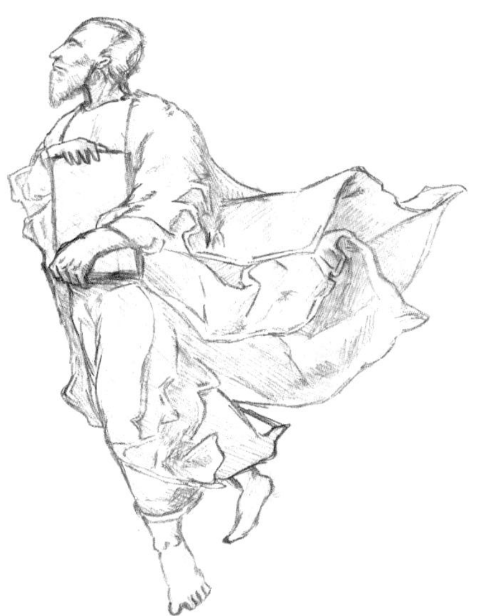

1.2 Copy from *The Transfiguration* by Raphael,
drawn at age 15

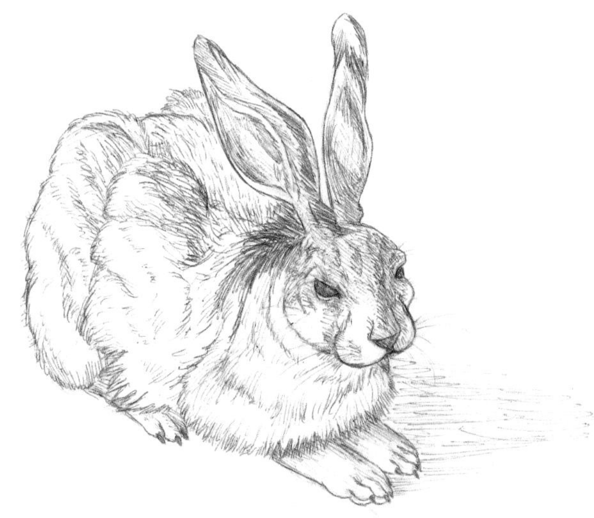

1.3 Copy from *Young Hare* by Dürer,
drawn at age 15

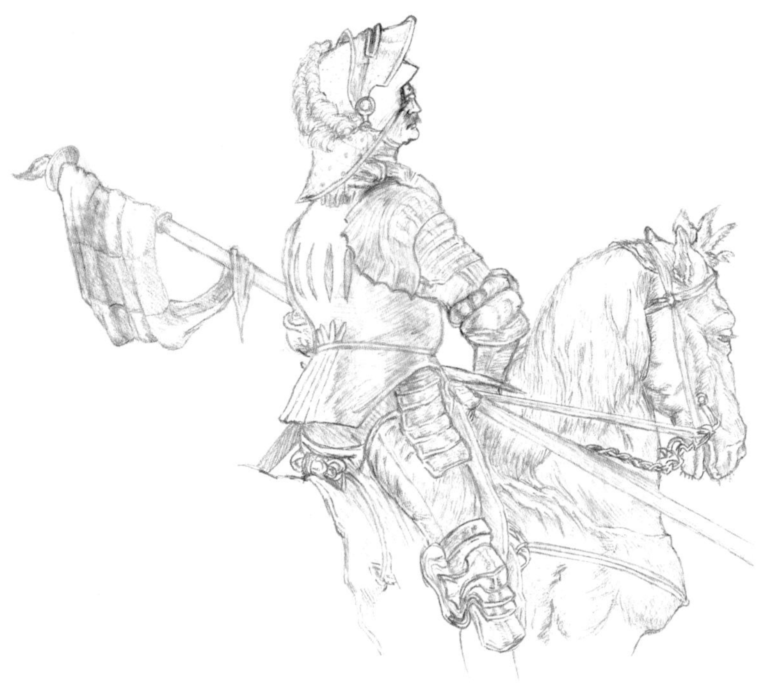

1.4 Copy from *St George on horseback* by Dürer, drawn at age 15

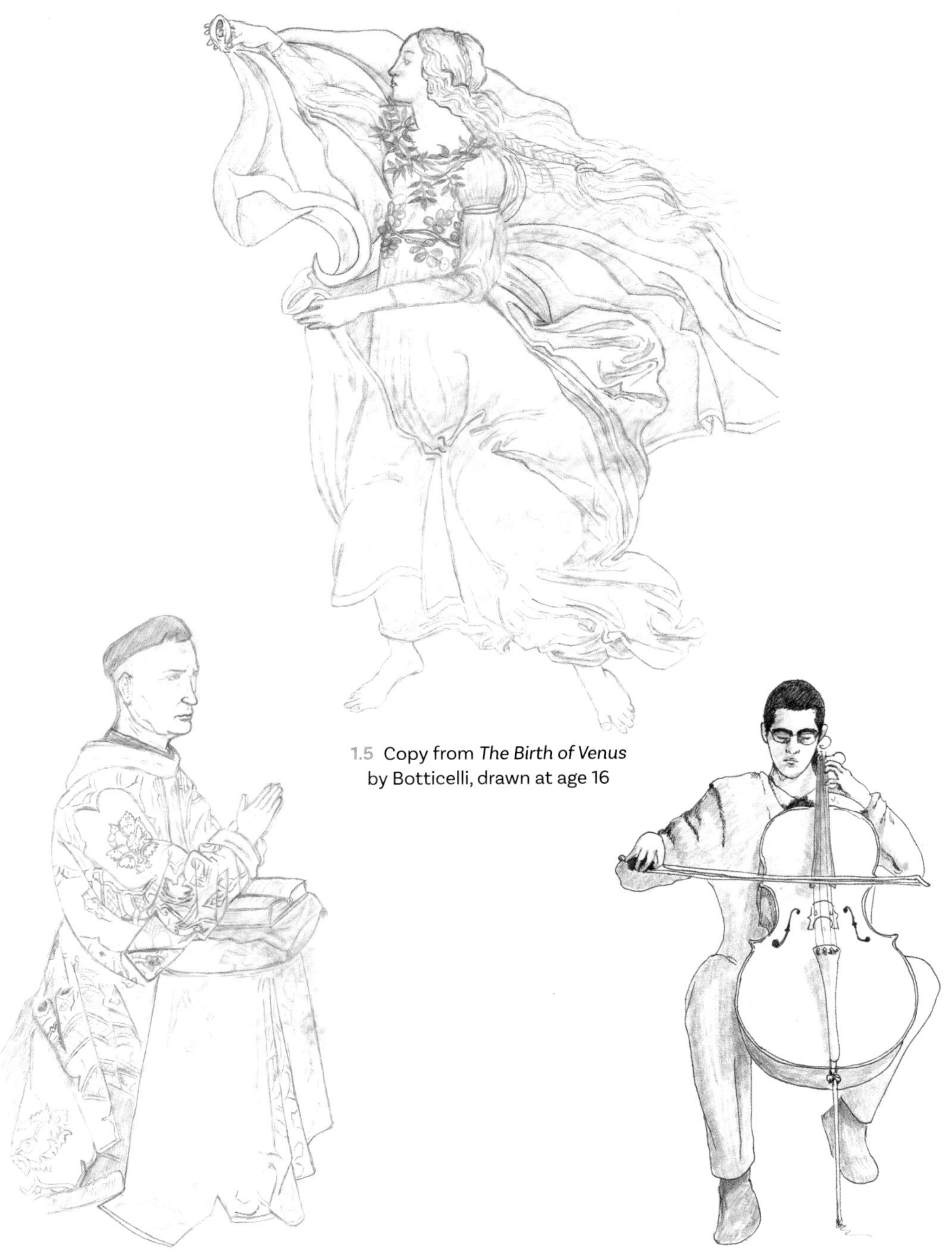

1.5 Copy from *The Birth of Venus* by Botticelli, drawn at age 16

1.6 Copy from *Madonna of Chancelor Rolin* by van Eyck, drawn at age 16

1.7 Self-portrait as a cellist, drawn at age 20

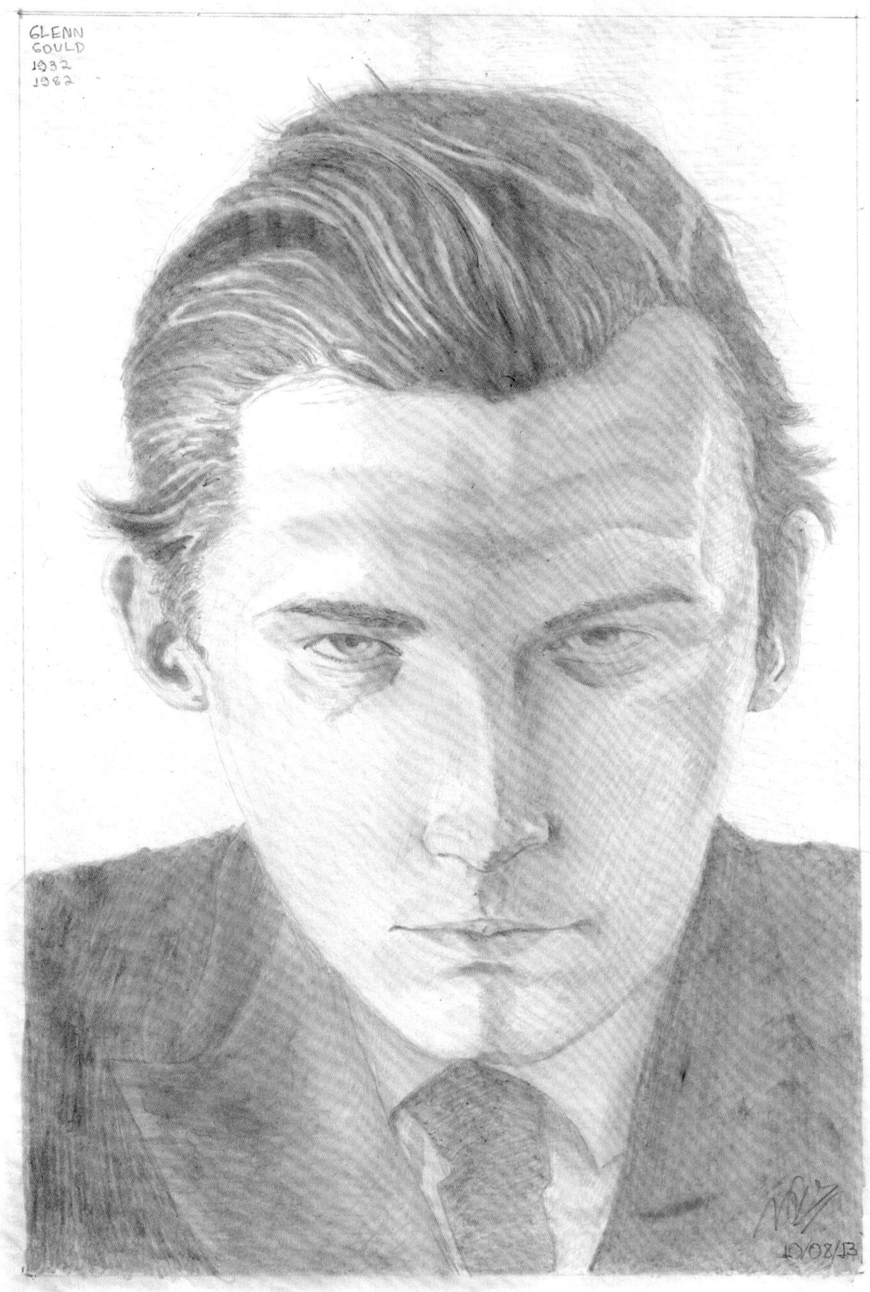

1.8 Glenn Gould, drawn at age 23

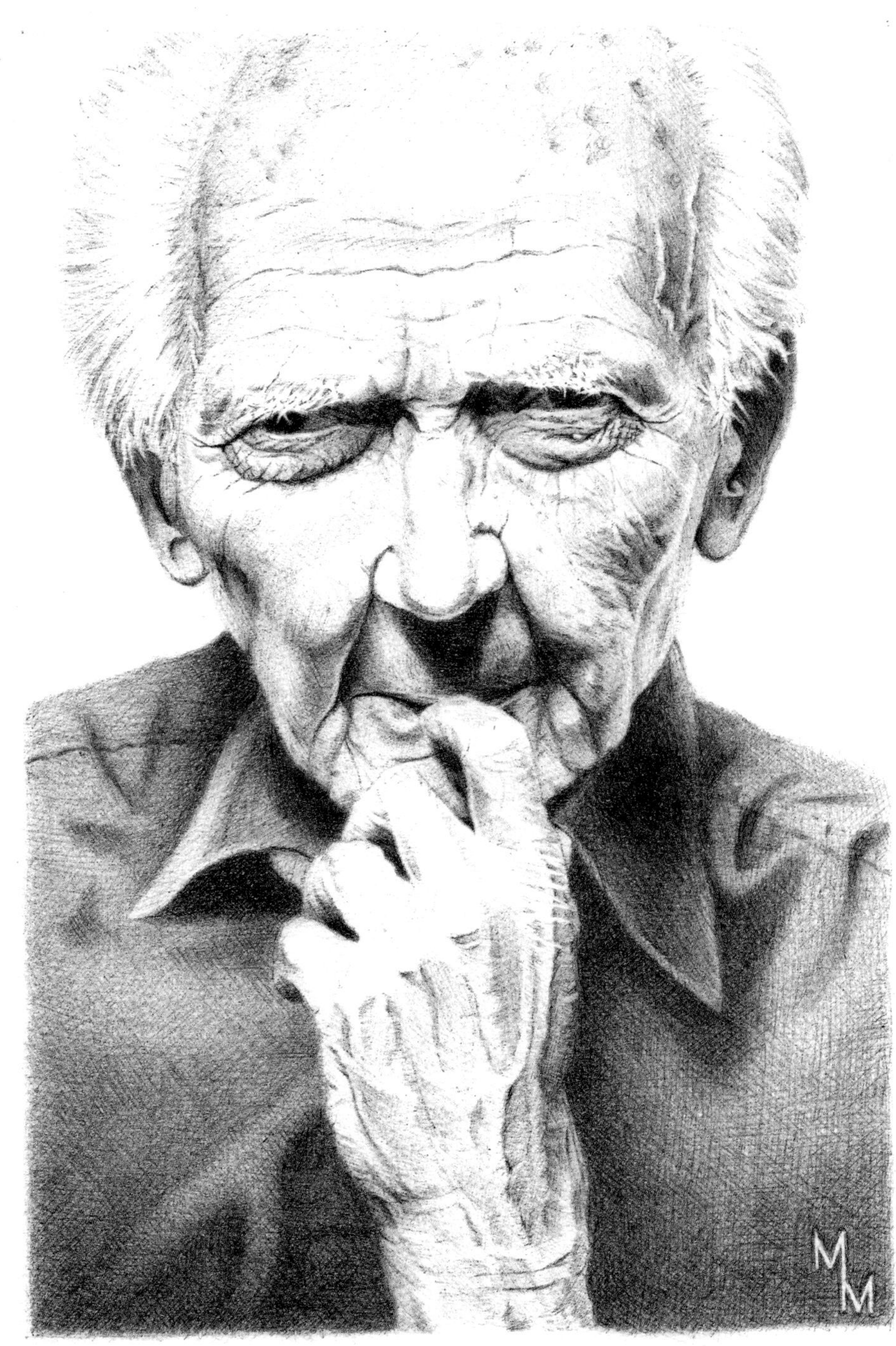

1.9 Zygmunt Bauman, drawn at age 25

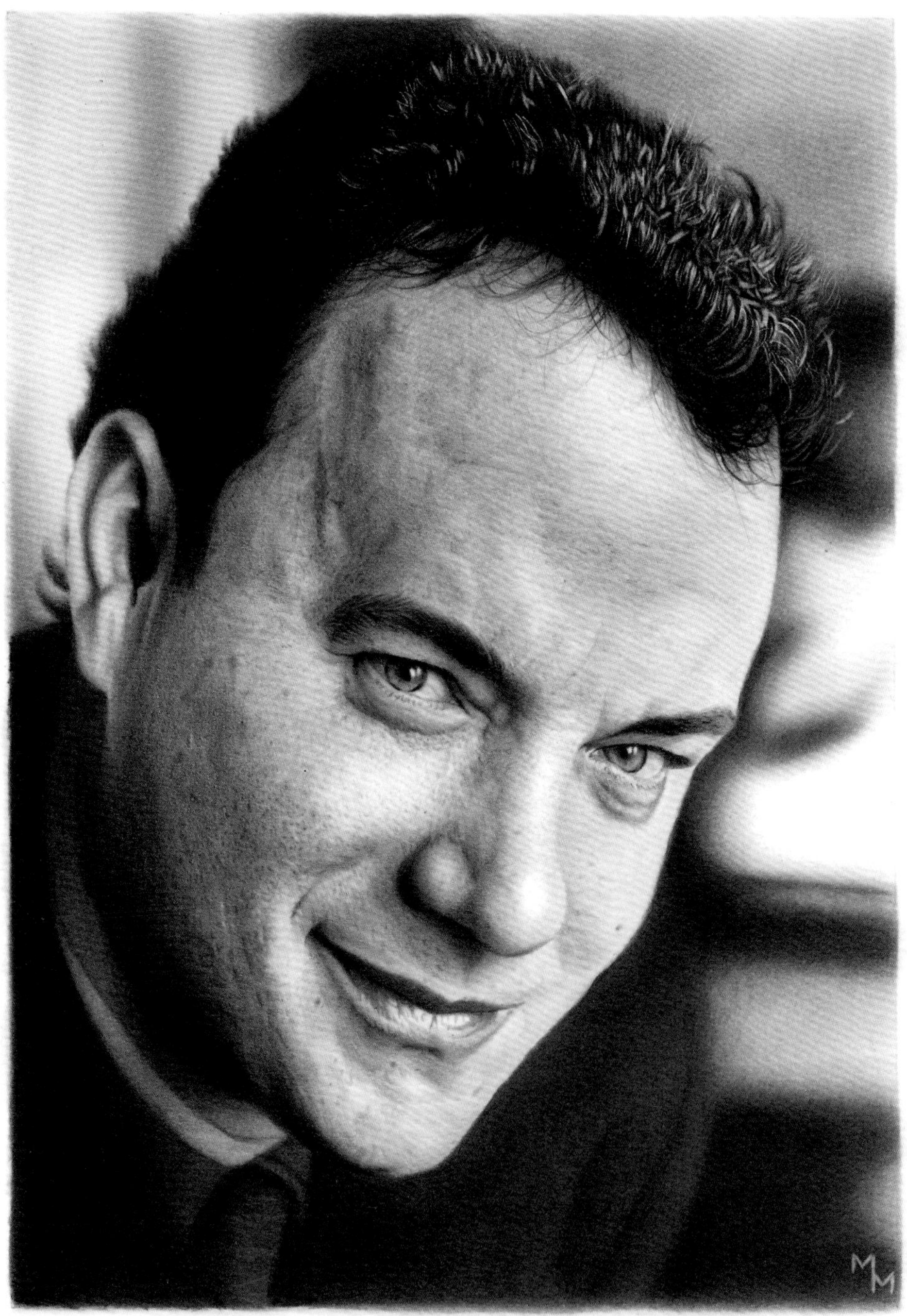

1.10 Tom Hanks, drawn at age 26

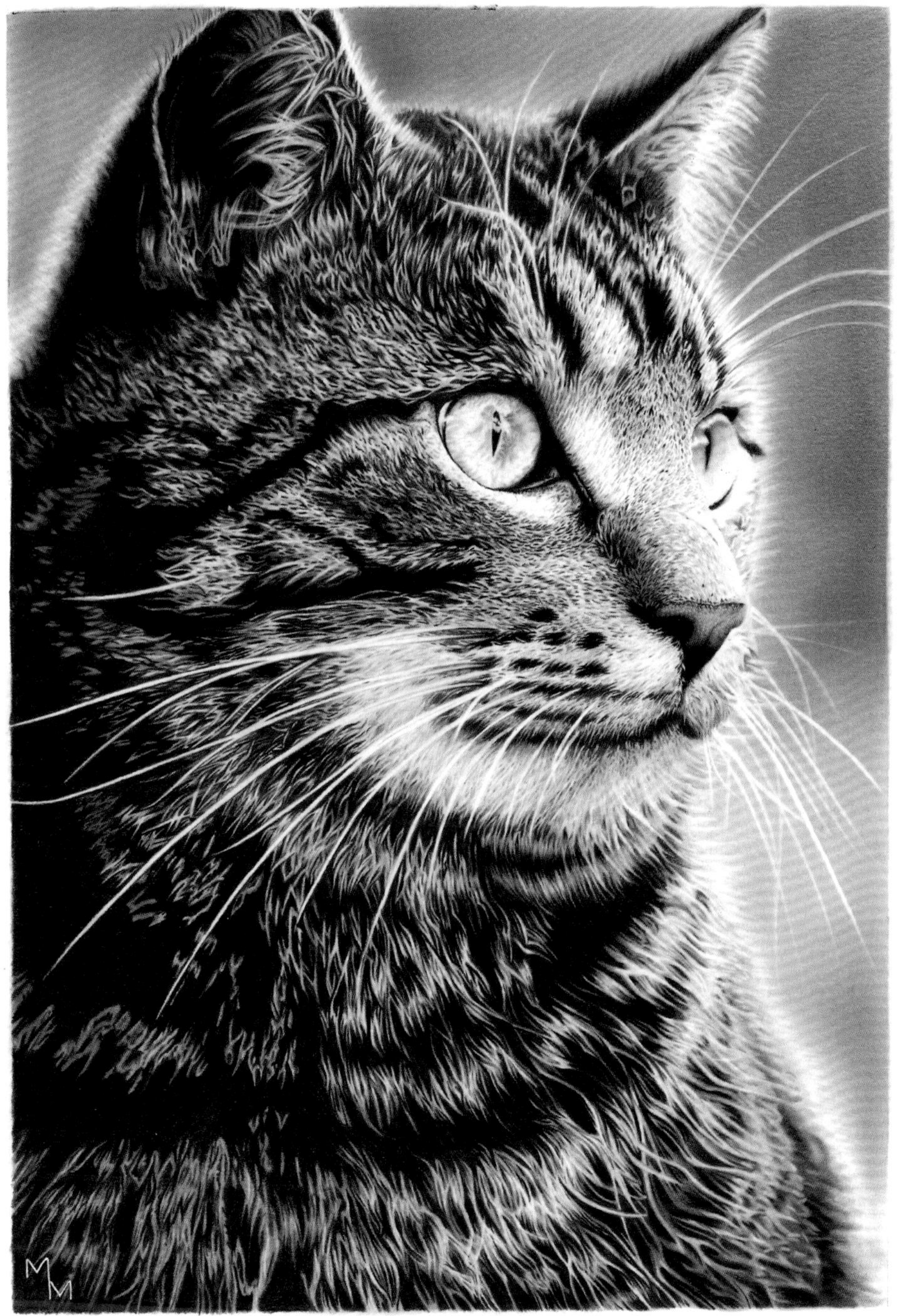

1.11 Cat, drawn at age 29

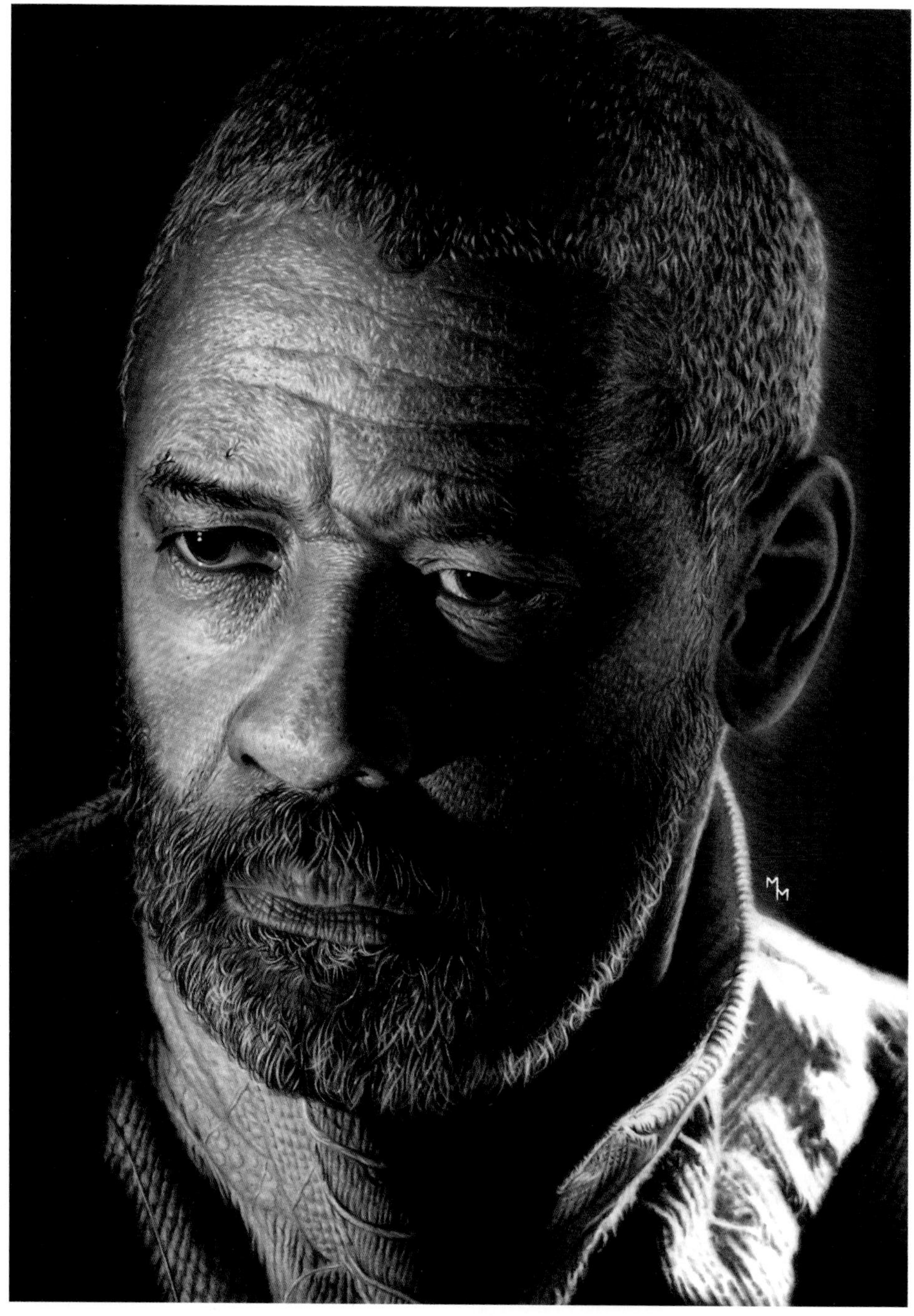

1.12 Denzel Washington as Macbeth, drawn at age 32

Be motivated

If you think about it, we've already been talking about motivation indirectly throughout the chapter. After all, don't you need motivation to start drawing? Or is it more important to keep up your motivation once you've started? Motivation is present at all stages of production, not just when we're actually hunched over a drawing board with a pencil in hand.

I've been preaching the importance of making drawing a habit in your life, but we're not robots. At any time you may wonder why you follow certain habits and not others. So, it seems to me that whether or not you succeed in developing a project or a skill depends not only on "how" you do something, but also on "why."

Let me give you a personal example. My relationship with the English language has been full of ups and downs. I was born and raised in Brazil, where Portuguese is the native language and English is a compulsory subject at school. I studied it for at least 15 years. Even though I was told that being able to speak English was important, at school my only motivation was to get a good enough grade to be approved. The lessons were boring, and to pass the exams I didn't need to become fluent, I just needed to fill in the blanks on the test paper with articles or correctly conjugated verbs. So why bother? Mastering English seemed distant, unattainable, and unnecessary to me.

> It does not matter how slowly you go as long as you do not stop.
>
> —CONFUCIUS

At the age of 21, I started a two-year college exchange program at the Politecnico di Torino in Italy. Having studied Italian for only six months before moving there, I arrived with many limitations in the language, but my progress was rapid for two reasons: I was immersed in the language, making it part of my daily life, and because Italian is a Latin language it has many similarities to my mother tongue. My classes were all in Italian, but in several situations, including group work with other international students, I had to speak English. I did so with great difficulty, and that discomfort made me decide that I would study the language again as soon as I could.

When I returned to Brazil, I also returned to studying English—but with a much more mature mindset and a clarity about what I wanted. I looked for a course that emphasized listening and speaking. I was especially motivated because I felt that these classes would give me autonomy and help me avoid embarrassing situations like my awkward attempts to communicate with my English-speaking peers in Italy. Luckily for me, I liked the atmosphere and teachers of my new English course, so I had fun and a strong sense of improvement as I progressed through the classes.

Thanks to those lessons, I was able to post in English on social media, which allowed me to attract people from all over the world who were interested in drawing, which in turn motivated me to record videos and courses entirely in English and write the book you hold in your hands. I hadn't planned any of this when I made up my mind in Italy, but the desire to be able to communicate with the world was there—and now I can.

What about you, dear reader? Try to remember when you felt very motivated to learn something, whether a complex skill or a specific subject. Why did you feel that way? Did you have a very well-defined sense of purpose? Were you making rapid progress in that subject? Or was it simply because you found it fun? Having identified the reasons that made you succeed at it, try to visualize how you could bring these elements and motivations into your drawing practice.

> Surround yourself with people who have the habits you want to have yourself. You'll rise together.
>
> —JAMES CLEAR

Find inspiration

When I discovered realistic drawing on the internet, I was very impressed. Over the years, I had experimented with different drawing styles and techniques—but never anything like this. How was that kind of drawing possible? The artists' work I found online was my inspiration, and I enrolled in a realistic drawing course as soon as I found one.

If you're still not quite sure what you can do with a handful of pencils and paper, look to other artists for inspiration. Many produce drawings with an absurd level of realism, and you can view much of their work online. For instance, you could search for Jono Dry, Emanuele Dascanio, Kelvin Okafor, Arinze Stanley, Leanne Bishop, Dirk Dzimirsky, Silvie Mahdal, Dylan Eakin, and Juliane Berge for excellent examples of realistic black-and-white portraiture. If you prefer to draw in color, seek out the impressive work of Clio Newton, Marcello Barenghi, Heather Rooney, Sheila R. Giovanni, Casey Baugh, Morgan Davidson, and the YouTube instructor drawholic.

Some of these artists didn't go to an art college but learned to draw realism on their own through in-person or online courses. These people inspire me every day to continue to improve in the art of realism, especially in portraits. I hope they inspire you too.

Keep hungry, keep learning

If at some point you find yourself on autopilot, drawing one piece after another but feeling like you're doing more of the same, try something different:

- **Vary the themes you're exploring.** Draw portraits, close-ups of faces, animals, plants, natural or urban landscapes, everyday objects, vehicles, buildings, or anything that isn't "the usual."

- **Change the dimensions of your drawings.** An A3 drawing is different from an A4 one, as a larger drawing may require more detail or simply be more challenging because it takes longer to complete.

- **Explore other art materials.** You can, like me, spend some time drawing with graphite only and then start using charcoal to achieve darker tones in your drawings. You can test the use of gel pens or white acrylic paint to add occasional highlights here and there. You can draw on toned paper, so that the light spots are made with white charcoal, if you wish. You can draw in black and white and add color details using colored pencils. And there's always the possibility of venturing into full-color drawings with colored pencils or pastels from time to time—why not? Don't rule out other possibilities if you're interested in them.

At some point you may finish a more laborious drawing and ask yourself "what's next?" So that I don't have to think too much or lose my momentum, I always try to get ahead and plan my next projects while I work on the drawing of the moment. To help, I keep a folder on my computer with photographs that make me want to draw and drawings by artists who motivate me. This strategy helps me to keep moving when the definition of what to do next isn't so clear to me.

> *Learning is the only thing the mind never exhausts, never fears, and never regrets.*
>
> —LEONARDO DA VINCI

Appreciate what you are doing

> ## Patience and time are the most powerful warriors.
>
> —LEO TOLSTOY

Appreciating other artists can inspire us, but it can also be intimidating at times. As a beginner, you may doubt that you'll ever be able to do anything remotely similar to some of the amazing work of artists you admire.

Stop, think, and change your perspective a little: How many people around you can draw like you? Probably not many; most may not draw at all. Even if you don't believe it, what you do has value, because what you see emerging on your paper is something that is yours alone. Just by having drawing as a hobby, you are already a special person.

Rather than compare yourself to other artists, learn to compare yourself to your past self. Keep your past drawings, and occasionally review how far you've come since you first set graphite (or whatever your medium) to paper. Your old drawings are a record of your life story. I still have drawings that I did over 20 years ago and plan to keep more as the decades unfold. While I hope to still be productive in my 70s, 80s, and 90s, I know I'll also be able to look back and appreciate what I've done throughout my life.

No one regrets having dedicated themselves to something that made sense to them. Appreciate your daily achievements, enjoy what you're doing, and let time do its work.

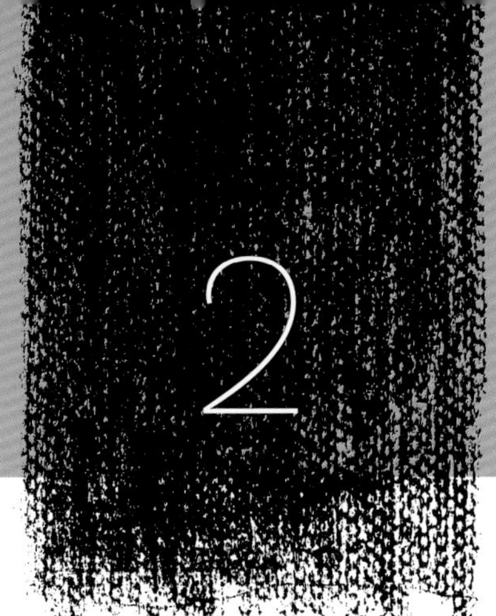

Materials

"What materials do I need for realistic drawing? What do you use?" I hear these questions a lot.

The short answer is paper, pencils, erasers, and something to blend with.

The longer answer fills the remainder of this chapter. I will share the art materials I used to make the book's example drawings, as well as discuss specific brands that I like best and why. Before we dive in, please know that I do not receive support from or have an affiliation with any of the suggested brands at the time of this writing. My choices are due to availability, price, and personal taste.

Many tools besides those discussed here can be used to make black-and-white drawings, too—so many that beginning artists may feel lost. At least initially, consider working with a limited range of materials and try to do the best you can with what you have at hand. As you gain experience with drawing, you'll learn what works best for you.

Paper

Good results start with good paper. When choosing paper for realistic drawing, pay attention to its weight, texture, and color. Your paper needs to withstand multiple layers of pencil, so look for weights of 67 lbs or 180 g/m^2 or more. Smooth paper, which I prefer, enables you to work with great precision and makes rendering details easier. Rough papers leave a more visible texture, but also generally support more layers of material on their surface, which makes it easier to achieve darker tones. Color is a matter of personal taste. Some papers have a colder tone, while others lean towards yellow.

Among the paper I've tried, Strathmore 300 Series Bristol smooth (**Figure 2.1**) is the one I liked the most because of its resistance, smoothness, which is not excessive, and pleasant tone. Fabriano Disegno 4 Liscio (smooth) and Lana Bristol are also good choices that I recommend and are similar to Strathmore's, but both are smoother, which makes it harder to achieve darker tones with them.

Pencils

Here we are going to talk about one of the most basic materials, if not the most important of all, the pencil. They can be found in the most varied forms, but for a beginner artist I recommend restricting the options to graphite and carbon pencils. In the case of graphite, you can also use mechanical pencils, but I would use them only for small details. I don't use them anymore, but they are still an option.

Graphite pencils

A good graphite pencil needs to be pleasant to use, resistant, and from a brand that offers a good range of tones. After all, it is the material we use most when drawing, and no one wants a pencil whose tip breaks every time it is sharpened or falls on the floor. Furthermore, a constancy of tone and gradation across a brand's range of pencils makes their behavior predictable.

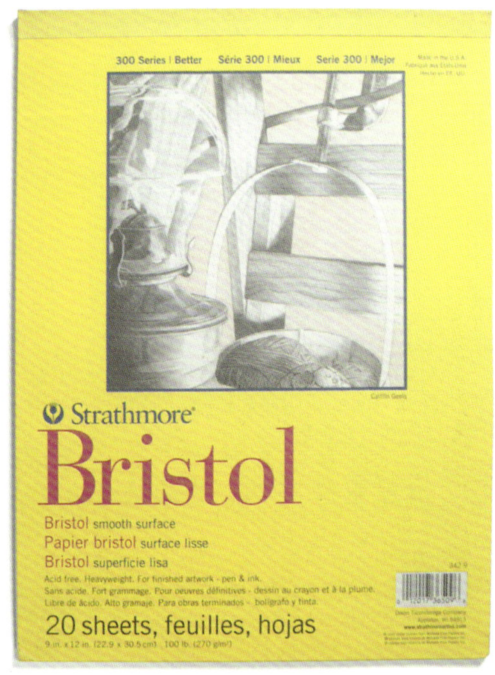

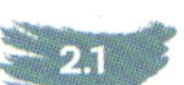

2.1

Staedtler Mars Lumograph pencils (**Figure 2.2**) certainly have these characteristics and are popular among professional and amateur artists alike. The tone scale I use is between HB and 8B. H pencils, which are very hard, are more suitable for technical drawings; grades beyond 8B are too soft and the gradations in tone no longer seem to make much difference. For darker tones, I prefer to use carbon or charcoal pencils.

An alternative to Staedtler Mars Lumograph pencils is the Faber-Castell 9000 line. Both brands also offer a dark matte version of their graphite pencils that enables you to achieve tones closer to black.

Carbon pencils

Carbon pencils can produce very dark tones like charcoals but without the fragility and dust. The binder added to their carbon makes these pencils easier to control, giving them a behavior similar to graphite. In short, carbon pencils are a middle ground between graphite and charcoal. The Staedtler Mars Lumograph Black pencil is the logical choice if you use that brand's graphite series and want to achieve darker tones (Figure 2.3). I have in my kit the 2B, 4B, 6B, and 8B grades. If you prefer Faber-Castell's pencils, the Pitt Graphite Matte series is a great option. (We'll delve deeper into the difference in tone between graphite, carbon, and charcoal in Chapter 4 and into blending issues in Chapter 5.)

Erasers

To the surprise of some, erasers are often used in realistic drawing, but less to correct errors and more to create lighting effects. To do this, you will need erasers that you probably never used in your school days.

Stick eraser

Pinpoint control is important for highlight placement, and a stick eraser will help immensely. In the realm of stick erasers, the Tombow MONO Zero Eraser reigns supreme (Figure 2.4) and is available in various sizes and tip shapes. I find the 2.3 mm round tip version most useful.

TIP: Use a craft knife to shape the eraser tip so you can draw thin lines or simply to clean it when it's worn out.

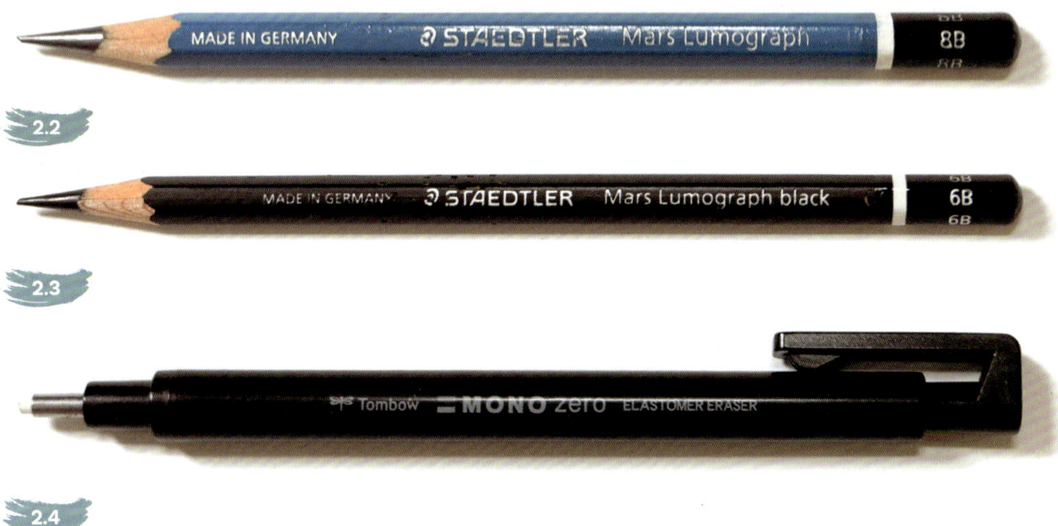

2.2

2.3

2.4

Eraser pencil

Cheap and very useful, eraser pencils serve a similar function as stick erasers but behave slightly differently. Because the Faber-Castell eraser pencil (Figure 2.5) is firmer than the Tombow MONO Zero Eraser, you can use it with more pressure and erase more aggressively. Despite its firmness, however, the eraser pencil has less precision than the stick eraser. You can use it for more discreet highlights where you want intermediate tones rather than very light highlights. Try both out to better understand the difference between eraser pencils and stick erasers.

Electric eraser

An electric eraser (Figure 2.6) is far from being an essential item, but it can be useful. Electric erasers can remove graphite, carbon, and charcoal more efficiently than stick erasers or eraser pencils, enabling you to make very light spots, almost in the color of the paper used—even in the middle of a stain (a blended area) already filled with several layers. I found one especially useful in Chapter 7's flower exercise.

Eraser pen

You may need a regular eraser at any time. An eraser pen isn't vital, but often comes in handy. I use one to clean the margins of my drawings when they turn gray from the graphite that spreads over them while I work, or simply to erase lines traced with rulers. But why not use a regular eraser? Because a pen eraser is more precise, reducing the chance of losing part of the work already done, if that's the case. The Pentel Clic Eraser (Figure 2.7) is a good eraser pen choice. It doesn't damage the paper, leave smeary traces (assuming it's properly cleaned), or shed too many crumbs along the way. Additionally, you can buy refills for it, which makes it extremely durable, despite being cheap.

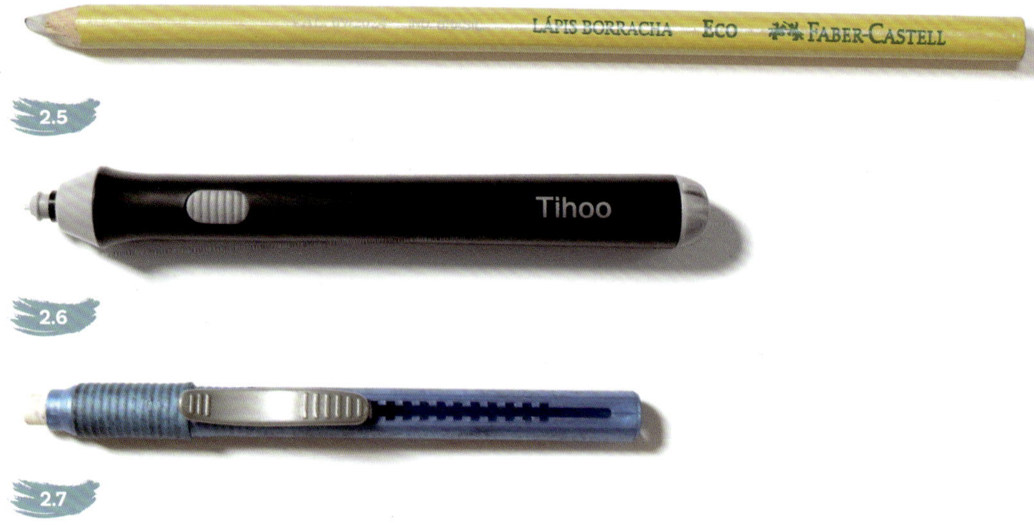

2.5

2.6

2.7

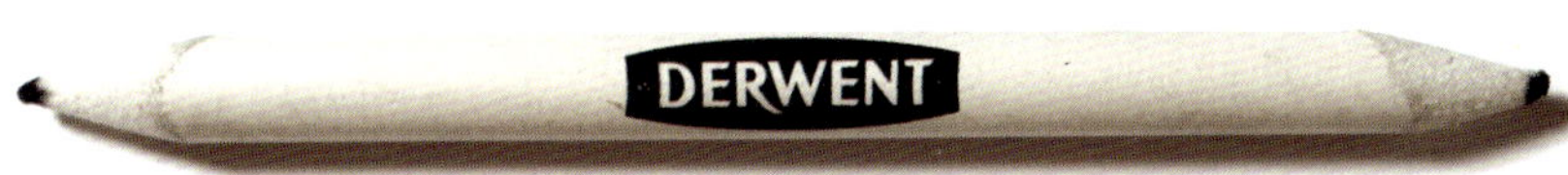

Blending tools

Blending tools are much less known than pencils, erasers, and sharpeners, and the simple fact of knowing them has made a huge difference in my drawings. Let's go to them, who will be protagonists from Chapter 5 onwards.

Tissue

The humble tissue is a highly accessible and useful tool for blending graphite, carbon, and charcoal (Figure 2.8). You can fold it into triangles or simply wrap it around your finger, then blend your material over a wide area where you don't need very small details. Tissue works especially well for making homogeneous coverage with graphite and carbon, because these materials are easy to control and are not very messy. A single piece of toilet paper is enough.

Blending stump

Blending stumps are the middle ground between tissue and brush in terms of effects it creates on a drawing (Figure 2.9). You can use this relatively cheap tool to blend like tissue, but in a more localized way, making it handy for smaller details. However, it will also undo all strokes that are visible; if you want to keep them, use a brush instead. It is important to clean its tip with sandpaper before using it for lighter details, as it accumulates dirt as it is used. Consider purchasing multiple sizes of blending stumps for more versatility when drawing. (We'll discuss working with the various blending tools in more detail in Chapter 5.)

Brush

Available in a wide range of shapes, sizes, and bristle types, brushes are also very useful blending tools. They are less aggressive in effect compared to the tissue and blending stump. You can use larger brushes for spreading the graphite loosely, and smaller ones for blending small spots without losing all the details done with the pencils.

I prefer flat brushes, whose bristles I cut with scissors to make them firmer, and cat's tongue brushes (**Figure 2.10**). The best size depends on the size of the drawings you intend to make. For A4-size drawings, I use brushes ranging from size 4 to 12. Having two or three sizes of each type of brush is enough. Pony hair bristles or similar are the best choice.

Sharpeners

In this section you will see that yes, there are different ways to sharpen a pencil depending on the type of sharpener you are using. If you have the opportunity to try other sharpeners, do so, as you will gain in terms of versatility and practicality when drawing.

Pencil sharpeners

Sure, you can find cheap hand-held pencil sharpeners practically everywhere, but there is no point in using a bad sharpener when you use good quality pencils. Make sure the sharpener you choose is ideal for your pencil. The sharpener hole should match the diameter of your pencil or accommodate pencils of different thicknesses (**Figure 2.11**). Also, don't persist in using a sharpener with a worn blade, as this will affect the quality of the pencil's tip. Some sharpeners come with replacement blades, and for others you can buy extra blades separately.

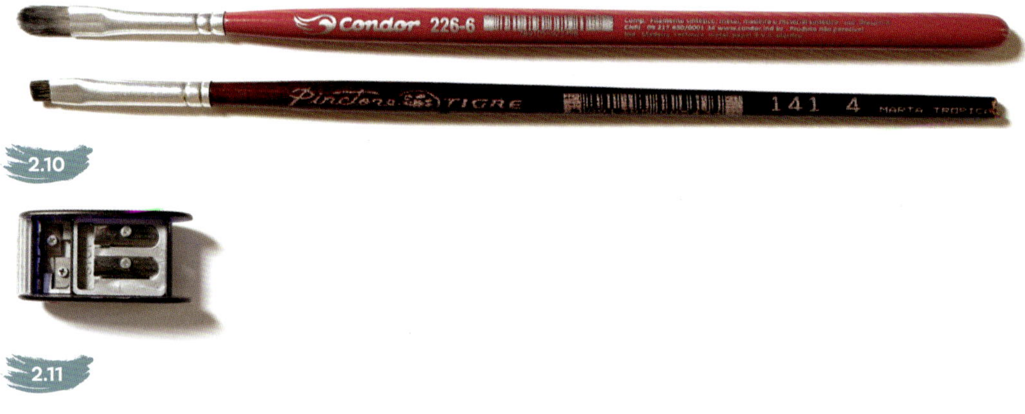

2.10

2.11

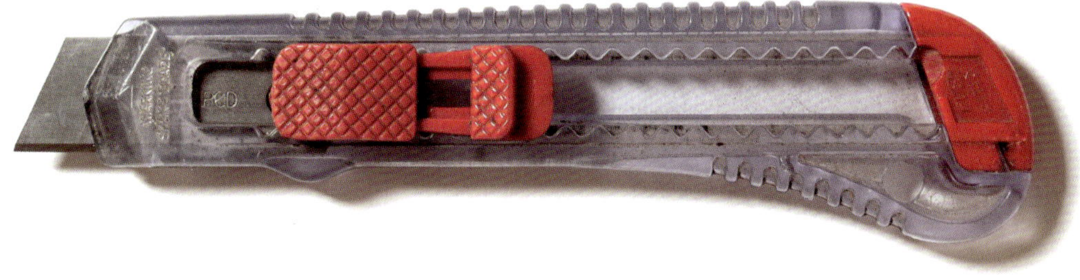

2.12

Craft knife

A craft knife is useful not only for cutting paper, but also for sharpening pencils in a more refined way (**Figure 2.12**). I use a craft knife when I need to draw very fine lines, such as for hair strands, and the tip of my pencil needs to be molded into a particular shape. Using a knife also helps to preserve the pencil for longer, as sometimes you can sharpen only the tip and not the wood. I don't sharpen pencils with a knife all the time, however, because it requires more time and care to make the pencil look good.

Crank sharpener

My life changed when I purchased a crank sharpener (**Figure 2.13**). Its practicality and effectiveness are outstanding, and that's why I now use a hand sharpener only with thicker pencils that don't fit my crank model. If you're willing to pay a little more, you can find options that offer multiple openings to accommodate a range of pencil sizes.

Crank sharpeners do come with tradeoffs. These relatively large and heavy objects aren't exactly portable. If you always draw

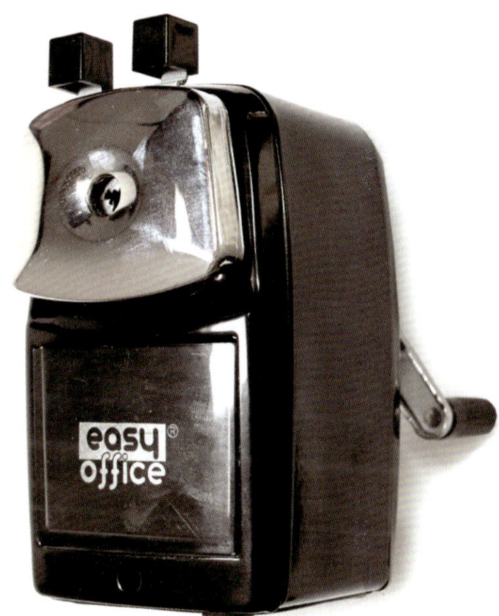

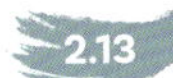
2.13

at the same desk, as I do, this isn't a problem; if you like to sketch outside, it could be. Another drawback is that removing broken tips from crank sharpeners can be difficult. Pencils with brittle tips, such as charcoal and pastel pencils, are more liable to break and should not be sharpened with crank sharpeners.

Extra tools

Here we will deal with some materials that are behind the scenes, but that make the drawing process easier. They are not essential, but consider having them if you can.

Embossing tool

The embossing or indenting tool (**Figure 2.14**) is not a tool I use very often, but it can be quite convenient for creating the white hair effect. It basically creates grooves in the paper and, when the pencil is used in that area, it will not be able to fill the grooves, but only what is around it, creating the effect of white threads. An eraser can be used to achieve this same type of effect, but it is unlikely that it will be able to remove the graphite in such a way as to restore the original white of the paper. It is in these cases that the embossing tool proves to be most useful.

I have a single embossing tool in my kit with a size 2 ball tip and it serves me perfectly whenever I need to create very light threads. I used it on the beard of the man on the cover of this book and in the animal fur exercise in Chapter 6.

Sandpaper

For me, sandpaper (**Figure 2.15**) has two main functions. I use it to clean the tips of blending stumps and shape the tips of pencils. If you need to use a blending stump in bright areas, you must sand any lingering charcoal or graphite off the pulpy tip; otherwise, the stump will leave unwanted stains on your drawing. When I want a chisel point on my pencil tip (Chapter 4), I reach for the sandpaper, too. You can use a piece of very fine grit (150-220) sandpaper available at hardware stores, but you can't go wrong picking one that is designed for artists.

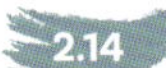

2.14

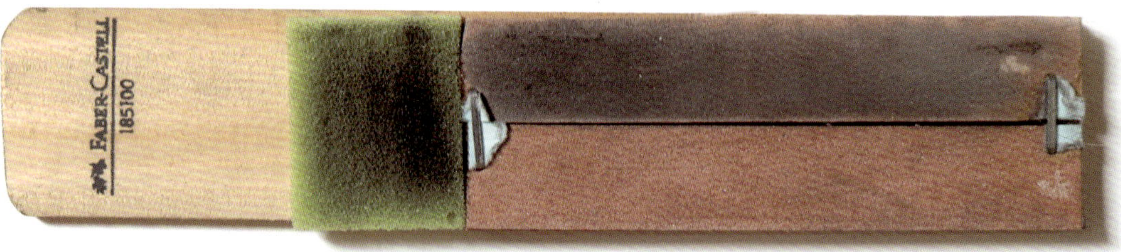

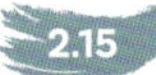

2.15

Table brush

Drawing is a little messy, especially when using an eraser. To remove crumbs without touching the drawing, use a table brush (Figure 2.16) or any large, very soft brush. Just be careful, because a brush can drag loose graphite or charcoal dust and end up smudging the drawing surface. In exceptional cases, you can blow the powder away. Blow sideways and gently, and swallow first so as not to get saliva on the paper. (Keep your drawing free from splashes of any type of liquid, by the way!)

Tape

I always draw on a sheet of paper taped on a drawing board to keep it from slipping and shifting. This is very important for realistic drawing, which demands so much attention to detail. Although you can use ordinary masking tape, better quality painter's tapes, like ScotchBlue (Figure 2.17), have greater resistance, tend to leave less glue behind, and are less likely to damage the surface when removed.

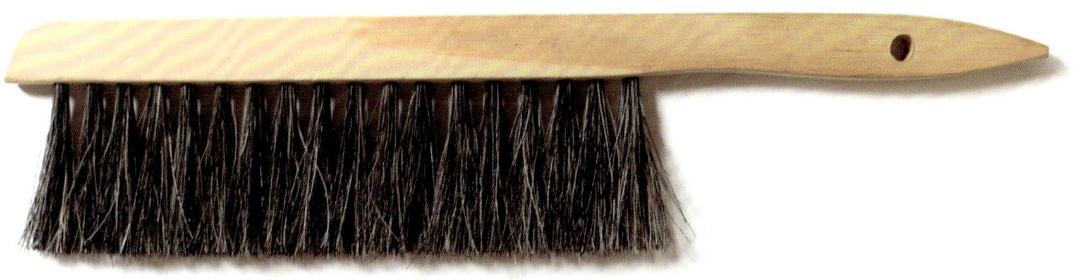

2.16

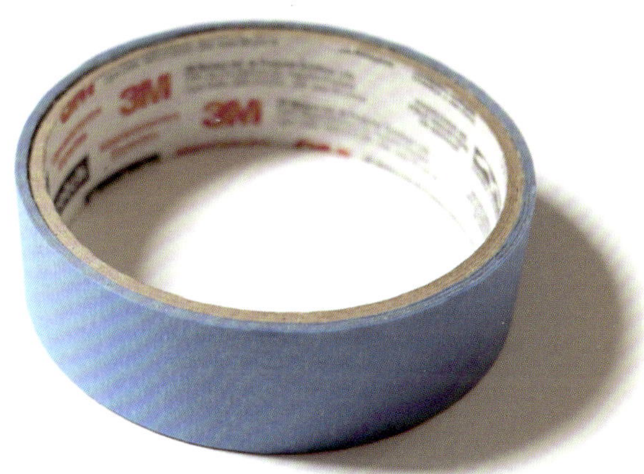

2.17

Fixative spray

Materials like graphite and charcoal won't stay completely attached to the paper surface unless you apply a fixative varnish over them. Sold in spray form, these varnishes are essential for preserving your drawing and storing them without dirtying everything they touch (**Figure 2.18**). Choose a varnish with a matte finish to reduce the graphite shine that can appear when your drawing is viewed from different angles.

TIP: Before applying it to your finished drawing, test the spray (and your technique) on a practice paper covered with the same drawing materials. Once applied, the varnish cannot be removed!

Always read the instructions before using these sprays and be sure you have adequate ventilation. Varnish is toxic and highly flammable. Wear a mask when applying it and be careful for your eyes.

Reference photos

Because realism consists of a faithful representation of a given subject, I often use reference images to draw. Choose high-resolution images with sharp and crystal-clear subjects so you can easily see details.

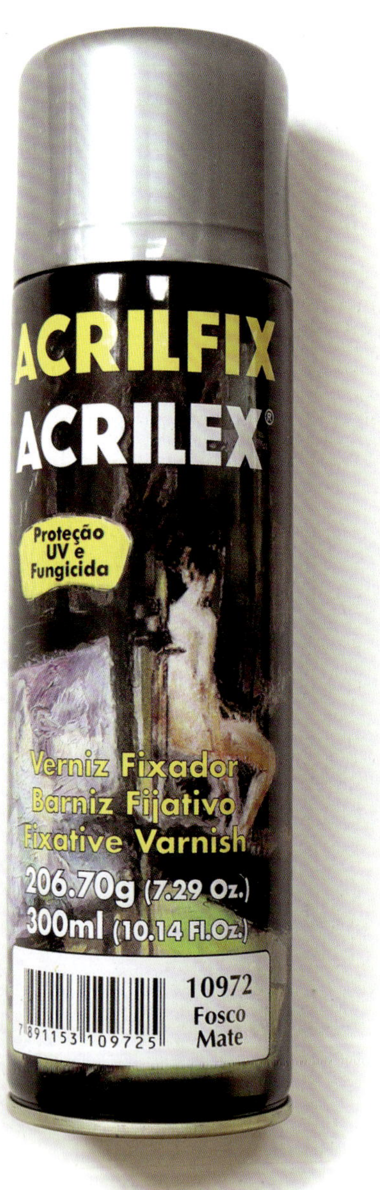

2.18

The internet holds an inexhaustible source of images. Pinterest is one of the best places to get inspired and find something that you like. Social media, especially Instagram, can also be a helpful source. In both cases, be mindful of image resolution; Instagram, for example, tends to compress images, which reduces quality. Google Images enables you to search for larger images by sorting by size on the search tab.

Stock websites are good sources of high-resolution photos. FreeImages, Unsplash, Pexels, Pixabay, and Freepik all offer many professional images for free, as well as paid subscription plans that provide access to more resources.

Another solution is to turn to websites that host images that can only be downloaded by purchasing them individually or through a subscription. Adobe Stock and Shutterstock are both good sources of high-quality royalty-free images, but all their images must be paid for either individually or through a subscription.

Wherever you find your reference images, be sure you are respecting copyright law and not violating any licensing rules. A good way to free yourself from that worry is to take your own reference photos. Practice taking multiple images of whatever you'd like to draw. Make sure the lighting is high quality and not casting unwanted shadows.

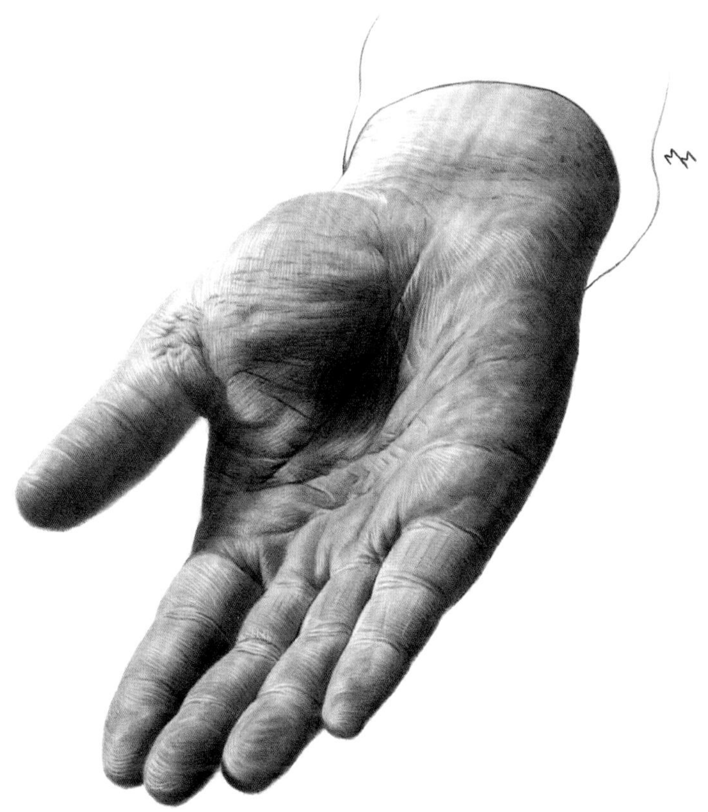

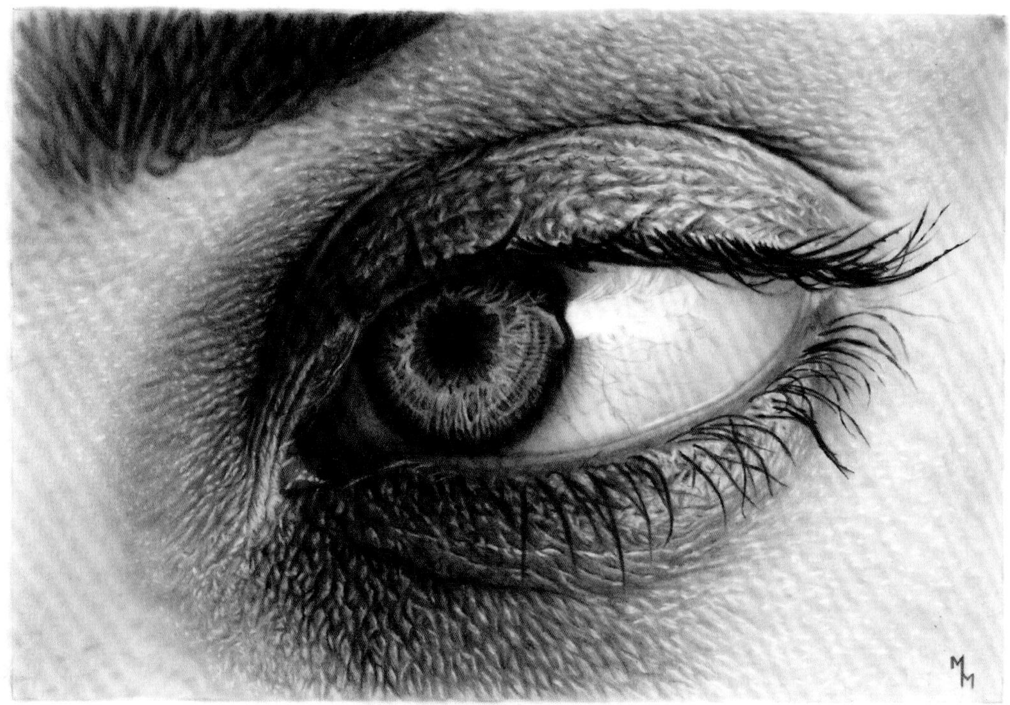

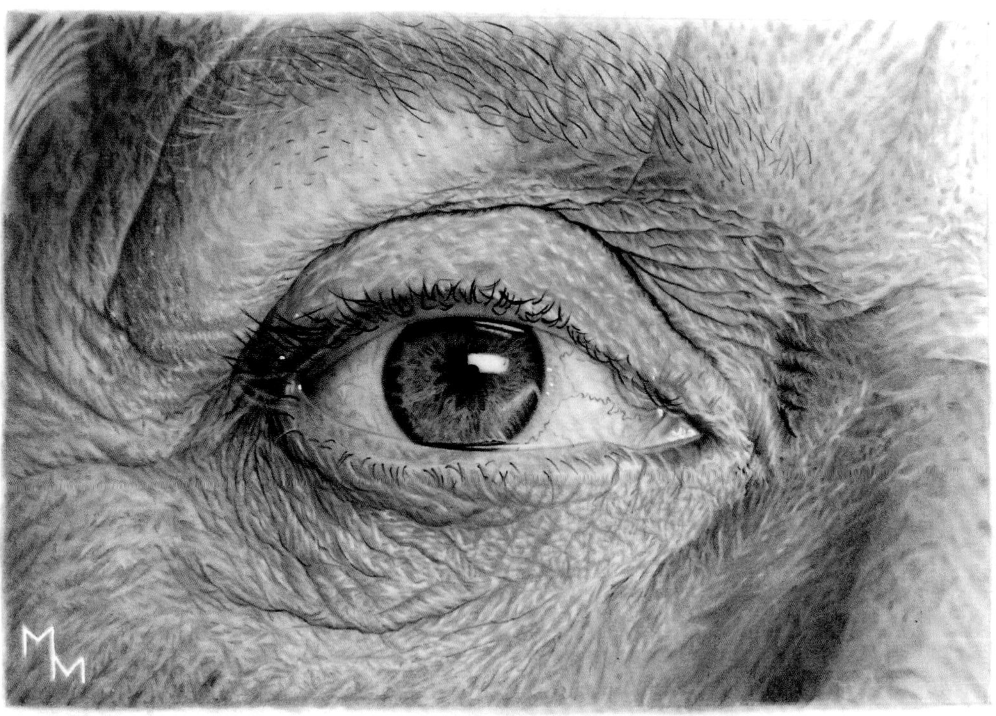

Drawing close-up pictures of eyes is one of my favorite things.

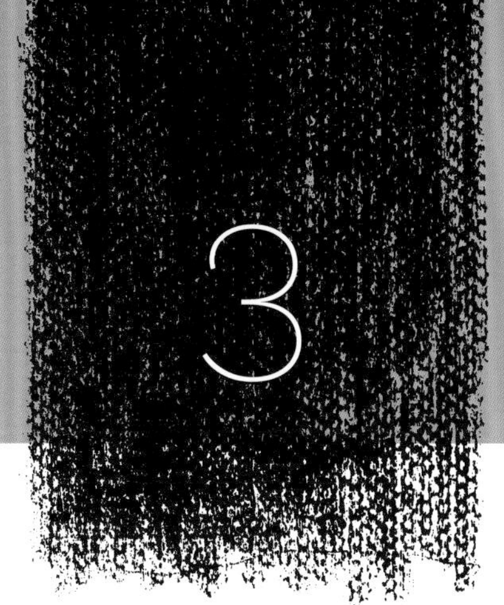

Sketching

You're motivated. Your tools are ready. It's time to draw! The first stage of any realistic drawing is the sketch. The function of the sketch is to place the reference image on your drawing sheet, so that from the shading steps onwards you no longer have to worry about the proportions of the drawing. In this sense, we must draw not only the contour lines, but also include references for shading and textures. A series of sketch examples in the following chapters show how this will be done in practice.

In this chapter, I will share some methods and tips that will help you make perfect sketches—even if you don't have any drawing experience. We'll start with the basics.

How to hold a pencil

Do you know how to hold a pencil?

Of course! When we learned to write, we were all taught to hold the pencil by positioning the thumb and forefinger close to the tip (Figure 3.1). This grip, however, is not always the best way to hold a pencil when drawing. It gives a firm and precise line, but when sketching we generally want greater freedom of movement and a lighter line.

So, let's talk about some new grips that are more effective for drawing. For instance, start with a traditional grip, but position your fingers a little further back, in the middle or at the other end of the pencil (Figure 3.2). This will give you more agility and lightness of stroke. You'll also be able to see better what you're drawing, as your hand won't be in front of you covering up your drawing. I use this grip to draw my freehand sketches.

Another way to hold the pencil is to pass your hand over it with the palm facing downwards and your fingers holding the pencil underneath (Figure 3.3).

You can also wrap your fingers around the pencil and extend your index finger over it (Figure 3.4).

Holding the pencil further back will give you more range of movement, allowing you to move your arm and elbow more. It will also enable you to make longer strokes without interruption, so you don't have to splice one stroke on top of another.

Try these ways of holding a pencil and choose the one that seems most comfortable while giving you both freedom and control. Despite what your primary school teacher may have taught you, there is no right way to hold a pencil, only the way that suits you best.

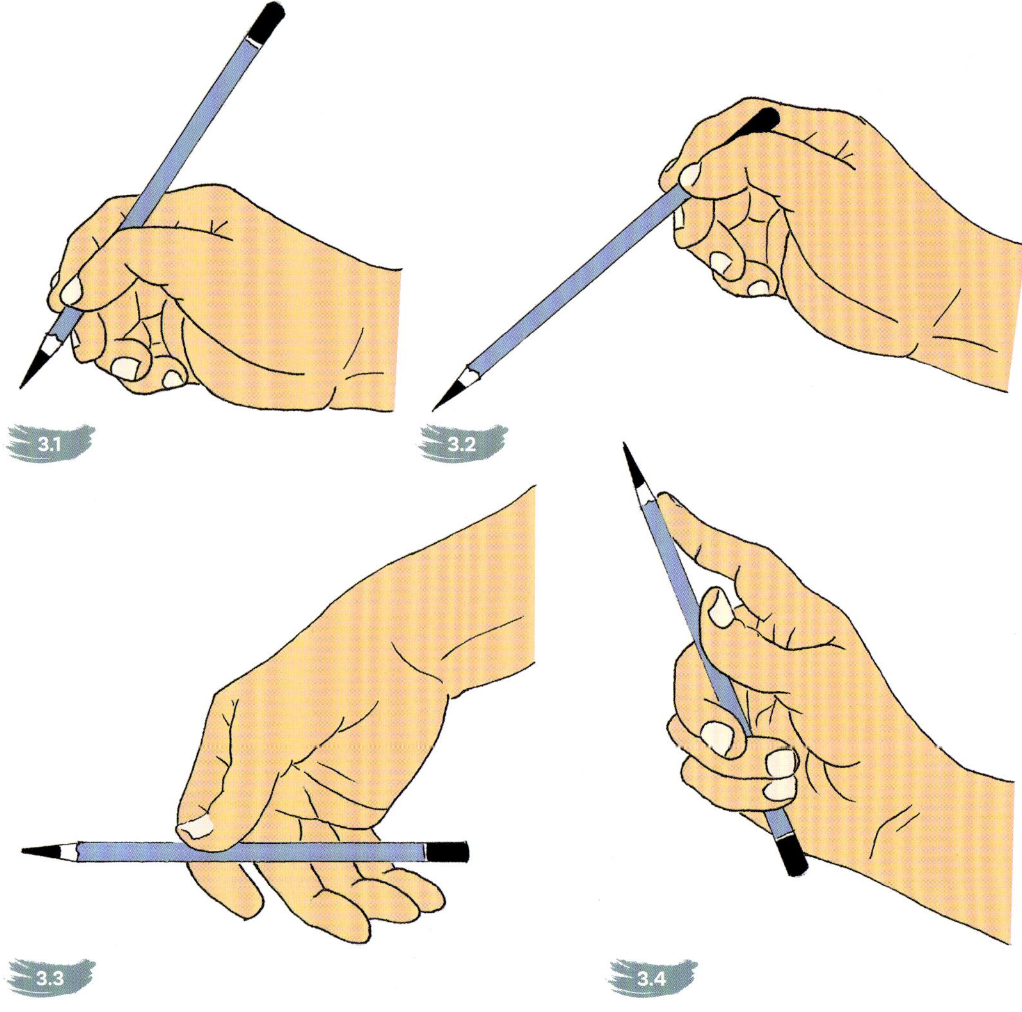

Freehand method

Freehand sketching is the most challenging method to begin a realistic drawing, but three guiding concepts will help you: simplification, proportion, and triangulation.

Your sketch defines the basic shapes of your drawing and how the figure or figures will be positioned on the paper. Normally, sketches are not used for details, and the strokes of the sketch are not meant to appear in the finished drawing. However, the lines of the sketch serve as a guide for the following stages, such as shading and blending. By identifying the underlying shapes in your reference image and *simplifying* them to geometric shapes, you can make them easier to draw.

Simplification

To demonstrate, let's draw a pear (Figure 3.5) on an A5 size sheet (148 x 210 mm) with a light pencil, such as one with H, HB, or B graphite. The first thing to decide is how the drawing should occupy the space on the sheet. Where and how big should it be?

Paying attention to the limits of the paper helps a lot when sketching. Bear in mind that the blank area is not just empty space but part of the composition of your drawing! In addition, if your drawing follows the same relationship between the figure and the background as your reference (if the distances from the edge of the paper are the same as those of the image you're using), you'll be able to compare the two as you sketch and judge your progress. If you are drawing a real-life object in front of you, how you place your sketch on the paper is totally up to you.

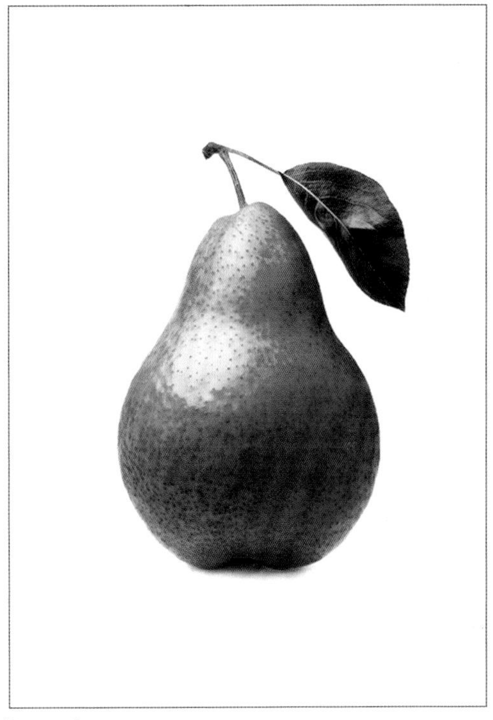

3.5

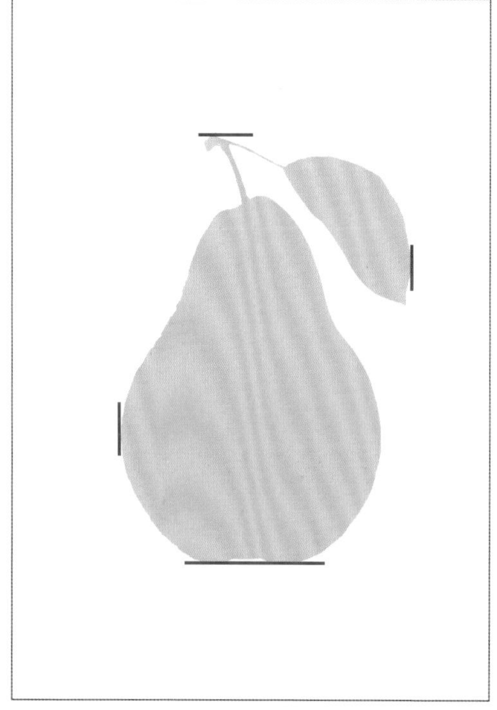

3.6

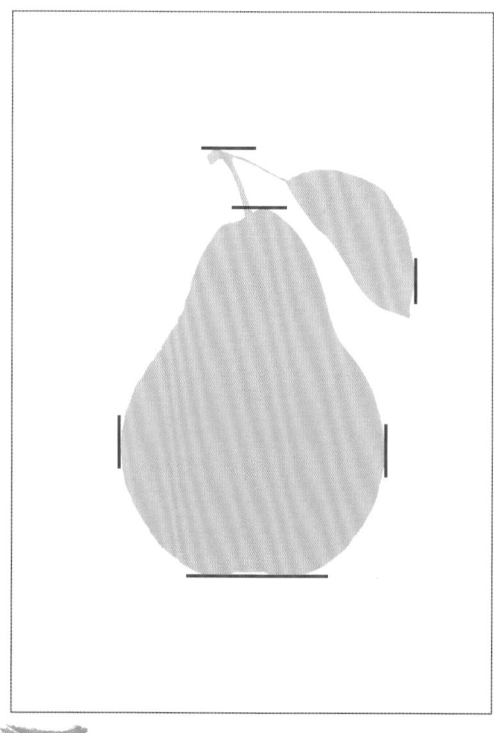

3.7

To set the position and size of the drawing, start by marking the edges of the figure on the paper; mark the highest, lowest, left-most, and rightmost points of the object (Figure 3.6).

Next, mark two more important points: the right edge and the top of the fruit (Figure 3.7).

Take a long look at the pear. How could you simplify it into geometric shapes? Studying the fruit, I imagined two main rounded areas, one above the other like two stacked circles. I added these to Figure 3.8 to sim-plify the shape of the pear.

Proportion

Using these points and shapes as a reference, draw the outline of the pear (Figure 3.9). Wasn't that easier? To draw the stem and the leaf, observe the gap between them and the fruit. This area is *negative space*, and it is also a great reference to use while sketching.

As you outline the pear or any subject, look for reference elements within the drawing itself so that you can check that you're going the right way. One element you can check is *proportion*. To obtain realistic proportion, compare the parts of the drawing with each other and with the whole. Take measure-ments between the key parts you identify in

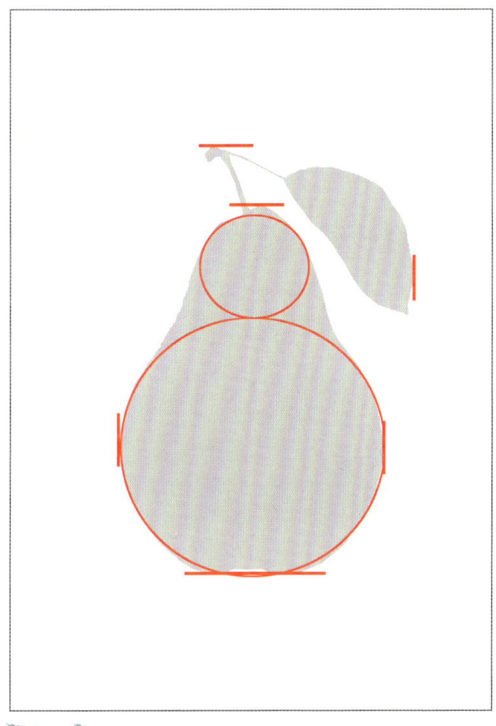

3.8

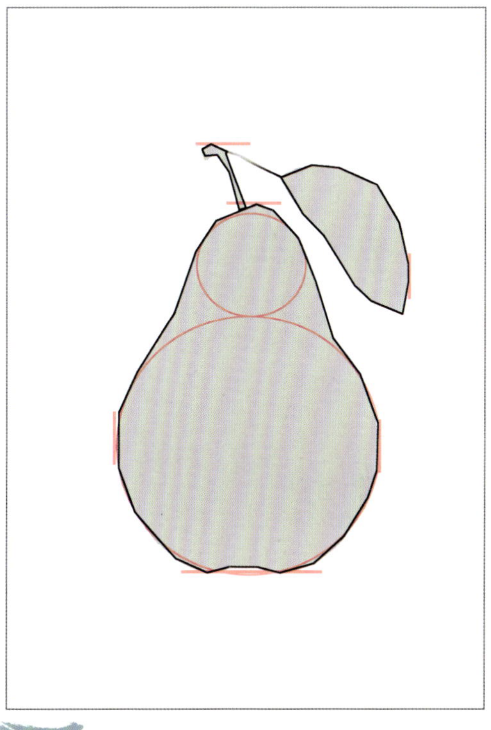

3.9

the drawing (Figure 3.10). For the pear, compare the width of the two circular shapes (A and B) with the height of the fruit (C). You could use a ruler, your pencil, or any other straight object to compare the measurements with each other. Of course, only a ruler will enable you to gauge the measurements precisely, but having a rough idea of the proportions between the parts is enough.

Triangulation

Another way of locating yourself in a drawing and having more confidence as you sketch is through *triangulation*. With this technique, you use two reference points to locate a third point (Figure 3.11).

Let's use the outline of the leaf as an example. After defining the extreme points of the pear's body, choose two of them to use as a reference. I chose the highest point (1) and the lowest point (2) of the fruit. Starting from your first point (1), look at the reference image and determine the angle formed between the high point on the fruit (1) and the location you want to find in your drawing. In this case, we want to find the midpoint on the top edge of the leaf (point 3). Draw a line (13) on your sketch at the same angle you see in your reference image passing through points 1 and 3. Finally, starting from the second point (2), draw another line (23) at the same angle that you see in the reference image, passing through points 2 and 3. The two angled lines in your

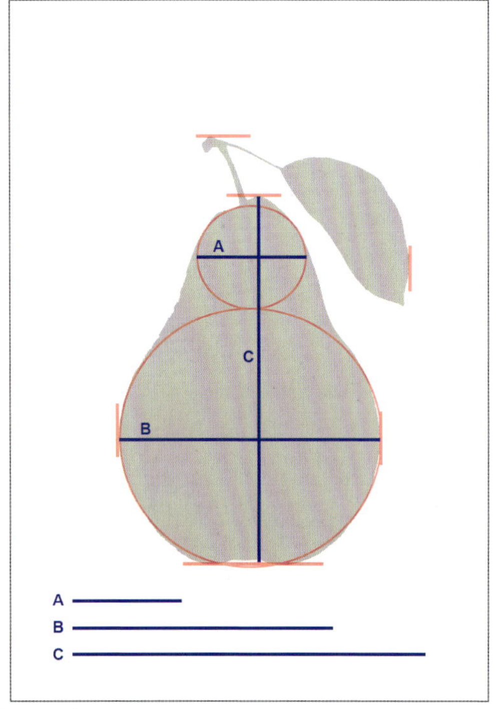

3.10

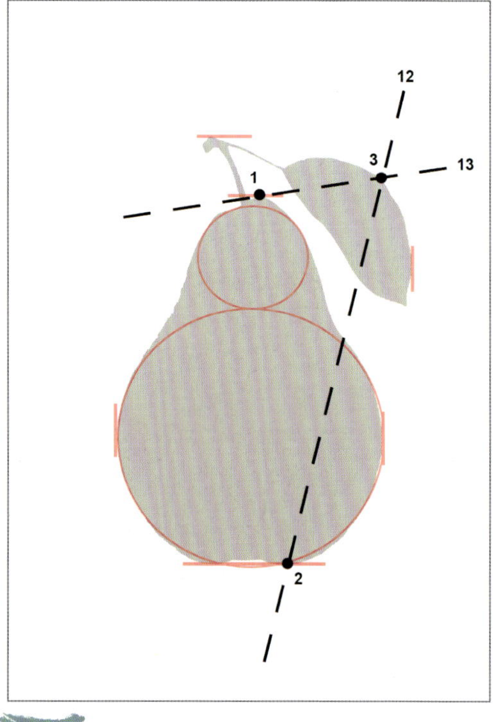

3.11

sketch will intersect at point 3, and you will have a new reference for the outline of the leaf. You can continue to use points 1 and 2 to locate all the other points on the pear, or you can also use the new ones you find as references for the additional points along the way.

The difficulty with this technique is transferring the angle you see in the reference image onto your drawing. The further away the target point is from your reference points, the greater the chance of getting the angle wrong. I recommend holding the pencil further back so that you have a clear view and can move your arm more freely.

The triangulation technique alone would be enough to sketch the entire pear, but combining it with simplifying objects into groups of geometric shapes, measuring and comparing the shapes, and considering the negative space will make freehand drawing easier. Plus, your results will be less likely to have distortions.

TIP: Before drawing the pear's outline with curved strokes, sketch the shapes using straight strokes; these are easier to draw than curves. When it's time to start shading, you can refine the strokes made in the sketch, if you want them to appear in the finished drawing. Or, you can simply erase the sketch if you prefer.

As you've seen, the freehand method involves knowing how to simplify, comparing the parts with each other, and not losing track of the whole in order to be successful. For realistic drawing, your sketch can include more details. If you want to achieve a higher level of fidelity to your reference, however, I recommend using one of the other sketching methods we'll discuss next instead of freehand drawing.

Light table method

If you prefer an easier approach than freehand drawing, the light table method is the simplest way to create a base sketch for your realistic drawing. Place a printed reference image on an illuminated surface, such as a light table, and place your drawing paper on top of the reference. Be sure to attach the drawing sheet to the reference image so they don't slip out of alignment, and then sketch the contour lines of the reference as seen through the paper (Figure 3.12).

A wide variety of portable and freestanding light tables for tracing are available, with an equally wide price range. When choosing one, consider the size of the lighting surface and the intensity of the light it emits. The light needs to be strong enough to pass through a sheet of paper weighing 67 lbs or 180 g/m^2 or more, which is recommended for realistic drawing.

If you're trying to keep expenses down, you can improvise a lighting surface instead. For example, you could place a lamp underneath a glass table and direct the light upwards. You could also use a window on a bright day, but I find it very uncomfortable to draw on a completely vertical surface.

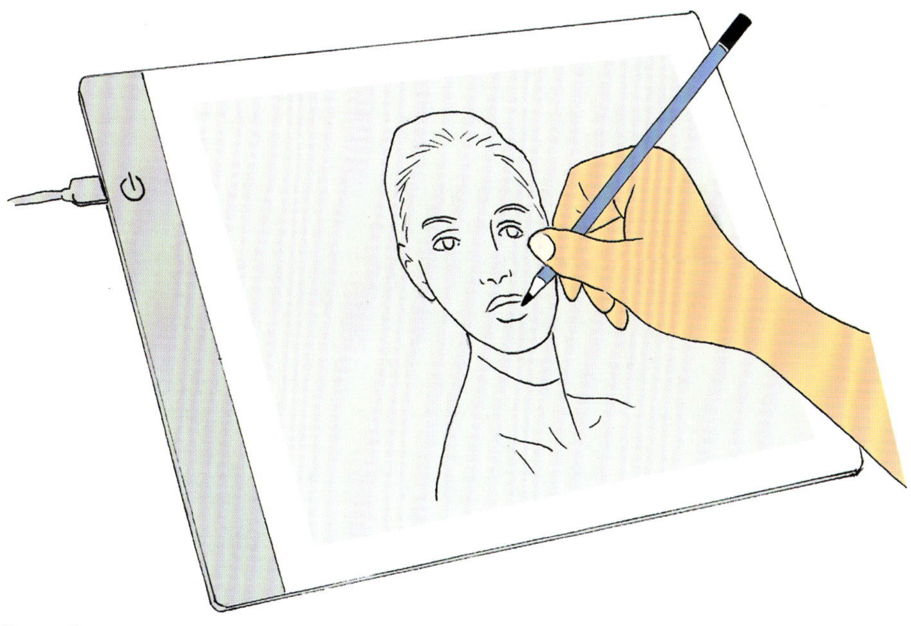

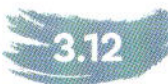
3.12

Besides, I tend to lean on the surface I'm drawing on, and the idea of leaning on and forcing a thin layer of glass doesn't appeal to me in the slightest. It's up to you, though. It works—as long as the clouds and rain stay away.

The screen of a monitor or tablet makes a good light source, as well. If the drawing you want to make is smaller than the screen of your device, you won't even need to print your reference. Be careful, however, with your device's screen. Depending on the strength of your stroke, you could leave marks on the screen. In addition, if you're working from a digital reference image, you'll have to attach the paper to the monitor or device screen, smearing it with glue from the tape. Again, it works, but I don't recommend doing this.

Grid method

The grid method is quite popular and doesn't require any special equipment, just a ruler and pencil. Use the ruler to divide your reference image into rows and columns, and then divide your drawing sheet into the same number of rows and columns. Then, draw the sketch using the points where the image crosses your grid lines as reference. Simply count the lines and columns to make the strokes in the correct place.

The area of the drawing doesn't have to be the same size as that of the reference image, but it must be in the same proportion. For example, if you're using a digital reference image that measures 1000 x 1500 pixels, your drawing must have the same 2:3 ratio but could measure 10 x 15 cm, 5.0 x 7.5 cm, or 20 x 30 cm, and so on. Likewise, the number of rows and columns must be identical for your reference image and drawing. In Figure 3.13, I made a grid with five rows and five columns. Notice that the distances between the rows and between the columns changes in the same proportion as the total width and height measurements change between the reference and drawing.

You don't have to create a grid in which the width of the columns and rows are equal, forming squares, although I prefer to do it that way. I always use digital reference images and do some quick tests to determine the optimum number of rows and columns, so the resulting squares are neither too big nor small. Several free mobile apps make this easy, like Grid Drawing, Drawing Grid, and Drawing Grid Maker. Yes, the names can all be very similar.

Nor do you need to divide each dimension of the reference into whole numbers. Simply use the same point, such as the top-left corner, to start the grid in the reference and in the drawing. If you set a value for each piece of the grid beforehand, it may be that the last row or column of the grid doesn't coincide with the edge of the paper, but there's no harm in that.

Suppose, for example, you plan to draw a 12 x 10 image (6:5 aspect ratio) and you want a grid made up of squares of 1.5 units per side (Figure 3.14). In this case, the width will divide into a whole number (12/1.5 = 8 columns) but not the height (10/1.5 = 6.667 rows). No problem: Just use the same starting point in the reference as in the drawing to draw the grid.

5
10
7.5
15
1.5
1
3
2

3.13

Starting point

1 2 3 4 5 6 7 8
1
2
3
4
5
6

1 2 3 4 5 6 7 8
1
2
3
4
5
6

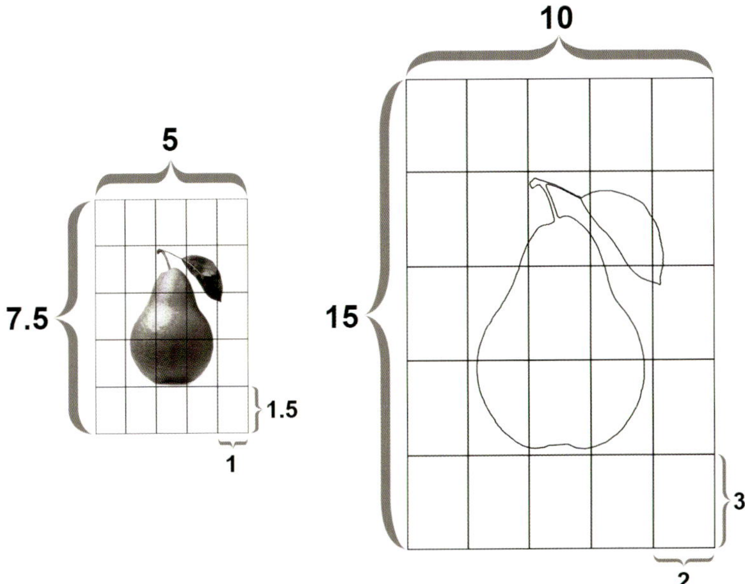

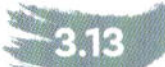

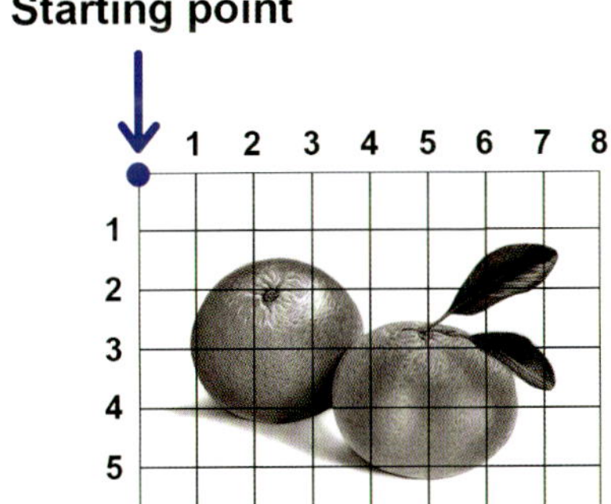

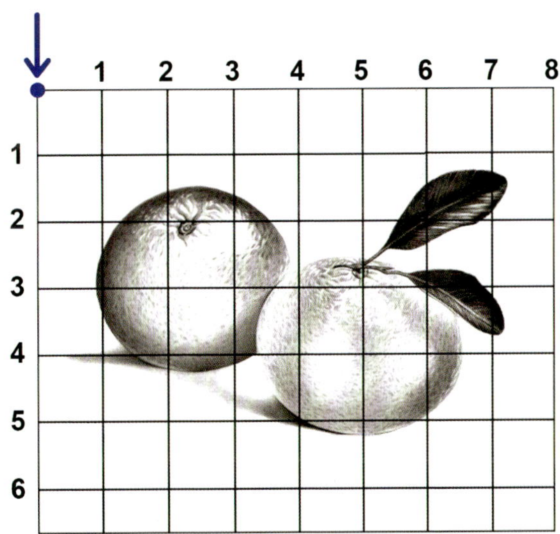

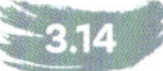

3.14

Finally, remember that grid lines are sketch lines. You probably don't want them to appear in the finished drawing, so use lighter pencils, such as H, HB, or B, and plan to erase them later. This is one of the disadvantages of the grid method: The more you erase a drawing, the more mess you make. To mitigate this problem, you can make the lines even lighter in empty areas of the drawing, such as a white background. On the other hand, in areas with a lot of details, such as those full of the tangerine's texture in Figure 3.14, grid lines are extremely useful, and they tend to disappear as you use techniques to blend the graphite (Chapter 5).

I use the grid method quite often and combine it with the transfer method.

Transfer method

The transfer method is one of my favorite techniques. Basically, you make a sandwich: Place your drawing paper on the bottom, layer a sheet of carbon paper on top of it (make sure the graphite side faces down), then position a printed reference image on top (**Figure 3.15**). Next, using a pen, pencil, or any tool with a firm point, trace the contour lines on your reference image to transfer them to the drawing paper.

To get the most out of this method:

- Fix the reference to the drawing sheet using two pieces of masking tape. This prevents the sheets from moving out of alignment while you're drawing.

- Trace over the reference image using a ballpoint pen so you know which lines you've already drawn. I like a red pen, so that I can better see what I've done.

- Don't apply too much force, as you could create grooves in the drawing sheet, damaging it irreversibly.

- Do make your strokes firm enough to make clear lines and avoid getting a bit lost when working on the drawing itself. In other words, find a middle ground in the pressure you apply to your strokes.

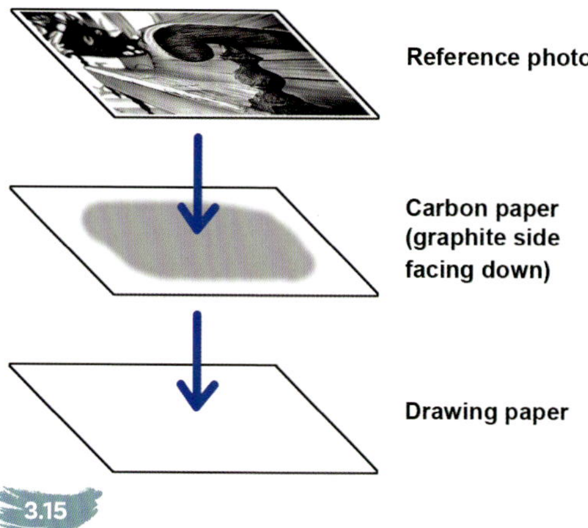

3.15

Carbon paper options

You can buy carbon paper sheets if you like, just make sure that the lines they produce are erasable. I've never bought carbon paper, however, because it's easy to make using regular printer paper and a dark graphite pencil, such as an 8B.

To make a sheet of carbon paper, fill one side of the sheet of common paper with graphite pencil and spread the graphite using a tissue, piece of toilet paper, or cotton ball. Repeat the process once or twice to get more consistent coverage.

> TIP: Leave a blank margin around the edges, so you can manipulate the sheet without getting graphite on your fingers (Figure 3.16).

You can use the same sheet for multiple drawings. As you use it, it will lighten, but you can apply new layers of graphite as often as you like. To store this sheet without smudging other things, fold it in half with the graphite side facing inwards. Simple, isn't it?

Some people fill in the back of the reference image with graphite instead of creating a separate carbon sheet. This method works in the same way, but you have to repeat the filling-in process for each new drawing. Do it on a separate sheet and save yourself some time.

3.16 My homemade carbon paper

Combining the grid and transfer methods

How do the grid and transfer methods combine? I insert a grid digitally into my reference image and print it that way. For drawing a complex reference image like Figure 3.17, both methods are useful. Be detailed when transferring lines, so you don't have to invent the details while shading and texturing. The grid is very helpful, because it's easy to get lost in the wrinkles and hairs of the reference. I suggest waiting until your skills are more advanced before tackling a drawing like this, but when you get to that level, you'll thank me for the tip.

If you want to combine the transfer and grid methods for simple drawings like Figure 3.14, add the grid lines only inside the subject so you don't have to erase them from the blank background.

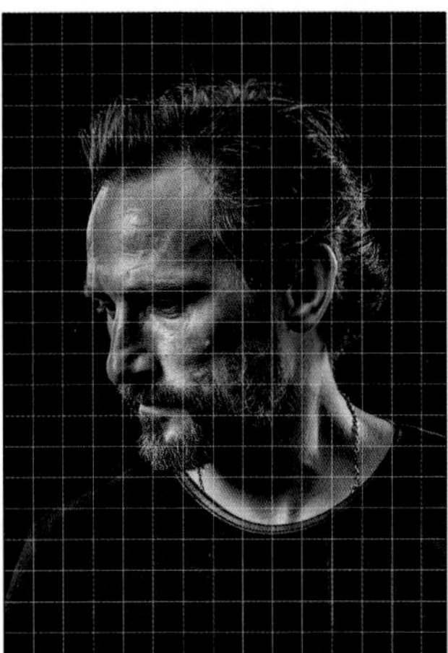

Reference photo

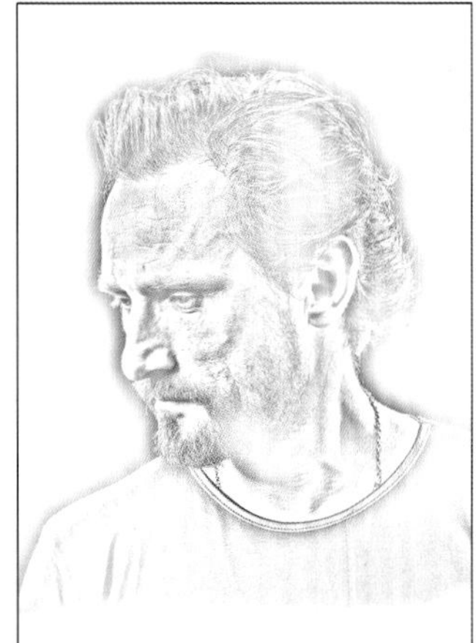

Transfer method

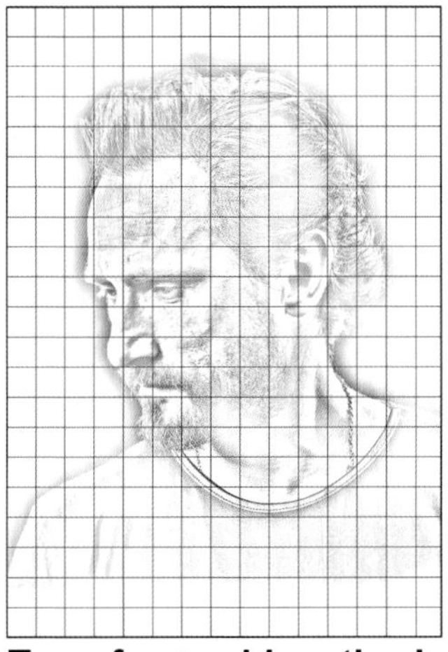

Transfer + grid methods

3.17 Combining the transfer with the grid method for a reference like this makes the task easier.

Stage 1 complete!

These four methods we've discussed are the main ways to prepare a base sketch from a reference image. In the next chapter, you will learn how to add volume to your drawing by using shading to represent general values of light and shadow. Let's get into it!

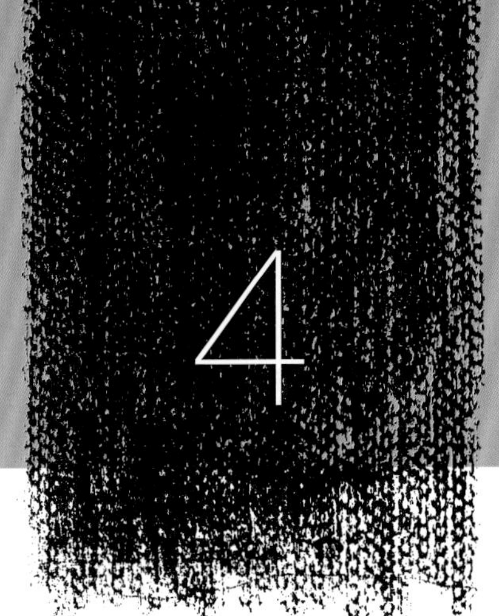

Shading

Have you ever thought how magical it is that a drawing can have such a feeling of depth that we forget it's a two-dimensional image? This illusion is created mainly in the shading phase, which is the next step after sketching. Shading establishes the general values of light and shadow that give volume to a drawing.

Although this chapter examines shading in isolation, the general values of light and shadow you create at this stage of the drawing process will be affected later in the blending and texture steps. So fear not, dear reader; these first few layers can be adjusted later. The better the quality of the shading you do now, however, the easier the process as a whole will become. After all, the goal of blending and adding textures is not to correct shading mistakes, but to make your drawing even more realistic.

In this chapter, I will demonstrate how to shade with graphite pencils, as these give you better control over the process. You can also add shading using a brush filled with graphite or charcoal powder, but these materials require greater dexterity and experience, and they can frustrate beginning artists.

Before you draw a stroke, I will show you how to optimize your pencil for both soft shading and firm lines, and then we'll discuss how to better perceive light and shadow values, as well as how a scale of values can help. Finally, we'll wrap up the chapter with some practical shading exercises.

Use a chisel point

As you've learned, the way you hold your pencil is important (Chapter 3), but the way you *sharpen* your pencil determines the quality of your stroke even more. To give yourself more flexibility and control, sharpen your pencil into a chisel point (Figure 4.1). The chisel point consists of a flat, angled plane, with which you can draw soft, broad strokes, and a sharp edge perfect for strong, well-defined strokes (Figure 4.2). The flat plane also provides more homogeneous coverage when shading, which you'll find useful for realistic drawings, while the sharp edge will help you create drawings using firmer, well-defined lines, which give a charming and more stylized finish.

To create a chisel point, first sharpen your pencil with a hand or crank sharpener, then tilt the pencil to about 45-degrees and lightly scrub the tip on a piece of fine sandpaper to flatten it. If you don't have sandpaper, you can scrub the pencil tip on scrap paper.

You can shape chisel points on pencils of any type or hardness. The softer the graphite, the faster the tip will wear out and need refreshing, however. Mechanical pencils with their thin lead are challenging, but you can create a mini chisel point, enough so that you can tilt it a little when drawing. Charcoal pencils can be more difficult to work with

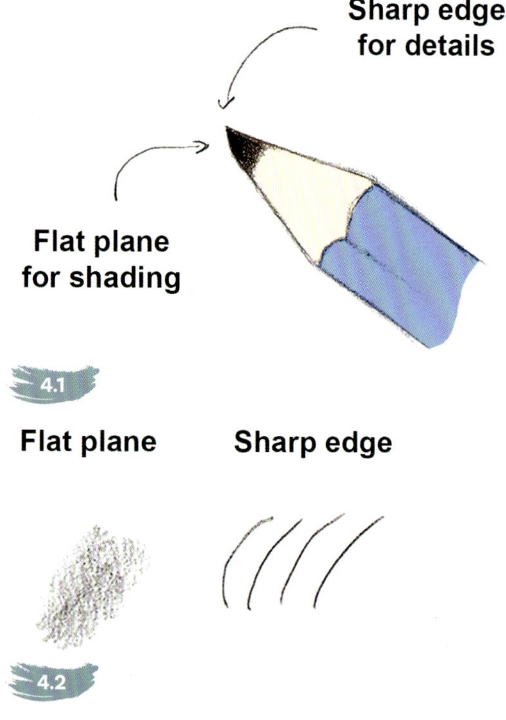

because their tips tend to be more fragile, breaking more frequently—one of the many reasons I use graphite more than charcoal. When I want shades closer to black, carbon pencils are an excellent choice; they are firmer, which makes shaping their tip easier too.

Speaking of values closer to black, let's now address the issue of shading light and shadow values rather than simply drawing lines.

Learn to see values

The line, like the point, does not exist in nature.

This statement may sound reckless and spark endless debate but think for a moment about trying to draw an object from life. You probably first draw a contour line to mark its limits in relation to the space around it. This line, however, is an abstraction, a trick used to represent that object from the position you observe it. If you rotate the object and look at it from another angle, the contour line that you "saw" before will no longer be there.

To achieve a greater level of realism, you need to learn to see things as they are, to see their values of light and shadow, and then use shading to illustrate what you actually see rather than drawing the abstractions, the lines, that your mind creates. As proof, go back to Chapter 1 and compare my drawings through the years. Figures 1.2 and 1.3 rely on contour lines, which make the subjects look cartoonish. In Figures 1.7, 1.8, and 1.9, the realistic-looking subjects stand out in relation to the background due to the differences of light and shadow values I used. Figures 1.4 and 1.5 represent my transition years, when I was gradually improving my perception of values and shading.

The more time you spend observing images and trying to reproduce their values on paper, the more your perception skills will improve. To help, you can create a scale of values to measure the gray tones of your reference images and thus be able to reproduce them more accurately.

For printed references, you can make a gray scale with your graphite pencils. For example, Figure 4.3 shows the scale I made using Staedtler Mars Lumograph pencils, ranging from HB to 8B, as well as some pencils from Staedtler's Black series. (My scale doesn't include all pencils of these series simply because I don't own them.) Notice I put two tones for each pencil, one very strong and the other lighter. Although this disrupts the light-to-dark gradient somewhat, it better helps me decide which pencil to choose by illustrating the different ways I can use them.

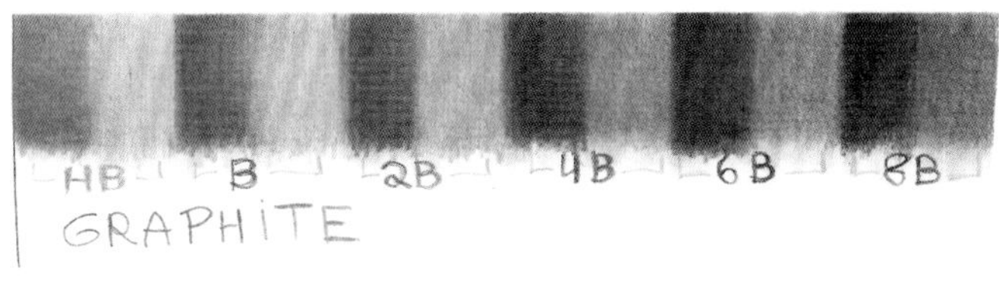

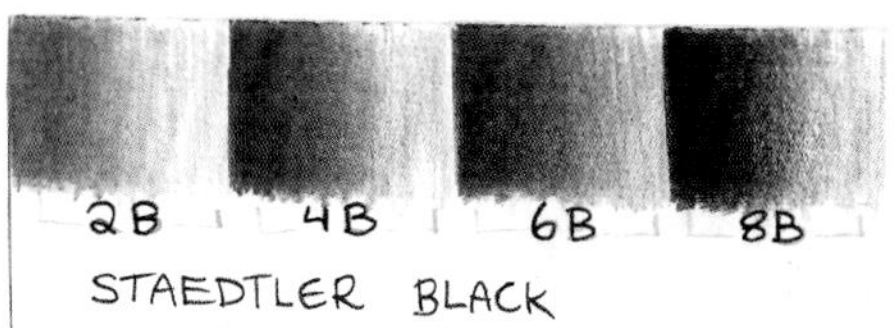

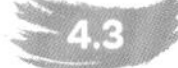

I included the carbon pencils because even the darkest graphite is a shade of gray that is still far from black, which limits the range of values possible. Being able to work with a wider range of values allows you to create drawings with more contrast, which gives the drawing a greater degree of depth. Charcoal enables you to reach even darker tones, practically blacks, which makes it an excellent option too, if you know how to handle them.

Compare the portraits in **Figure 4.4**. I did the portrait of Tom Hanks (left) entirely with graphite pencils; for Joaquin Phoenix (right), I also used dark carbon pencils. The difference between the darker tones of the two drawings is clear.

To use the scale, position it on the reference image in the area you want to check, and then compare which shade comes closest to the gray you see in the photo. It may seem counterintuitive, but choose a pencil a little lighter than the one whose shade matches the one in the photo. For example, if you think a certain area should be done using a 4B pencil, start with a 3B or 2B. As you cover the drawing with graphite, it will get darker. If your coverage is lighter than it should be, just switch to a darker pencil. On the other hand, if you use a pencil darker than you should, the only way to go back is to use the eraser to remove that graphite, which will mess up your drawing and take more time to fix. In the case of **Figure 4.5**, for example, I would pick my 4B pencil to shade that background. It's common to overlap different pencil grades in a given area, but the scale will help you get an idea of which pencil to start with.

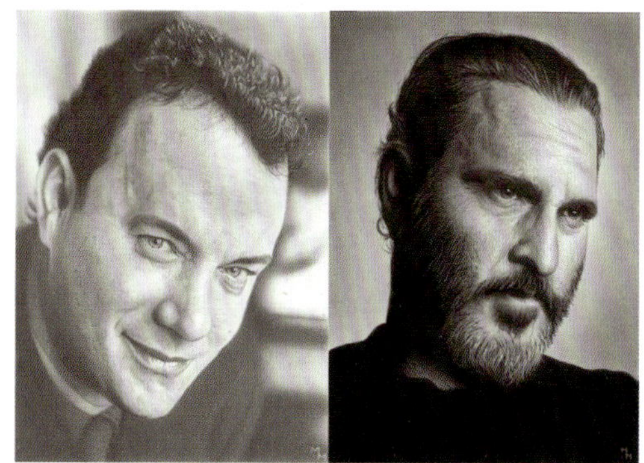

4.4

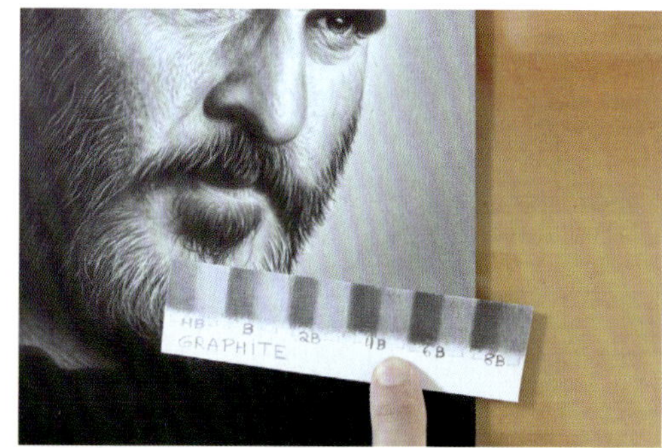

4.5

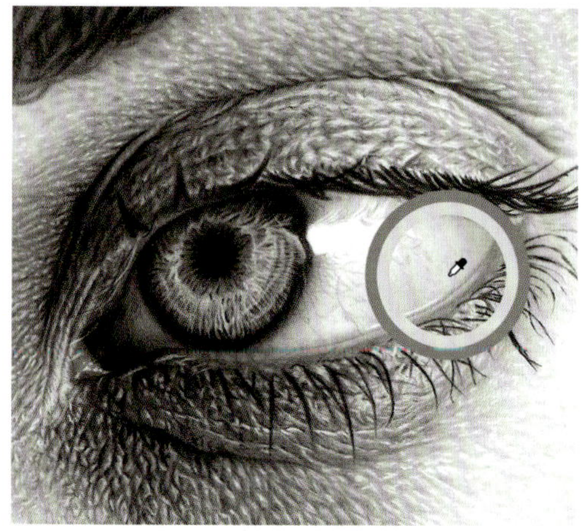

4.6 Analyzing the white of the eye reveals that it is not exactly white! The inner ring around the eyedropper shows the selected color.

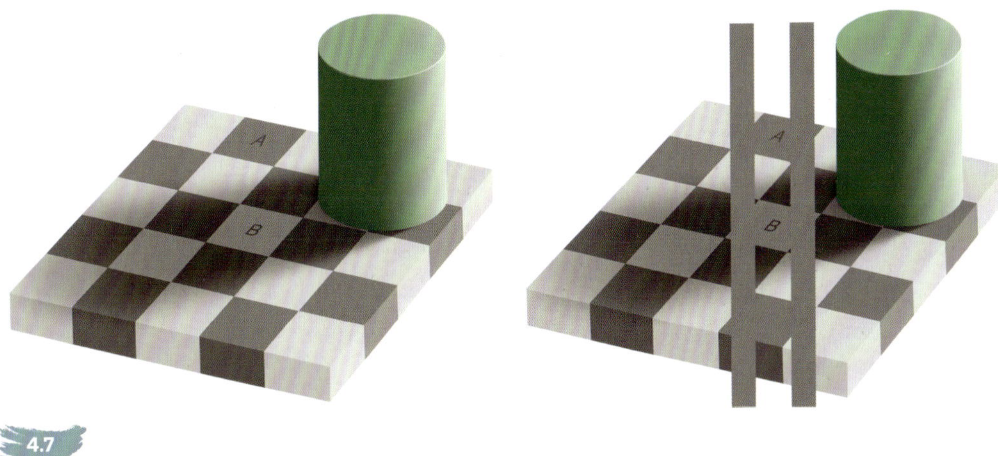

4.7

For digital references, most image-editing apps have a tool, usually identified by an eyedropper, to select the color of a given area (**Figure 4.6**). You could use your handmade graphite scale over your device's screen, but this will be of no use if you change the brightness of the screen between one check and another. As the process of making a realistic drawing can last hours or even days, you're better off using your app's tools.

No matter which scale or tool you use and how much you practice, remember, as humans we all have inherent limitations in our perception. Our eyes can be tricked by optical illusions because of the way we perceive contrast, shadows, and light. **Figure 4.7** shows a prime example of an optical illusion relating to the perception of light and shadow: the Checker Shadow Illusion, published in 1995 by Edward H. Adelson, a professor of vision science at MIT. At first glance, the image on the left looks like a checkerboard of light and dark squares with an object partially casting a shadow on it. Look closer. On the left, square A appears to be darker than B. On the right, however, the bars connecting both squares prove their tone is the same! This is an exceptional case, but it illustrates that, yes, our perception can be deceived.

Shading exercises

Now, let's get our hands dirty and do some shading exercises! Although quite simple, these exercises are of fundamental importance. If you are not able to control the fluidity of your strokes, you will have trouble with any drawing you make. On the other hand, if you master the shading techniques, your drawings will have a noticeable leap in quality. Practice these exercises not just once, but repeatedly until you feel satisfied with the results. For these and the remainder of the book's exercises, I recommend that you use paper suitable for realistic drawings: smooth and weighing at least 67 lbs/180 g/m^2. (Refer back to Chapter 2 if you need more advice on the materials.)

Stroke strength

Let's start with drawing light strokes with a pencil. Compare the lines made in Figure 4.8. The strokes on the left are strong strokes, the kind you don't normally want when drawing. The strokes on the right are light and your goal when shading. Your light strokes should be firm, short, and quick; do not touch and drag the tip of the pencil across the paper as if you were writing. If you do, you will get the result on the left.

To get the feel of what it's like to do lighter strokes, you can start doing strong strokes and gradually reduce the force applied, as in Figure 4.9. I've included some lines made with a blue ballpoint pen to show how you can get a lighter line even when drawing with a pen.

Small gradients

Now try creating gradients. Start small (I make them 2 x 2 cm) and use only a 2B pencil for the first gradient. The goal is to make a slight transition from dark to light. For each step, the arrow on the left of its corresponding figure indicates the direction of the strokes.

To begin, make light horizontal strokes from left to right along the entire left side of the frame (Figure 4.10). Each line should start out light and end even lighter, until it disappears.

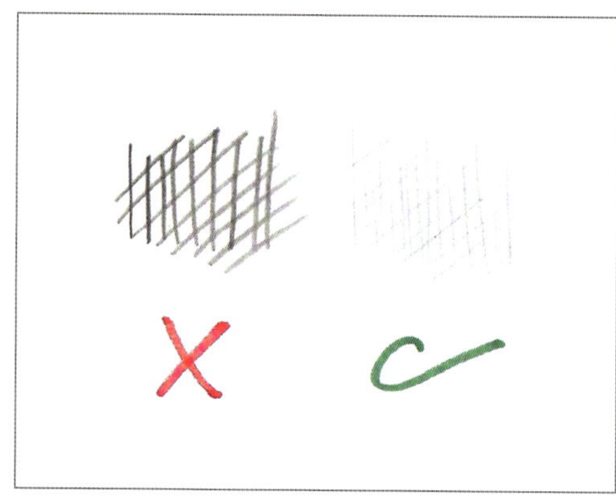

4.8

4.9

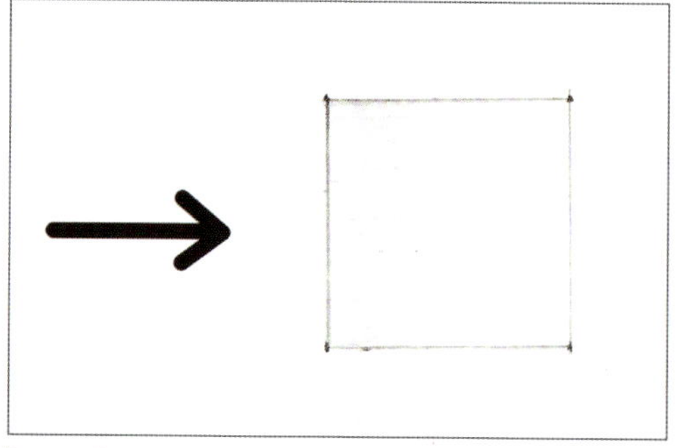

4.10

Add another set of strokes in an upwards diagonal direction using the same decreasing pressure from left to right (Figure 4.11). Repeat the procedure, now on the downward diagonal (Figure 4.12).

Finally, add vertical strokes, from one side to the other, trying to maintain the homogeneity of the coverage and making increasingly lighter strokes as you move to the right (Figure 4.13). I prefer to do the strokes from bottom to top, but you can do them in the opposite direction if you find it more comfortable. Practice both, because sometimes one direction will work better depending on the area you're shading. Crossing the lines is a way to make the coverage more even and is a common technique in realistic drawings.

Good work! You just completed the first layer of our gradient. Now repeat the process, gradually increasing the pressure on your hand to create more consistent and strong strokes on the left corner of the gradient. The goal is to adjust what was done in the first layer, filling in the gaps left by the pencil and achieving the desired effect. Thus, you want shorter and more concentrated strokes on the left side of the square, pushing the darkest values.

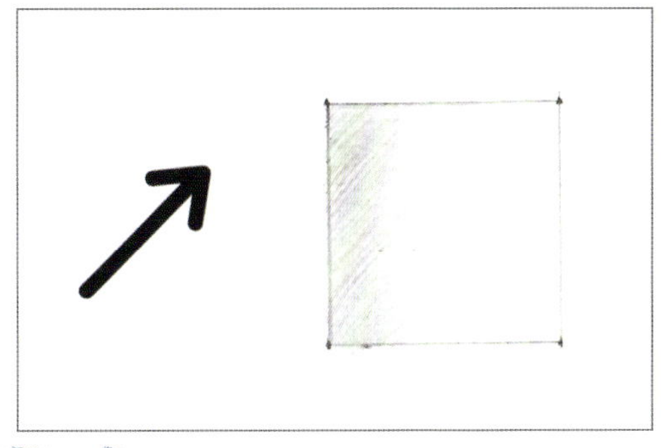

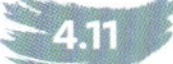

4.11

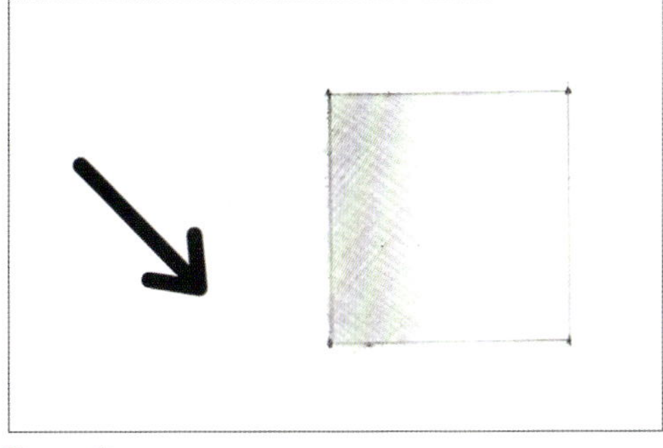

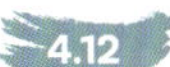

4.12

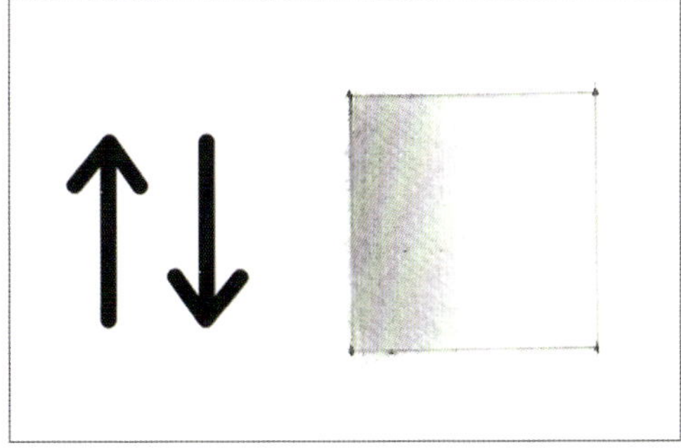

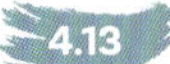

4.13

Figure 4.14 shows what my gradient looks like. Continue making other gradients like this, but change pencils and the direction of the gradient, as suggested in Figure 4.15. Rotate the paper if that helps you feel more comfortable. As you gain more confidence, try a circular gradient: Make the lines from the outside to the inside, crossing the lines and decreasing their intensity as you get near the center of the gradient. Figures 4.16 to 4.23 illustrate the stages of this gradient. I used a 4B pencil for this example.

Repeating the exercise while varying the direction of the gradient and changing pencils will help you to better understand the tools you have and practice moving your hand in different directions.

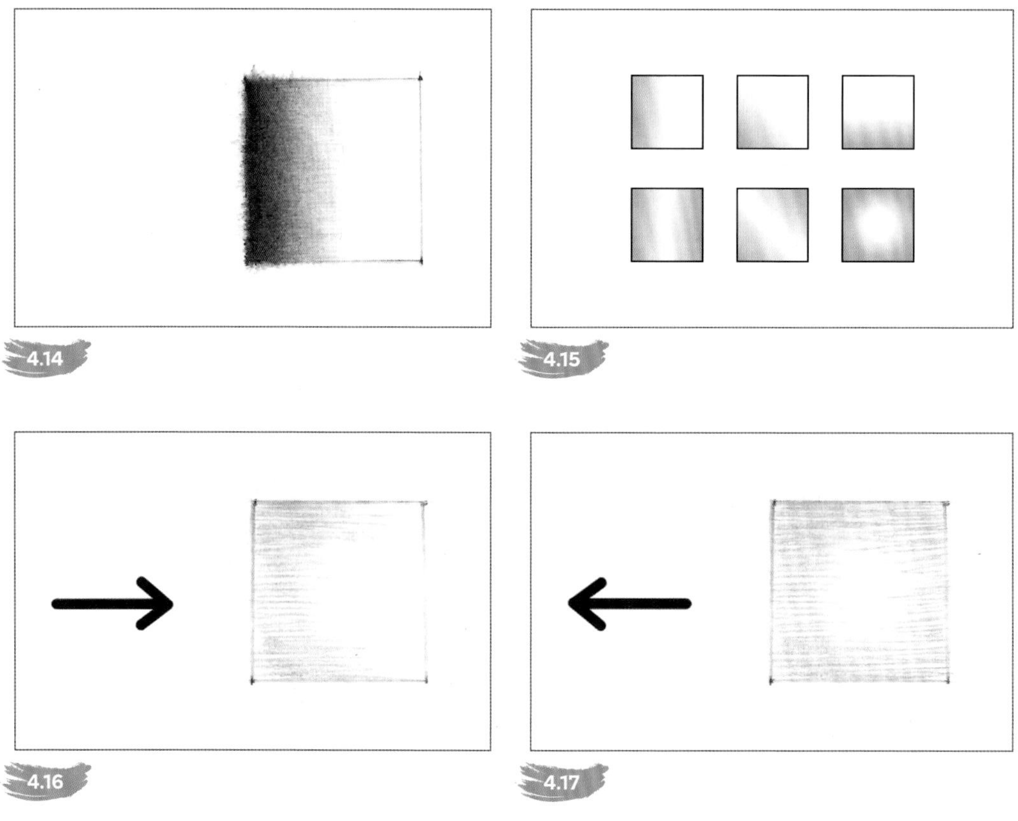

4.14

4.15

4.16

4.17

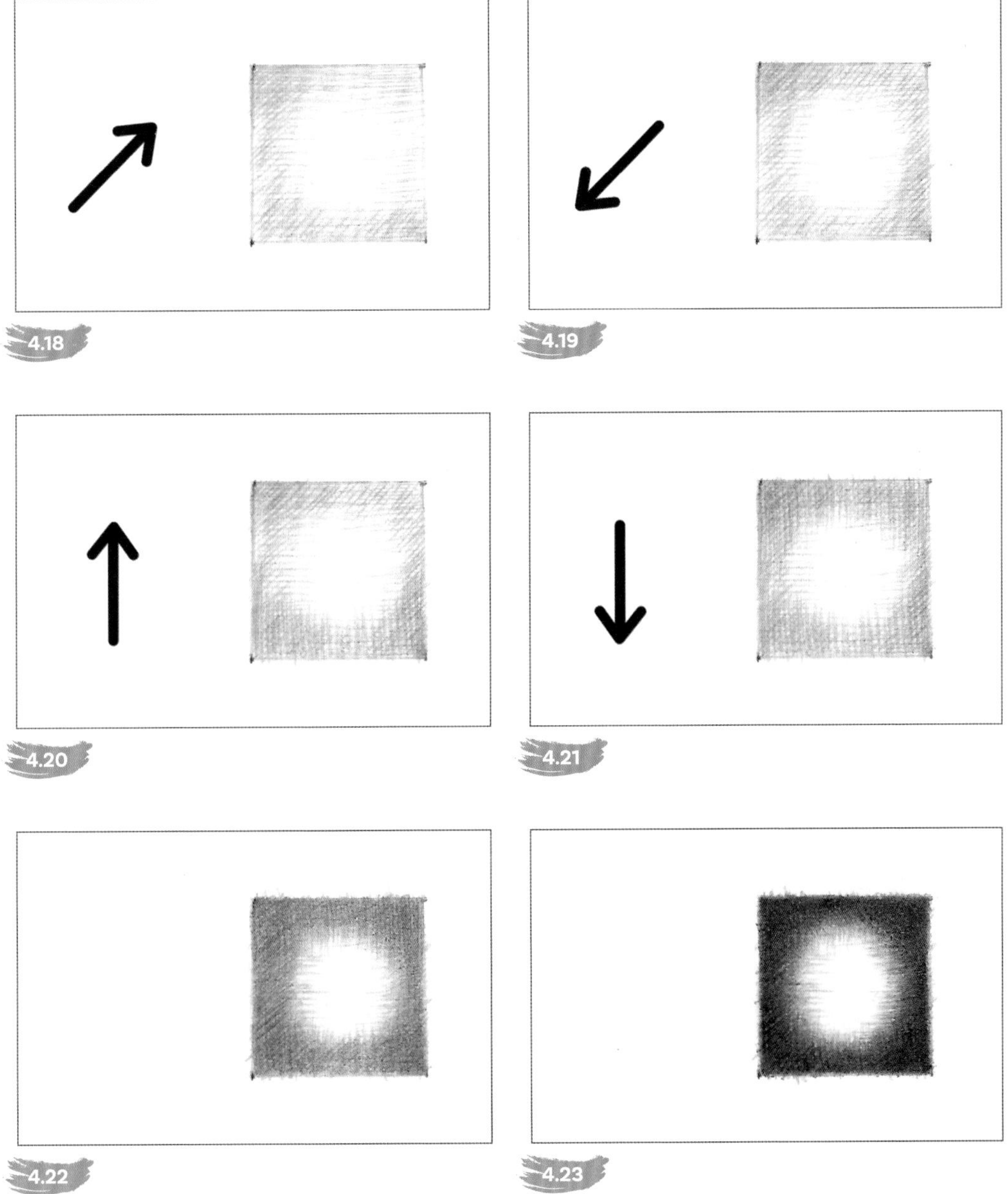

4.18

4.19

4.20

4.21

4.22

4.23

Large gradient

Let's expand what you just learned into a larger gradient that will take you more time and require more patience and control using the pencil. To begin, draw a rectangle in the proportion of 4:1. I suggest 8 x 2 cm. Divide the rectangle into four equal parts along its length; that is, mark outside the long edge with a pencil every 2 cm. Now you have four squares of 2 x 2 cm inside the rectangle (Figure 4.24). Once again, you will create the gradient using just one pencil (I chose a B).

Start shading with light horizontal lines, always going from left to right. Make the strokes advance beyond the first mark outside the rectangle and finish them lightly, as seen in Figure 4.25. This will be the darkest area of the gradient, so you don't need to keep the pressure light, but don't exaggerate your stroke's force either. You will later add other layers to darken the region more.

Cross the lines as you did in the small gradients; that is, fill in with diagonal and vertical strokes to create a homogeneous coverage (Figure 4.26). As you can see, the coverage is no longer so light, reaching an intermediate shade of gray.

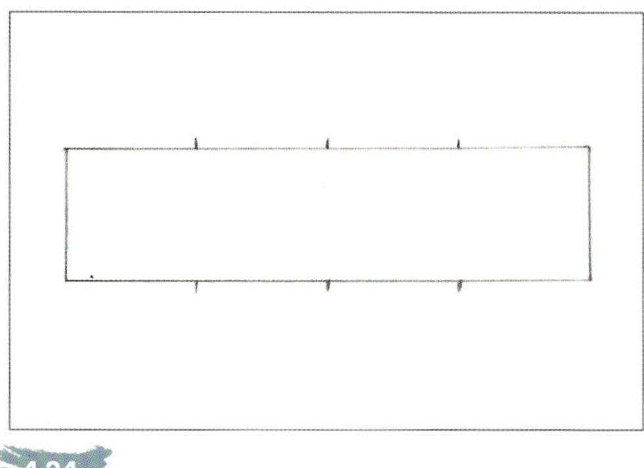

4.24

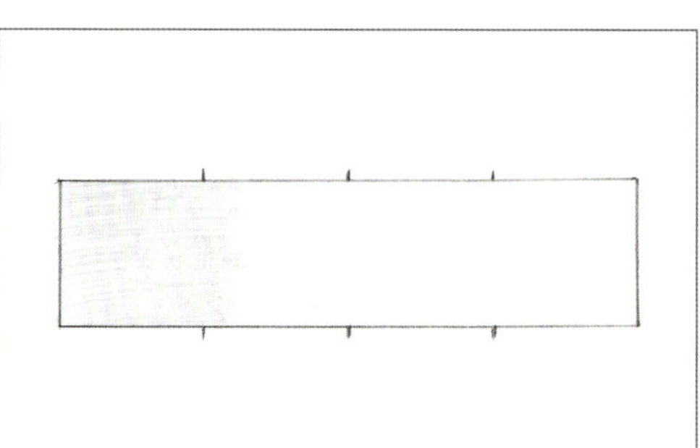

4.25

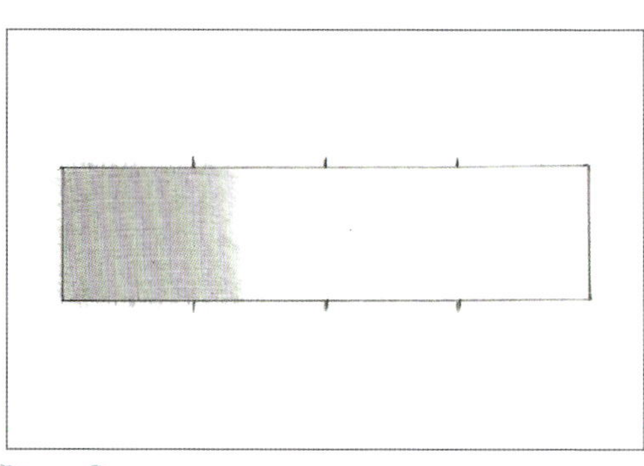

4.26

Move on to the other areas, repeating what you did in the first square but in a lighter way to achieve a lighter shade of gray. From left to right, the second square should be lighter than the first one, and the third should be lighter than the second. Leave the last, right-most square blank for now (Figure 4.27).

At this stage, you can adjust the tones so that they are more balanced by adding new layers of graphite (Figure 4.28). The act of overlapping layers until you reach the value you want is called *layering*. As the first square is the darkest of all, repeat the coverage in here, applying more and more pressure on the pencil until the square is saturated. Keep going until the paper no longer supports new layers of graphite on this area. When you get one part of the drawing super dark, you may feel the need to darken the rest to keep the balance.

Now that the values are better established, you can more easily focus on improving the transitions between them. Figure 4.29 shows the result of this exercise after pushing the darkest values more and balancing them again, moving from left to right. Try this exercise with other pencils. The more large gradients you practice, the better your technique will become.

Although this exercise is simple, it's not necessarily easy. The secret is to be patient. Take some breaks to calmly observe the gradient and notice where to adjust. Your first attempts may not yield what you were expecting, nor do you need to do it with absolute perfection to move on to the other exercises, but it is interesting to return to it from time to time to practice how to control your hand and hone your ability to perceive the various shades of gray graphite produces.

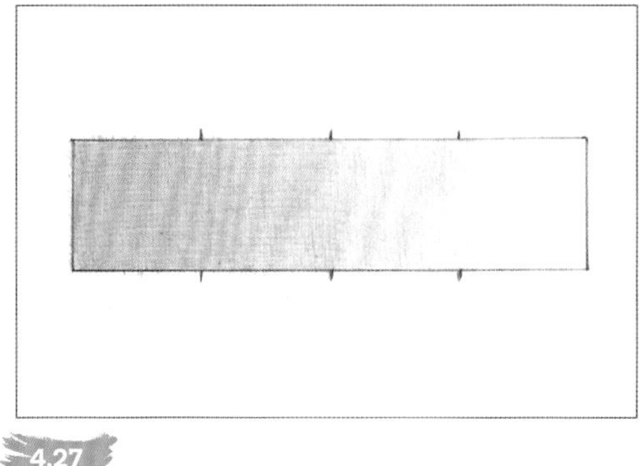

4.27

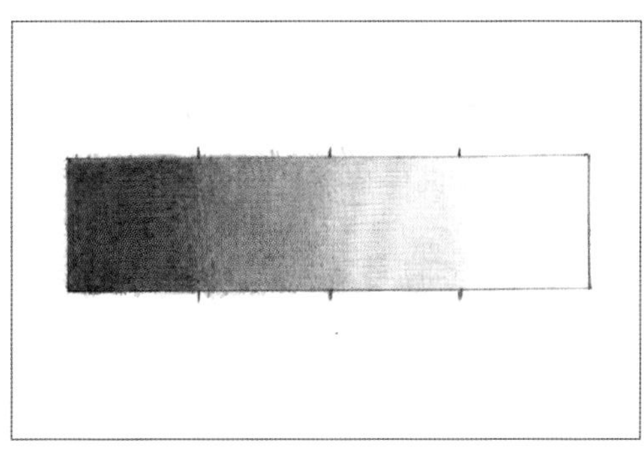

4.28

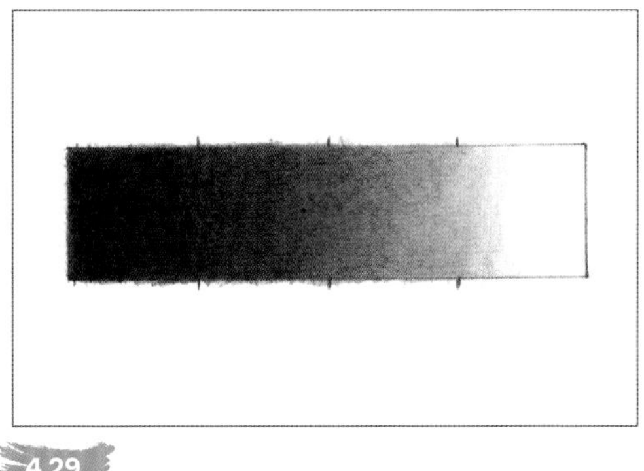

4.29

Sphere

Now let's try something that is closer to a real situation: a sphere, which is a classic study of light and shadow. Your challenge is to apply the gradient techniques to drawing a three-dimensional object. In this exercise you'll learn about how light and shadow help you create the illusion of volume in two dimensions. Before you begin, take a long look at Figure 4.30. It illustrates the sphere you'll be drawing, as well as some terms that I will use in my instructions.

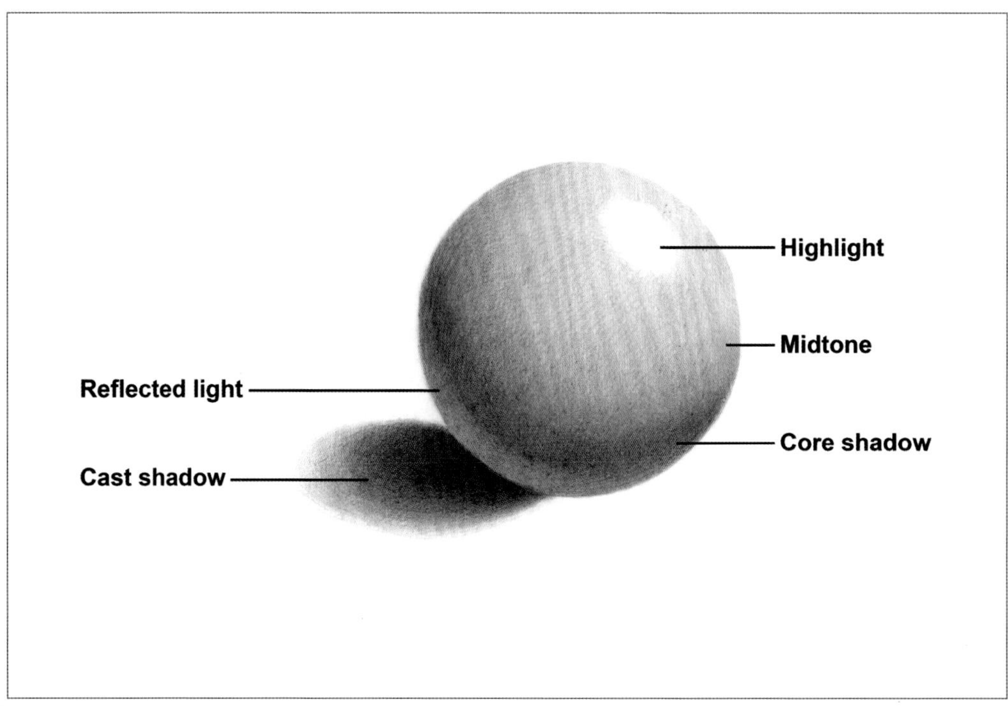

4.30

First, you need to draw a perfect circle—a difficult task for humans. If you find it easier, trace around a roll of masking tape, the rim of a glass, or any other perfectly circular object to sketch the outline of your sphere. I used a roll of masking tape with a diameter of 7.5 cm (Figure 4.31).

Once the sketch is done, start shading using a B pencil. Use the same method as you followed for the gradients: shading by stroking crossing lines. Remember to change the direction of the strokes every 45 degrees with the goal of achieving a homogeneous coverage. This time, however, leave an empty space for the highlight on the top right corner of the sphere. As shown in Figure 4.32, reinforce the core shadow using a 2B pencil, as shading only with the B could make the sketch lines disappear in that area.

Now that you've done some sort of zoning of the light and shadow areas, continue adding new layers of graphite, especially to the coverage with the B pencil. On the core shadow area, add more layers using a 2B and darken it to the area that is below this shadow ring (Figure 4.33). This area is a little less dark than the color shadow because there is a light that reflects from the surface where the sphere rests, creating this subtle effect. (Check back to Figure 4.30 to better identify the reflected light, if you need to.)

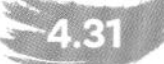

4.31

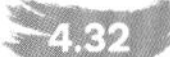

4.32

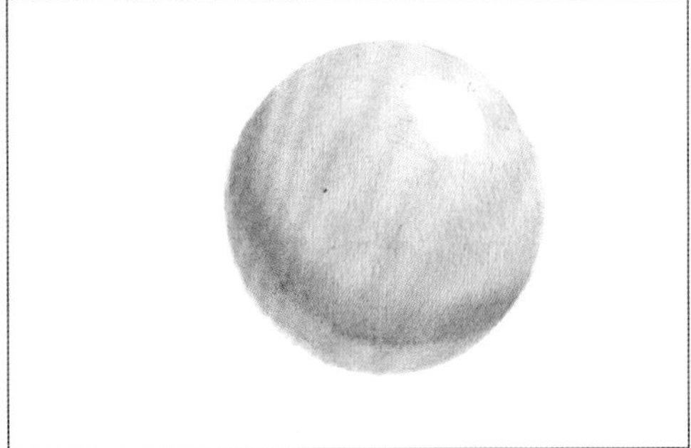

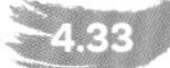

4.33

Continue deepening the coverage you did with the B pencil. To push the core shadow, use a 4B pencil, which gives a more intense contrast, leaving the drawing more vivid and with a greater sensation of volume. Now that the core shadow is darker, work on the transition of this darker shadow to the adjacent areas, both above and below the ring, using pencils B and 2B. As shown in Figure 4.34, you can also make a base layer for the shadow cast on the ground.

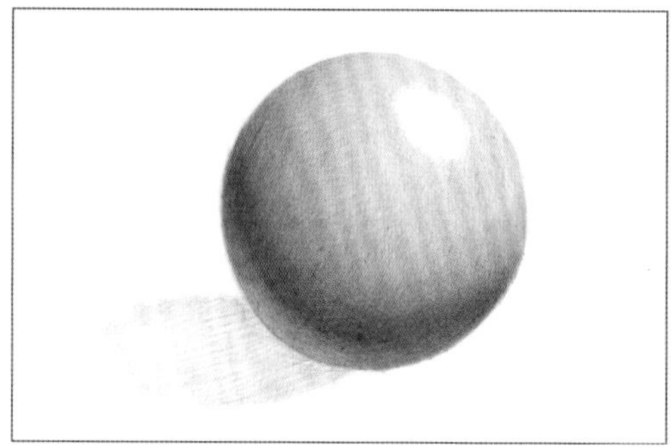

4.34

Now, it's a matter of making some adjustments to the sphere and darkening the cast shadow (Figure 4.35). Using the 4B pencil, don't just fill in the area of the cast shadow— make a kind of gradient, darkening the tones near the sphere and decreasing its intensity as the cast shadow moves away from it. It is very important that this area does not have a sharp outline, as this makes all the difference in the level of realism possible.

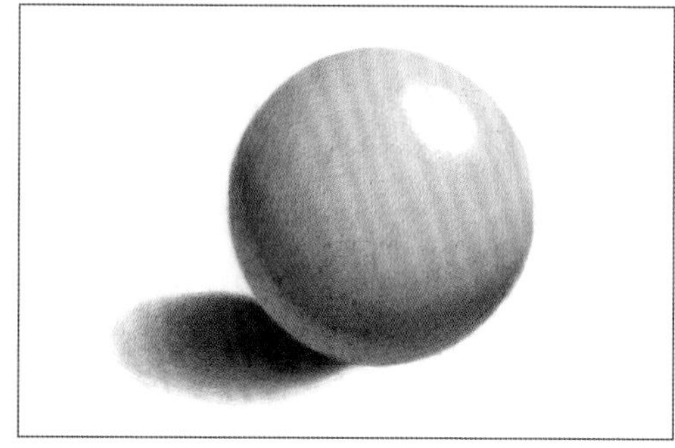

4.35

And thus, we finished the sphere! Although it's a little more laborious than the gradients, I hope you didn't find it too hard. The key is to vary the tones to suggest the curvature of the sphere.

Covering a sphere this way, even a small one, does take some time, partially because you are not using any blending. As you'll see in the next chapter, blending methods tend to speed up the process, making it easier to obtain smooth transitions and a homogeneous look. Not only is blending graphite and charcoal one of the most interesting stages of realistic drawing, the techniques you'll learn next will make a huge difference in your drawings. Trust me, dear reader, they are really game-changing.

Practice your shading before you move on, though. Good shading makes good blending!

5

Blending

In monochromatic drawing, blending is a technique used to soften lines and fill in areas in a blurred way, without sharpness, to create *stains* of tone instead of lines. Blending is an essential technique for realistic drawings, because it tends to hide the strokes left by the pencil, unlike shading. **Figure 5.1** compares a stain made with a pencil only (left) and one made by blending the graphite with tissue (right). I used the same 4B pencil for both, but the effect is very different!

The blending techniques you will learn in this chapter build on and enhance the volumetric shading effects you learned to create in Chapter 4. Specifically, you will learn about various tools and methods to blend graphite and charcoal. These techniques are not mutually exclusive, either. In my work, I frequently combine all of them in the same part of a drawing. You'll have a chance to practice yourself in the chapter's exercise of drawing a water drop.

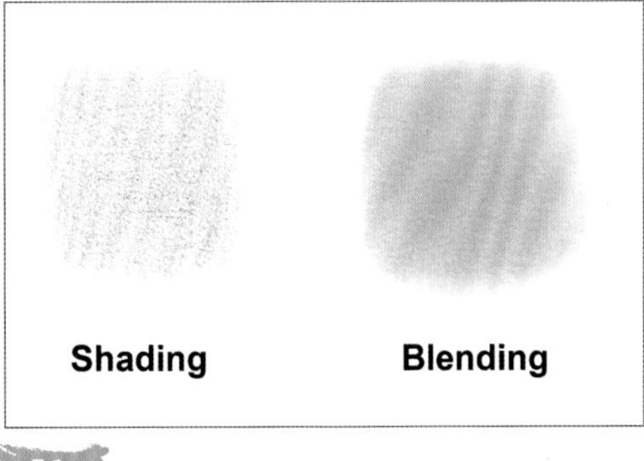

5.1

Graphite, carbon pencil, or charcoal?

For blending, graphite, carbon pencils, and charcoal each has distinct advantages and drawbacks.

- **Graphite.** Although it's also available in bar and powder form, I use graphite most often in pencil form, because it gives me a lot of control over the process. Such control is desirable especially for areas that are not very large, as often found in A4- or A3-size drawings, for example. A limitation of graphite is that it always retains a gray tone, which makes obtaining values close to black impossible and reduces the range of values with which you can work. Another drawback is that it shines, depending on the angle from which you observe it. If you haven't noticed this phenomenon yet, take your shading practice results from Chapter 4, position yourself close to a light source, and observe them from different angles.

- **Charcoal.** Charcoal, which is available in compressed bars and powder form, blends out much more easily and can produce deep blacks. On the other hand, it is difficult to control and can end up causing a mess on hands, surfaces, and other inconvenient places as you work.

- **Carbon pencil.** Combining the best characteristics of both, carbon pencils offer the practicality and control of graphite pencils and the capacity to achieve the darker values of charcoal. The tradeoffs are that the strokes of these pencils do not blend as easily as graphite or charcoal due to the binder used in their composition, plus they reflect light like graphite, albeit to a lesser extent. A matte setting spray can minimize the shine (Chapter 2).

Figure 5.2 compares the results of a graphite pencil, carbon pencil, and charcoal bar on the page. Notice how opaque the charcoal is and the slight shine of the other two. Graphite and carbon pencils are my favorite materials for making monochromatic drawings. Although they do not reach values as dark as charcoal, carbon pencils are still very dark and can be combined easily with graphite pencils to extend their tonal range and deepen blends.

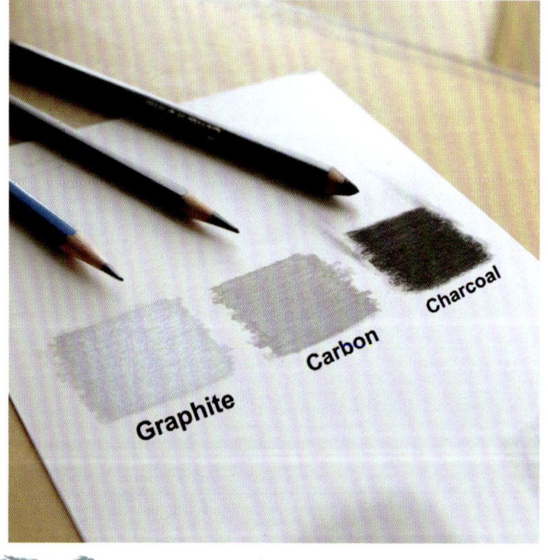

Blending tools and methods

As I mentioned in Chapter 2, you can use a variety of tools to blend graphite and carbon. Let's delve a bit deeper now and examine the different effects the various tools produce, as well as the situations when they're most useful. For easier comparison of the results, I will use the same pencils for all the examples: Staedtler Mars Lumograph B and 2B Black.

Conspicuous by their absence among the blending tools are the fingers. Why? Because you shouldn't use them. In addition to being less precise, your fingers deposit oils from your hand on a drawing, producing unwanted stains. Marks from your fingerprints may also remain—not what you want in a realistic drawing. Besides, a variety of tools can do the same task more accurately and at low cost, so use them instead.

Cotton

Although I don't use cotton for blending very often, it can be useful, and its effect is very soft compared to other blending tools. Cotton balls, for example, are great for covering large areas in really big drawings. Their disadvantage is their low level of precision. Shading over a specific area without messing up its surroundings can be difficult.

To gain a little more control for working on smaller areas, you can wrap the cotton around a thin object, like a blending stump, or use a cotton swab. From time to time I use cotton swabs to apply graphite or charcoal powder to the drawing, but I don't use them much for blending pencil strokes.

Homogeneity is not cotton's strong point, because it usually leaves a characteristic mark behind. Depending on the effect you want to create, you could use this to your advantage. If you want to create spots with some irregularity, such as for aged skin or an object with a rougher texture, a cotton swab would work particularly well.

In Figure 5.3, observe the effects created with a B graphite pencil and 2B Black, either by rubbing a cotton swab over strokes done on the paper or by applying powder directly to the surface (simply rub your pencil on sandpaper to create powder). I suggest you experiment with your materials to understand how they work with cotton.

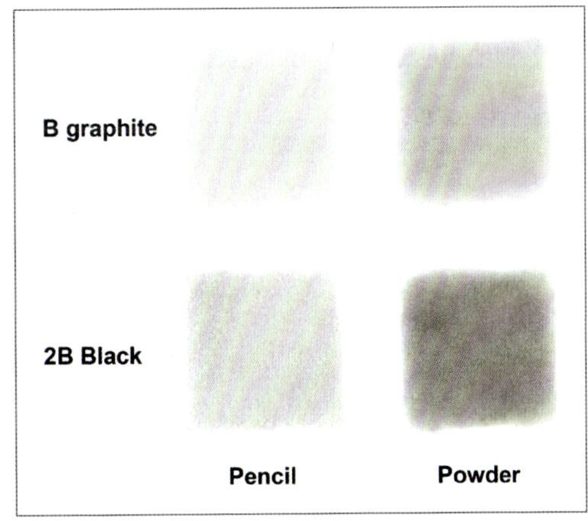

5.3

Tissue

The humble hero of realistic drawing, tissue is one of my favorite blending tools. It can create a smooth and homogeneous effect like no other, plus it's cheap and plentiful. I especially like to use it for blending the base layers of a drawing.

Some people use tissue wrapped around their finger, but I prefer a folded trapezoid. I start with a piece of toilet paper (**Figure 5.4** A), which is practically square, and then fold it into triangles successively (B, C, and D). Finally, I fold one of the ends (E) where I place my index finger, and I place my thumb underneath (F). This sequence of folds helps to firm the paper and gives it a greater degree of precision. Still, it is not the best tool for small details; I find it more useful for blending graphite over larger areas.

I use tissue primarily to blend the graphite pencil strokes done beforehand. For example, I would use it to blend Chapter 4's sphere between each of the steps (Figures 4.32 to 4.35). You can use tissue to directly apply powder also, but I don't. **Figure 5.5** shows the results of blending with tissue.

Blending stump

A blending stump is a cylindrical drawing tool, typically made of soft paper that is tightly wound into a stick and sanded to a point at both ends (**Figure 5.6**). Although it is possible to make your own stump, I don't recommend it. You can easily find a range of sizes at art supply stores for affordable prices.

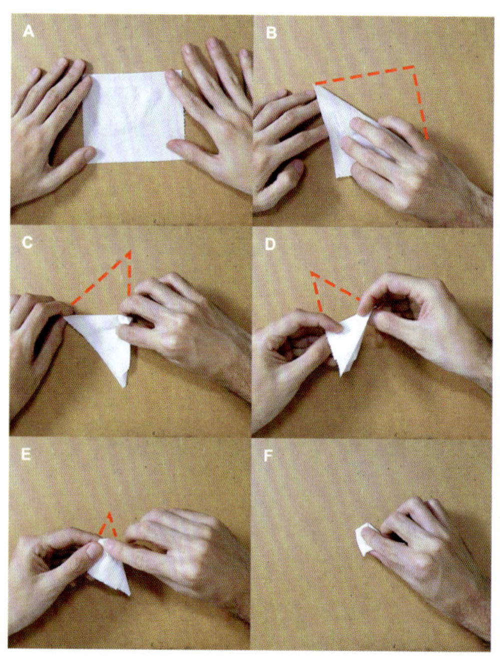

5.4

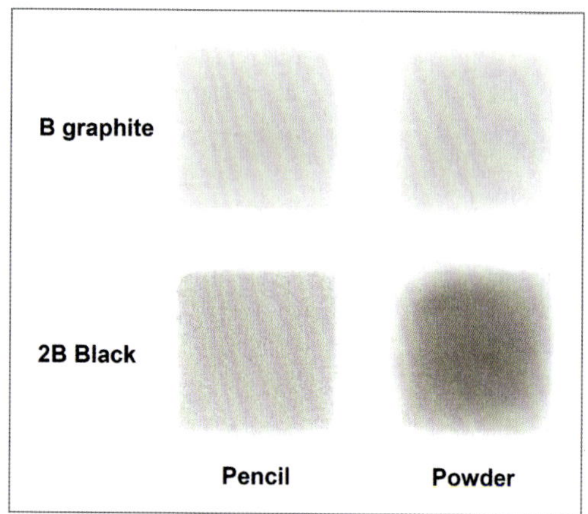

5.5

Stumps can blend lines very smoothly, and their sharp points make them well suited to working at levels of greater detail. If you need to produce smooth and homogeneous effects in large areas, however, blending stumps will require greater skill (for these situations I prefer tissue). **Figure 5.7** shows the results of blending with stumps.

A caveat to using blending stumps is that they must be clean to be most effective. Dirt, whether graphite or charcoal, accumulates on the tip of a blending stump while you use it and can be transferred to the drawing unintentionally. Be aware of the buildup and sand it off occasionally. Because stumps have two ends, I reserve one for graphite and the other for charcoal to avoid cross contamination.

Brush

Brushes are some of my favorite blending tools. A collection of brushes in various sizes and shapes gives you immense versatility: You can easily blend large areas, small details, soft looks, and intense effects. Not to mention that brushes are equally useful for softening pencil strokes and applying powder directly to a drawing.

My kit contains round brushes, flat brushes, and brushes with cat's tongue tips. I prefer pony hair bristles because they're soft and flexible. The brush sizes you need depends on the size of the drawings you intend to make; most of mine are small. To start, I recommend a size 4 (small) and 12 (larger) brush for each type of tip. You don't need to

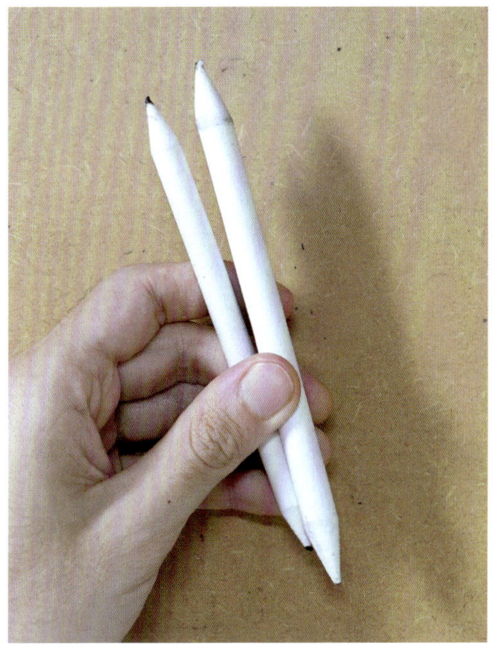

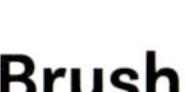
5.6

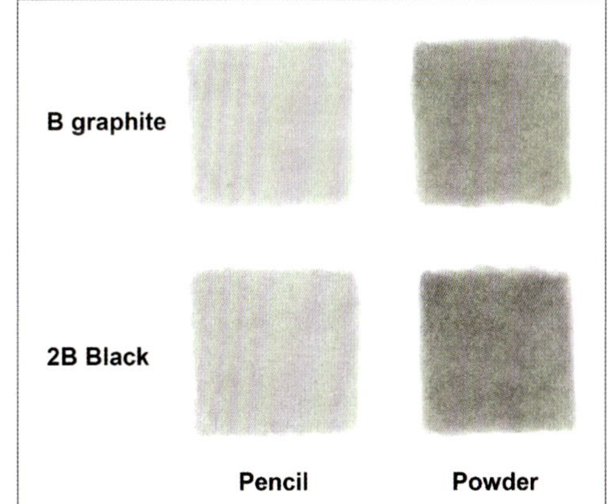

5.7

buy a lot of brushes right away—good ones can be expensive. Start with flat brushes, then try out some other options and little by little acquire the styles and sizes that work best for you.

When should you use each type? Let's look at cat's tongue brushes first (Figure 5.8). These flat brushes with a curved end are very good for creating very smooth effects, with an above-average level of delicacy. They create a subtle effect you can use to cover areas where a light gray tone is desired. Using a cat's tongue brush over pencil strokes will keep the strokes visible while blending some of the graphite, which is very useful for texture work. Their

lightness is also great for applying the graphite in powder form.

I prefer my common flat brushes to have firm bristles, so I cut their bristles in half with scissors. Compare the original (left) and trimmed (right) brushes in Figure 5.9. The firmer bristles help the graphite or charcoal powder to better penetrate the pores of the paper, which enables you to achieve darker shades and provide a more homogeneous appearance in a smaller area. As you can see in Figure 5.10, stiffer flat brushes provide a more aggressive effect than a cat's tongue brush, but the results are equally useful for creating textures, as you will see in the next chapter.

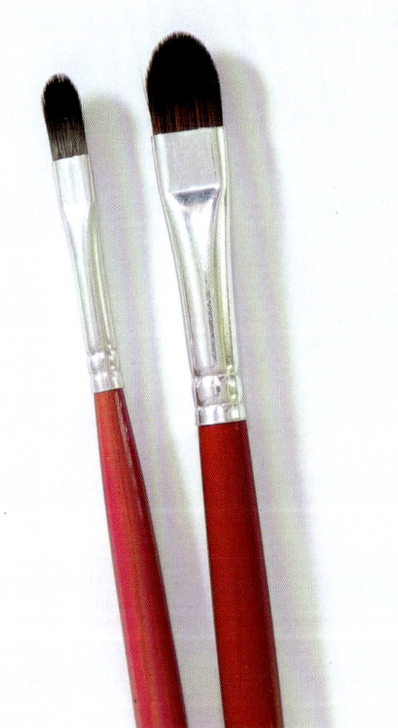

5.8

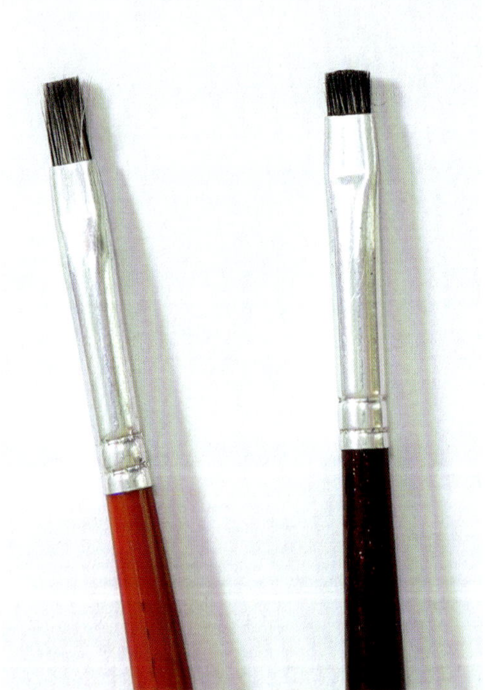

5.9

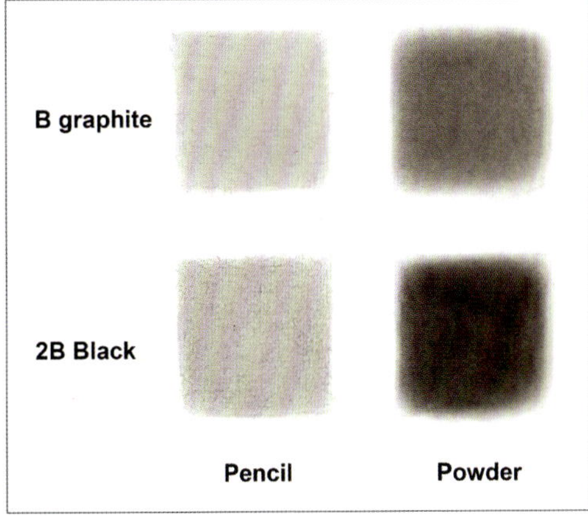

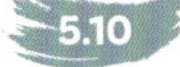

5.10

While optional for beginners, a round brush may eventually be useful. I like to use a round makeup brush with cut bristles to spread powder from a carbon pencil (**Figure 5.11**). The firmer bristles help make carbon pencil powder (and its stubborn binder) a bit easier to spread, while the round shape spreads the powder over a larger area, which would be more difficult with a flat brush.

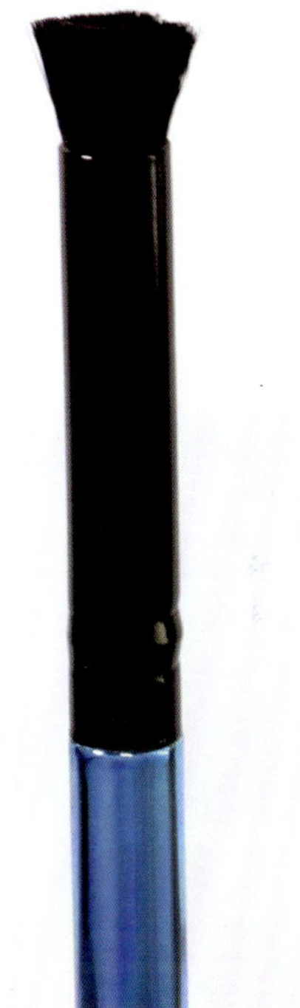

5.11

Water drop exercise

The best way to learn blending techniques is to practice, so collect your B, 2B, and 4B graphite pencils and get ready. In this exercise, you'll draw a water drop, add shading, and then enhance the highlights and shadows through blending. (Skip ahead to Figure 5.18 if you want to preview what you're aiming for.) As well as the pencils and blending tools we've discussed, you will need a thin stick eraser. I recommend a Tombow MONO Zero Eraser with the 2.3 mm round tip.

Begin by very lightly sketching a drop of water in a circular shape with your B pencil. Don't draw it too small, otherwise you will have problems with the light and shadow details. My example drop is about 6 cm, which allowed me to draw more loosely. Be careful that the outline of the drop is not too strong when it is finished. Draw a highlight with the B pencil to delimit the light reflection (**Figure 5.12**), too.

Still with the B pencil, shade the drop, creating the first layer of a gradient from top to bottom, left to right. Next, spread the graphite over the entire drop by rubbing tissue in the same direction, pulling the graphite from top to bottom and left to right until it looks similar to Figure 5.13. Remember I said tissue is a low-precision tool? When you spread graphite this way, it is normal to go a little overboard and "dirty" the outside of the drop. But don't worry, you can use an eraser to clean up the excess graphite later.

Use the stick eraser in the upper-left corner of the darkest side where the light is reflected to keep the highlight light.

TIP: To give you more precision, you can even sharpen the tip of the eraser using a craft knife.

Repeat the steps for the first layer (shade, spread with tissue, clean up the highlight) a few more times to obtain a greater consistency in the coverage. Figure 5.14 shows a new, second layer of shading over the blending, and Figure 5.15 shows the layer after using some blending tissue again.

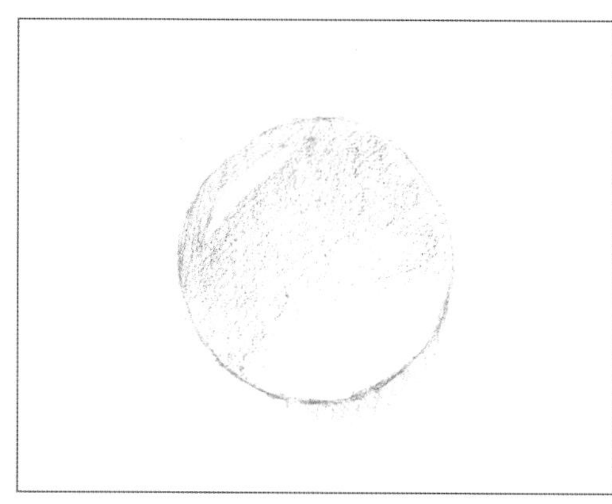

5.12

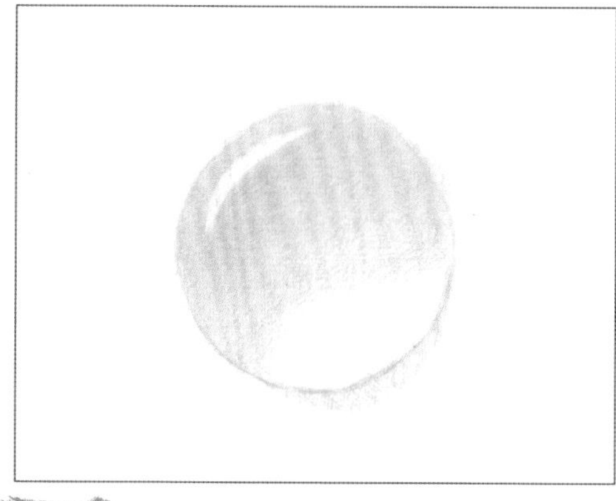

5.13

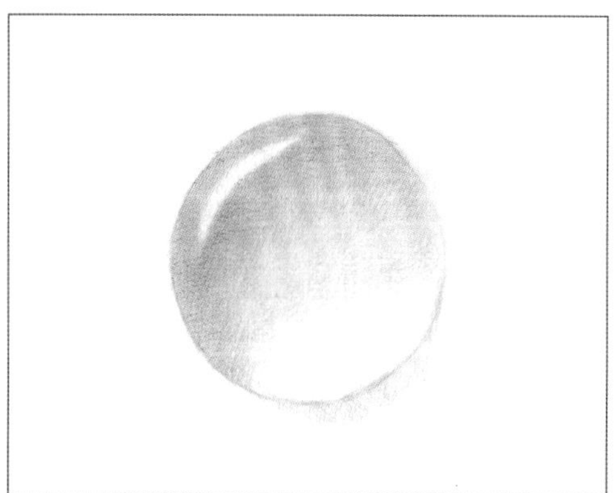

5.14

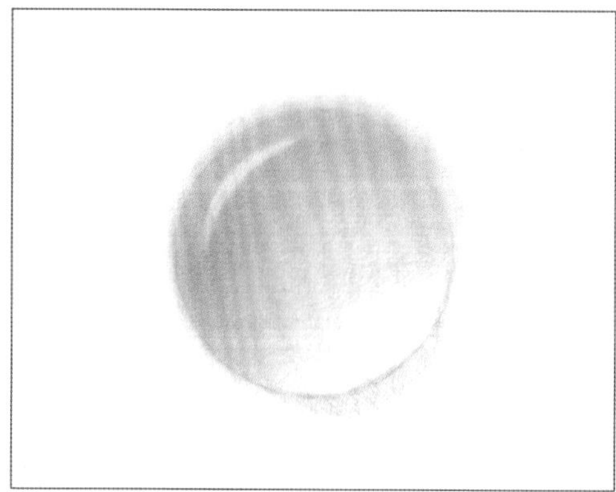

5.15

To create an area of intermediate tone, add the next layer of graphite with a 2B pencil, focusing on shading a smaller area, as you did for Chapter 4's sphere. Next, blend the intermediate tone with tissue (Figure 5.16).

Use a 4B pencil to achieve a darker tone in the drawing. Because this pencil is softer, its strokes look more textured, grainier. To get softness with darker pencils like this, I use the firm-bristle brush on their coverage. The brush is excellent for making the graphite penetrate all the nooks and crannies of the paper (Figure 5.17).

Now it's a matter of deepening and adjusting the tones established by the pencils and using the eraser for the highlight. For example, try using your 2B pencil to intensify the shadow cast beneath the drop and soften it with a blending stump. If it looks grainy, also use the brush.

Much of the graphite will spread outside the drop, but this is not a problem: Just use the eraser there, giving definition to the drop's contour. In these cases, I use an eraser pen, whose tip I shape with a craft knife. Where I need to erase with more precision, I use a Tombow MONO Zero Eraser with a 2.3 mm tip. Figure 5.18 shows my finished water drop.

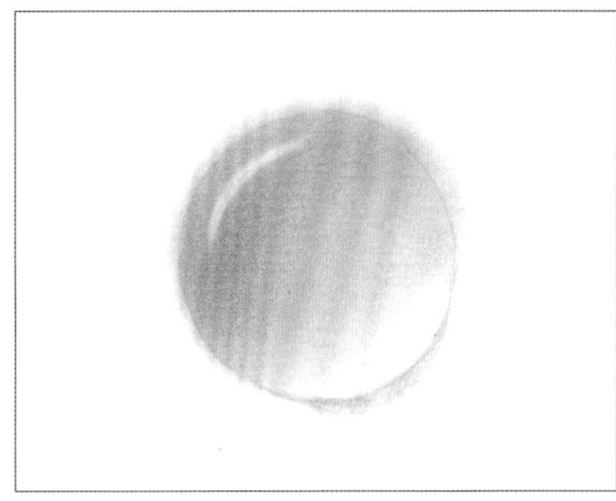

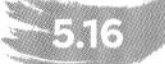

5.16

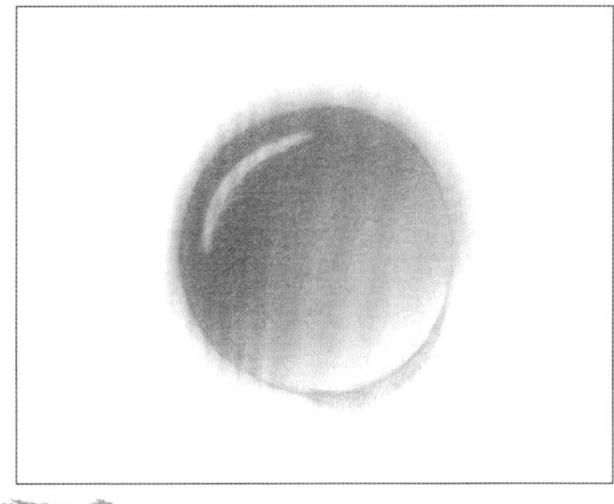

5.17

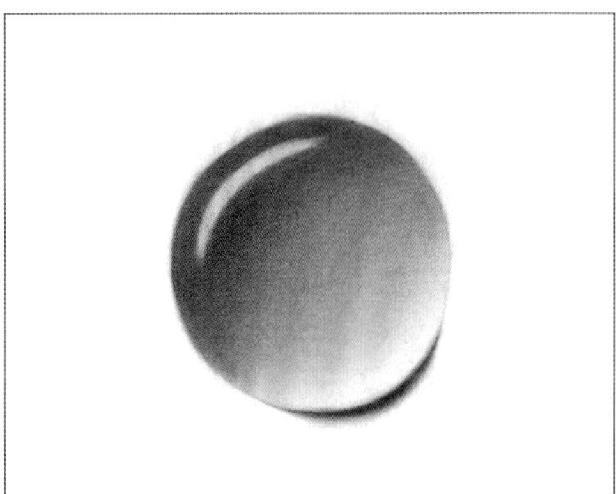

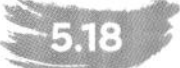

5.18

I hope you enjoyed this exercise! For more practice, you can draw other water drops with more complex shapes, like those shown in Figure 5.19. If you're unsure when to use cotton, tissue, a blending stump, or a brush for blending, experiment with the various tools to get to know them better through practice. I guarantee that, over time, you will better understand when each of them can be useful to you.

In the next chapter, you will have more opportunity to practice with different subjects, progressing from simple blending to creating textures.

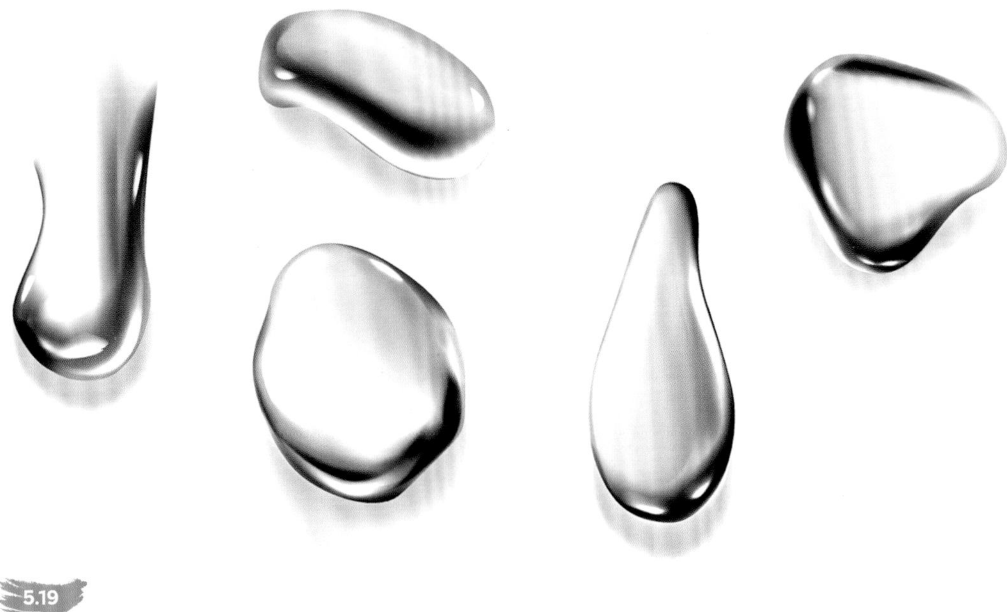

5.19

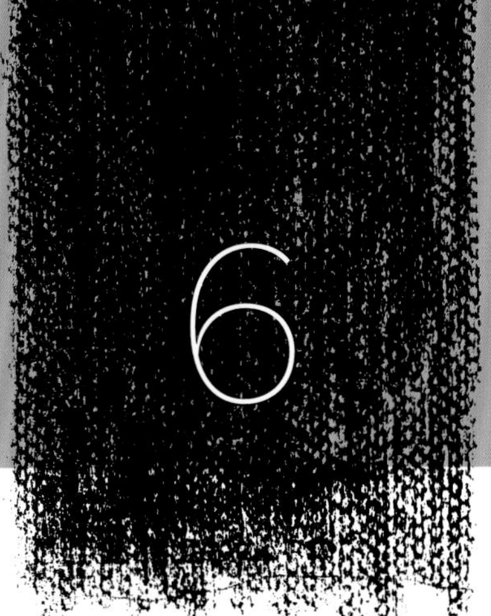

Texture

Texture is a key component of realistic drawing because no other drawing style addresses it in such a detailed way. Through careful manipulation of light and shadow, we can create effects that simulate skin, fur, metal, and a host of other textures. That may sound daunting, but don't worry, dear reader. Our goal is not to draw a perfect copy of a reference image, but rather an approximation of it that evokes a very similar sense of depth, tone, and volume.

Different textures require different approaches, but there is a series of tricks you can apply to emulate textures more easily. This chapter will be a hands-on look at these techniques, offering you the opportunity to practice rendering various types of textures with me. Along the way, you'll practice shading and blending, which will make you an increasingly experienced and confident artist. In fact, you will notice that the steps you learned in Chapters 4 and 5 can actually be mixed together, and you can start a drawing based on the texture.

For the exercises that comprise the rest of the chapter, you can use my drawing as a reference or use your own image of the same theme. If you plan to do the same drawing as I did, always skip ahead to see how the example looks when finished. Knowing where you're headed before you start drawing will give you guidance and a better understanding of how to go through the steps to get there.

Have fun!

Human skin

If you want to draw portraits, you will need to know how to simulate the texture of human skin. In this exercise, we are going to draw a greatly enlarged area. The truth is that you will encounter a situation like this only if you set out to make a really large portrait or draw part of the face seen very close-up. Still, it's worth tackling, because the texture is not as difficult as it might seem and scaling down the effect is easier than enlarging it.

Specifically, we'll draw an area of the cheek, just next to the nose. This can be seen by the play of light and shadow, which adds volume to the image. I made the drawing in a 7.5-cm square. To start, give the drawing some volume with its first layer of graphite (Figure 6.1). I used B, 2B, and 4B pencils for this first layer to achieve the desired tones. Blend the graphite with tissue. Do this first layer slowly, as it is one more chance to practice shading and blending.

One of the keys to this texture is the pores. Because the pores vary in tone (see the finished image, Figure 6.8), I used different pencils in different areas. Start with your lightest, the B pencil, to mark all the pores in the drawing. Note their shape is more oval than circular. After marking them, use tissue to blend the graphite once again and produce a diaphanous, very light effect. (Figure 6.2).

6.1

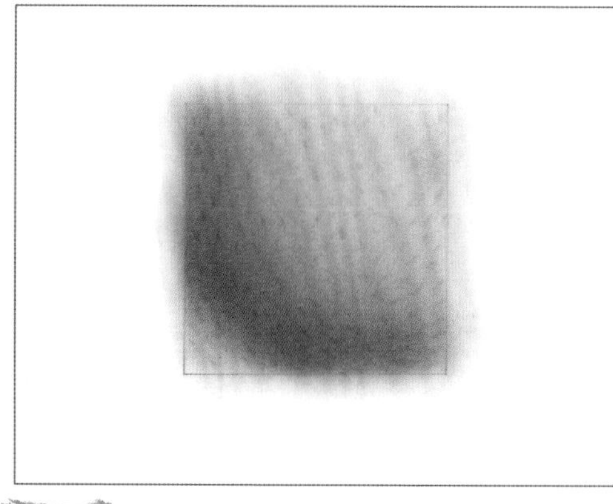

6.2

You've just created the texture's base layer of texture. Going forward, you will continue deepening these marks little by little, as if you were sculpting this area of the skin. The pores in the upper-right region are lighter, and those further away from this area are less illuminated, so gradually darken the less illuminated ones using a 2B pencil first (Figure 6.3).

I used a 2B and 4B more often to darken the pores on the left and below, in this arc of shadow that we formed in the base layer of the skin. I even wanted to deepen this shade a little more, adjusting it according to my taste. After you add your shading, you can blend the graphite in either of two ways. If you want to untangle the pores more and also work on the skin as a whole, use tissue. If you want to blend the pore in a more localized way, use a blending stump. For Figure 6.4 I used both tools.

Adding new layers of graphite, continue working with the 2B and 4B pencils in the pores to achieve the shade you want for them. Try not to make them all the same: Darken some and leave others lighter, always obeying the general logic of light that comes from top to bottom, right to left. With a B pencil, I shaded the skin again, leaving it a little less regular (Figure 6.5).

Now, let's add the light! For this, I opted for an eraser pencil. An excellent tool for creating textures, an eraser pencil leaves a mark that's clear but not too intense if you use moderate pressure. Furthermore, you can sharpen an eraser pencil like a regular pencil or use a craft knife to customize the tip for the creation of specific effects.

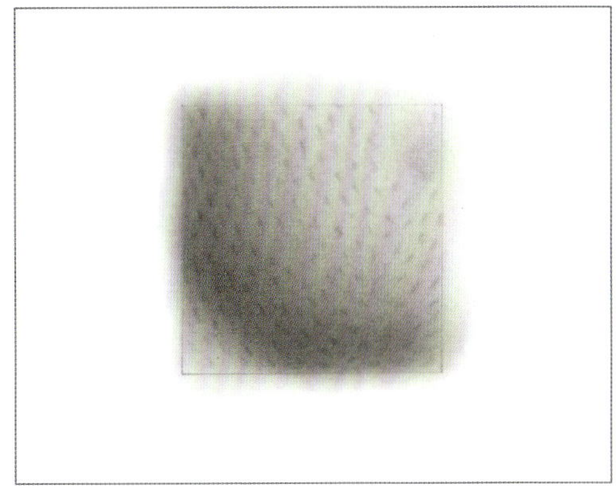
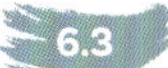

6.3

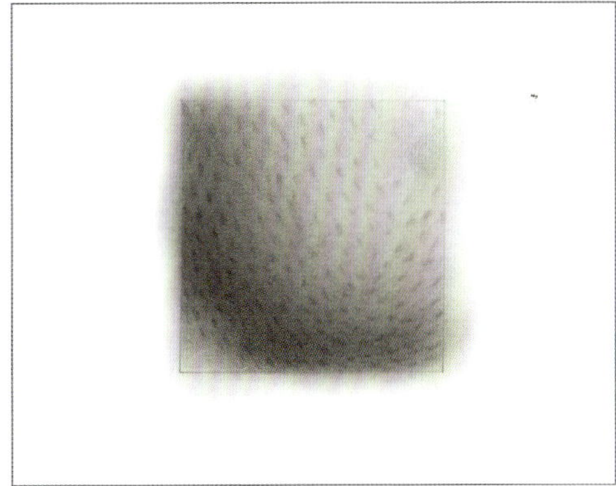
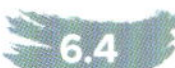

6.4

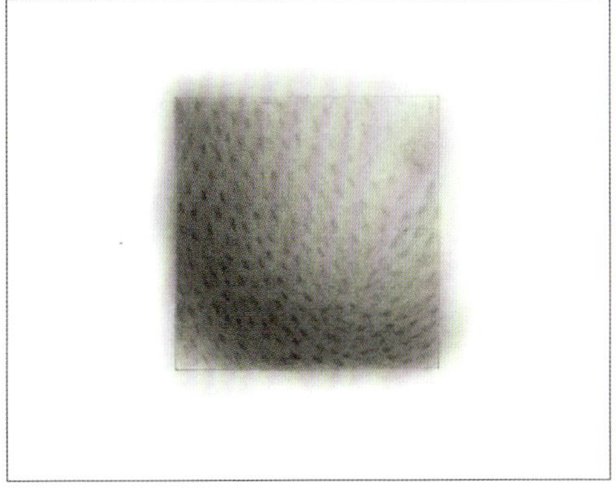
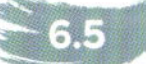

6.5

Pay attention to where I made the highlights in Figure 6.6. They are next to the pore marks made with the pencil, but on the opposite side to where the light comes from. As the light comes from top to bottom, from right to left, I used the eraser pencil to the left of the pore, below it, or both, depending on the location of the pore. Use the figure as your guide to add your own highlights with an eraser pencil.

To give greater complexity to the skin, use a Tombow MONO Zero Eraser to add a new layer of light. The objective here is to give the skin a more natural appearance, which is unlikely to be as neat and organized as it has until now. Figure 6.7 shows my results.

Finally, use a soft cat's tongue brush to slightly reduce the intensity of the highlights made with the erasers. This is a very subtle effect, but it reduces the artificiality of the drawing. Don't forget to erase the graphite that "escaped" out of the square. All that's left to do is admire your finished drawing. It doesn't have to be an exact replica of Figure 6.8, but should approximate the look of skin.

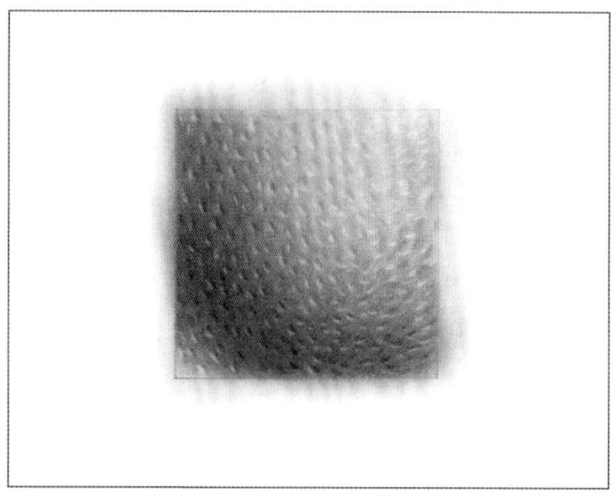

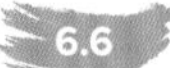

6.6

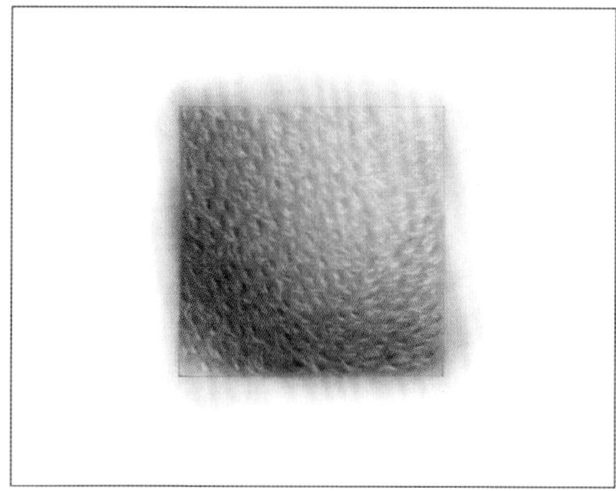

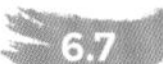

6.7

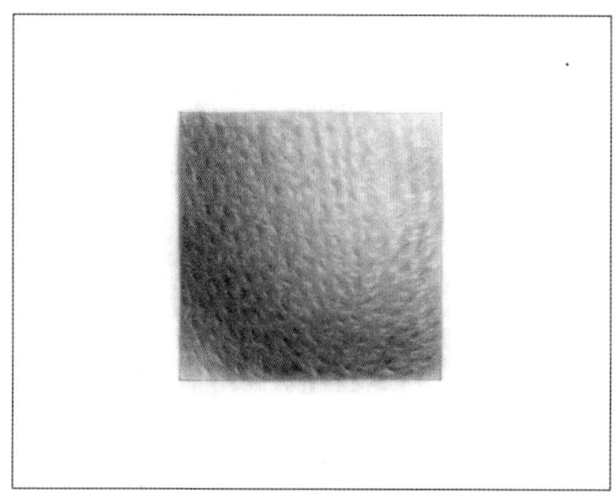

6.8

Hair

The approach to realistic drawing can be varied and still bring excellent results. For this exercise, we will follow a different path to draw a lock of hair than we did to draw the skin. Once again we'll work with layers, but I have no intention of using tissue this time.

Begin with a traditional sketch—it doesn't have to be large—to define the general shape of the lock and mark the points of light and shadow. Use a B pencil and be sure all your strokes follow the movement of the hair as in Figure 6.9.

Using a 2B pencil, add a first layer of graphite to clearly mark the darker areas of the strand (Figure 6.10), always following the movement of the hair. Leave the brightest area in white.

Next, I used a flat brush with firm bristles to blend the graphite. Why a brush? Because it enables you to blend the graphite without completely undoing the traces left by the pencil. Notice how these traces remain visible in Figure 6.11. The lighter areas were filled by the graphite dust brought by the brush, meaning there are still no pencil marks in the light areas.

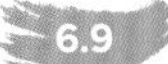
6.9

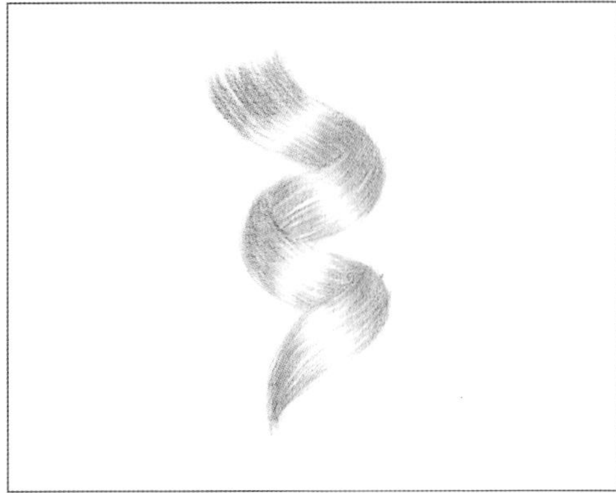

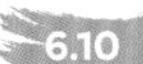
6.10

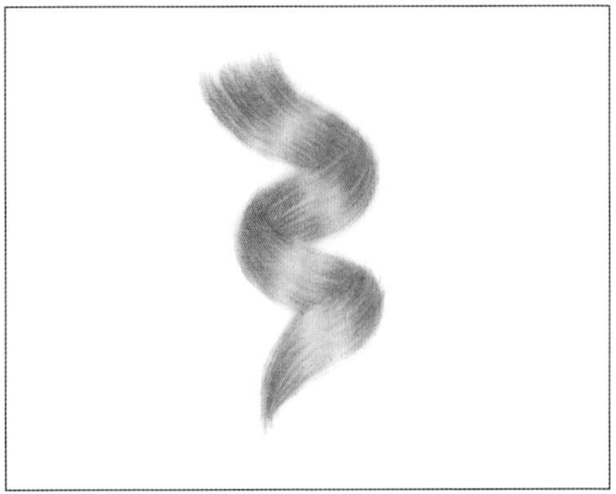

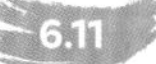
6.11

To convey more dynamism and contrast, use a 4B pencil in the same way you used the 2B. The combination of these two pencils gives a certain variability in the darker tones of the hair. You can advance a little with this pencil, even making some strokes pass through the bright area (Figure 6.12).

Because the 4B pencil is somewhat porous, apply the brush afterwards to smooth the result (Figure 6.13).

Add highlights with a stick eraser. I used a Tombow MONO Zero Eraser whose tip I sharpened with the craft knife. This enabled me to make very fine marks for an interesting effect (Figure 6.14).

By now, the hair should look quite realistic. Whether you choose to stop or to continue adding refinements is a matter of taste. I decided to do a few more touches with B and 2B pencils, advancing a few more strokes over the shine area. I also used a soft cat's tongue brush over the highlights to soften them a bit, turning the white of the eraser into a light gray. This way the work with the eraser and pencil was not disturbed (Figure 6.15).

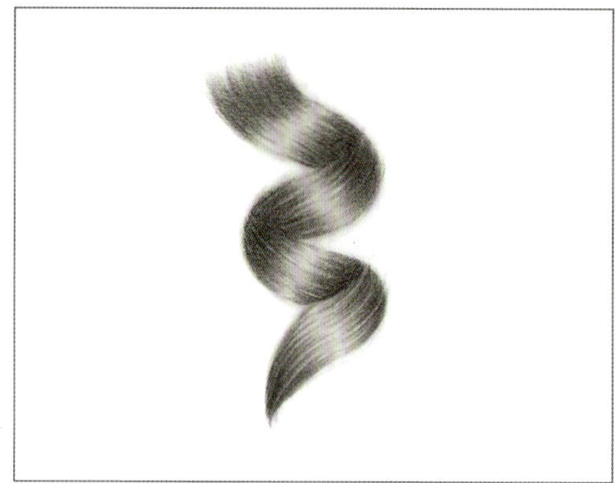

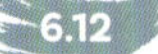

6.12

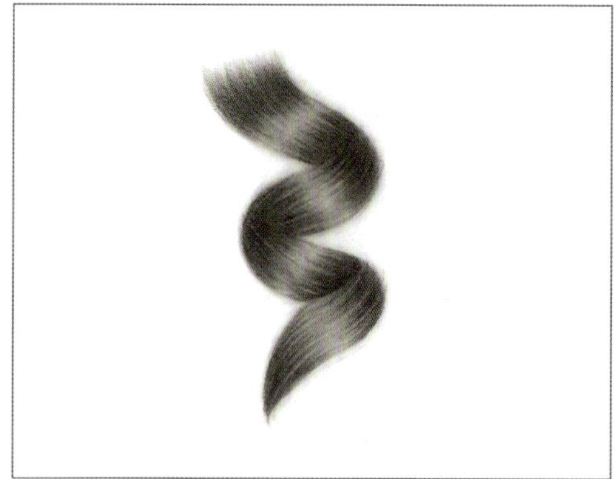

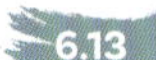

6.13

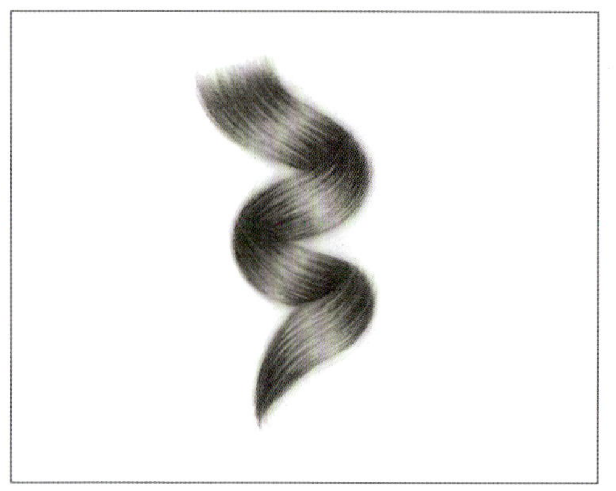

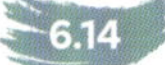

6.14

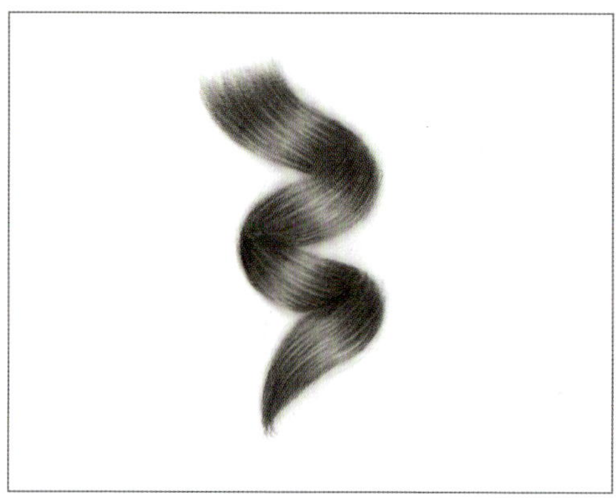

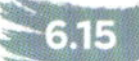

6.15

To finish, I once again used B and 2B pencils to push the shadow spots of the hair lock as well as draw some strands outside of it (Figure 6.16). Make these strands with firm (not necessarily strong!) and agile strokes, so that your hand does not shake when drawing them.

Finally, I used a stick eraser on the highlights again but in a more restrained way. I didn't use any brush afterwards. The idea was to make one or another strand of hair brighter, practically white, expanding the range of tones used.

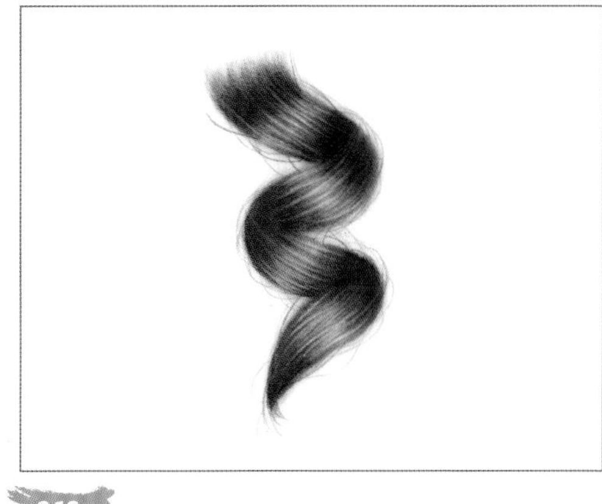

6.16

Mustache

Let's continuing exploring techniques to create hair. In this exercise, you'll draw a mustache with blond strands. How do you create the effect of light strands when working on white paper? You need to create a context that contrasts with them.

First things first, though, sketch the mustache with an HB pencil. Draw it with clearly marked and visible lines (Figure 6.17), making them a little darker than you would usually do for a sketch. In a moment, you will make a gray base for the entire drawing, and you don't want these lines to disappear in it.

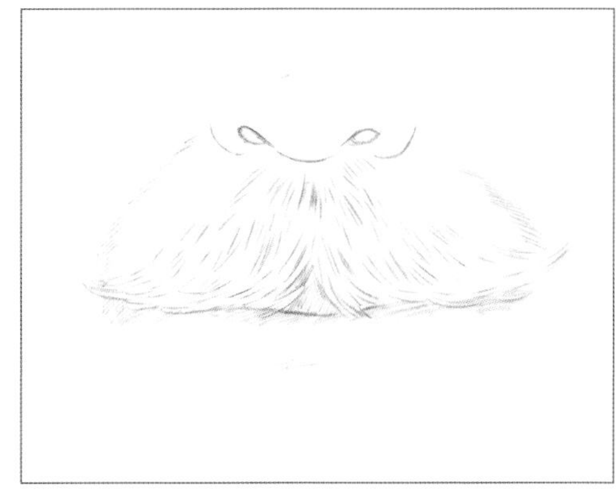

6.17

Prepare for the gray base using the same HB pencil. Vary the intensity of the strokes to add a little context to the mustache. The hair will be visible due to its contrast with the skin around it. Add some shadow to the mustache itself, especially below and in the middle of it, which gives it volume and depth (Figure 6.18).

Next, spread this graphite well and with tissue to create a gray base layer. In Figure 6.19, note how the pencil strokes practically disappear—that's why I recommended slightly stronger lines. The more experienced you become, the easier it will be for you to naturally anticipate solutions like this to eventual problems that might appear later in your drawings.

Before working on highlights, reinforce some features of the mustache using a B pencil (Figure 6.20). These lines will serve as a guide for the work you will do with the stick eraser. Also reinforce the nose features and the shadow the mustache would cast in the mouth area.

Next, start tracing the blond strands with a stick eraser. Have a brush on hand to remove the eraser crumbs, otherwise your drawing will become a mess.

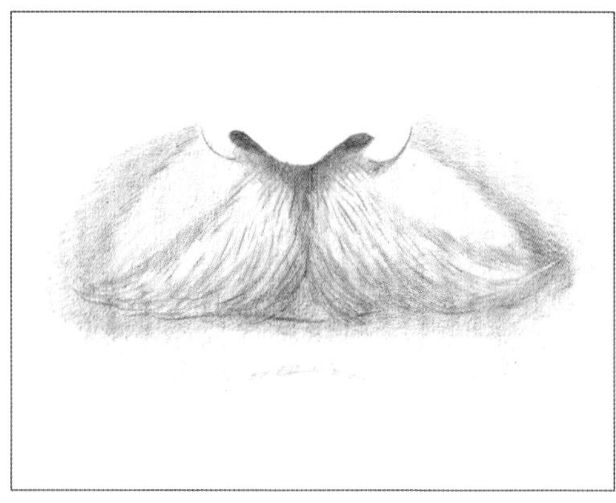

6.18

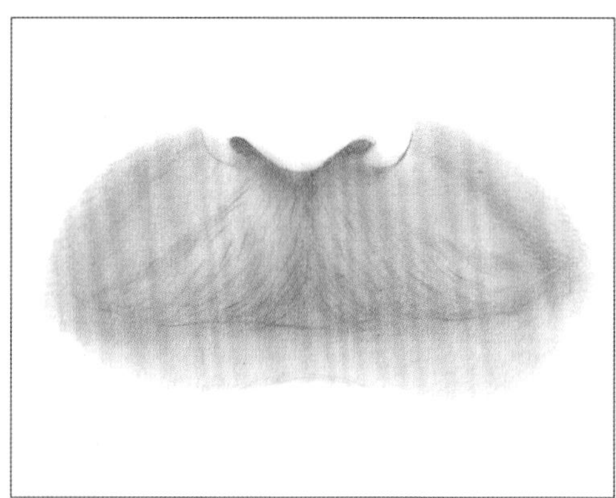

6.19

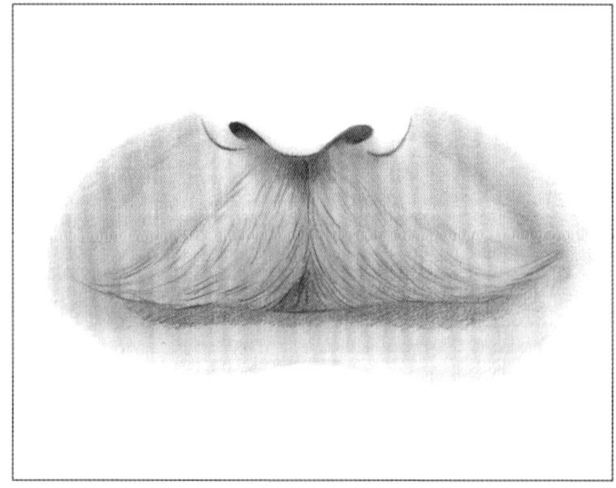

6.20

Try to work with the corners of the eraser to produce thinner strands. If the eraser is very worn, sharpen it using a craft knife. For me, this step is one of the most enjoyable, so have fun tracing thin strands in different shapes and directions. Aim for a result like in Figure 6.21.

At this point, the general values are already well established, but you need to deepen these values to create greater contrast, give your drawing more depth, and help the strands stand out more. To achieve that, use darker pencils in the shadows and a fine eraser for the lighter strands.

Choose a darker pencil (I used a 2B), and reinforce the more intense shadows, which are below and in the middle of the mustache. To smooth the transition between light and dark, use a B pencil between the two tones. Next use a brush with firm bristles to soften the shading while preserving the marks left by the eraser (Figure 6.22). Continue reinforcing the shadows until you're satisfied.

For the example, I used a 4B pencil to produce even more intense shadows, especially on the mouth, in addition to applying more 2B pencil. Using a B pencil very gently, I also made lighter shadows above the mustache hairs, again with the intention of preparing a base to intensify the contrast afterwards. You can use the same B pencil to fill in small shadows between the mustache strands, as well. Remember to blend with the brush. I even used tissue very lightly over the entire mustache to soften the strokes. Notice how much darker the drawing is in Figure 6.23.

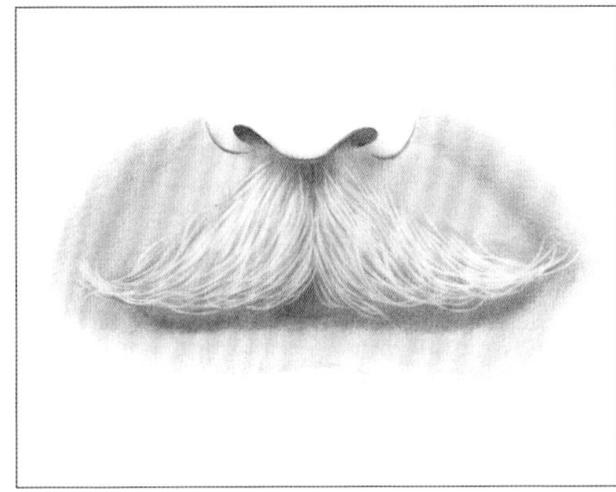

6.21

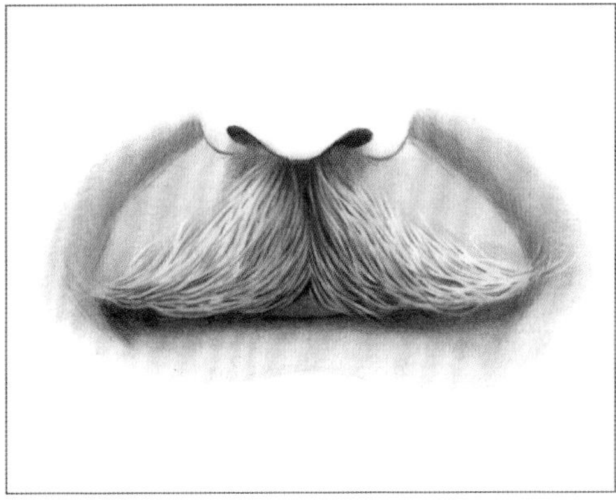

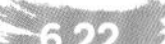

6.22

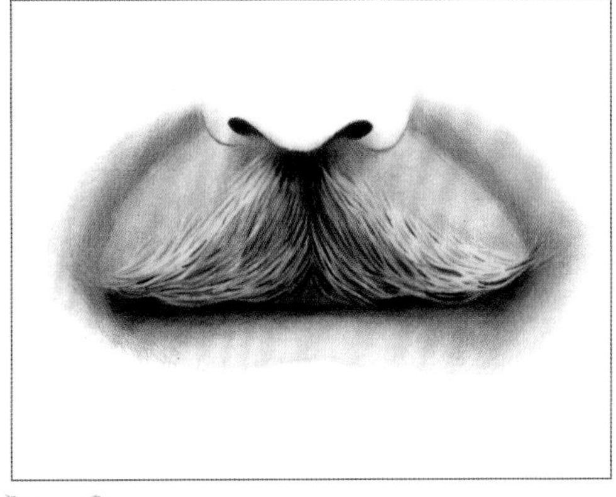

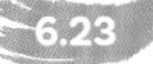

6.23

Thanks to this overall darker tone, the eraser effect will tend to stand out more. When you're finished darkening the surrounding skin, draw the mustache strands more carefully using a well-sharpened fine eraser. Add a little variation within the general direction that the hairs follow, as well. Compare **Figure 6.24** with the previous image to see which strands I added to the example, especially at the extremities.

You've reached the final stage of the drawing, which is always a matter of comparing your work with your reference to identify and make final adjustments. For instance, I still wanted to intensify the shadows a little more with a 4B pencil in the middle and under the mustache. I used the brush once more and made a few last touches with the eraser here and there until I was satisfied. **Figure 6.25** shows my results.

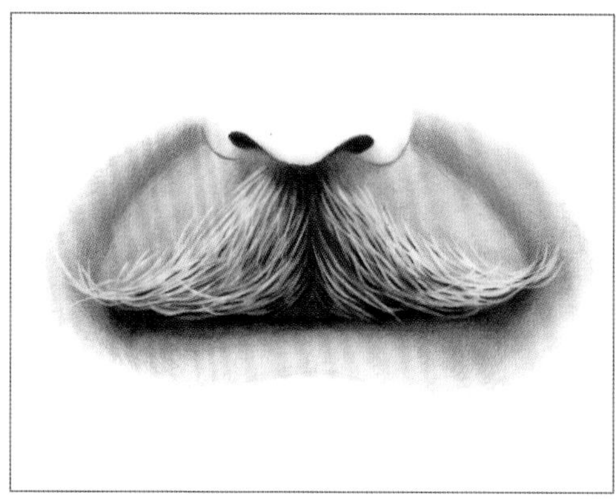

6.24

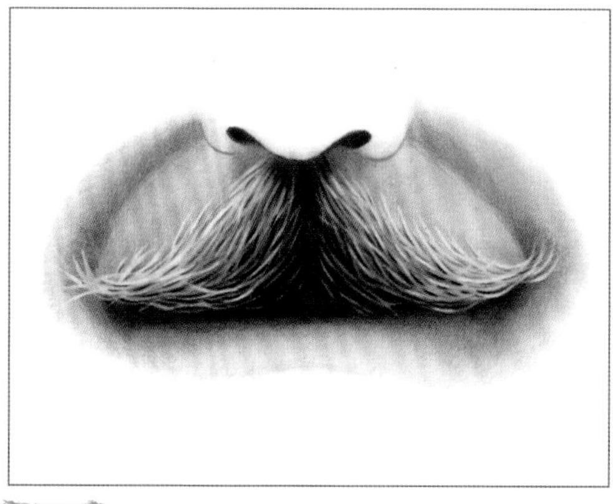

6.25

Eyebrow

Drawing an eyebrow is an excellent exercise for practicing stroke quality. After all, for it to look realistic, you need to know how to use the pencil to trace each strand of the eyebrow, bringing out each of the subtle variations that occur from one strand to the next. As with drawing hair, the tips for drawing eyebrows are also valid for drawing animal fur in most cases.

Before focusing on the details of your reference image, however, take a look at the eyebrow as a whole. Is it more curved or straight? Thick or thin? Longer or short? Pay attention to the tone of the strands: Are they dark, light, or mostly dark salted with unruly white ones? Observing the reference for a few minutes before starting to draw will help guide you once you pick up your pencil.

You can draw eyebrows in successive layers of graphite, starting with harder pencils and moving on to darker pencils. So, with a H or HB pencil, draw some strands, following the direction they grow with your strokes. You don't need to draw every single strand seen in the reference, but do observe and try to capture the general movement of the strands. Some of them may be going in different directions, and these tend to give the drawing a more natural look.

In this first layer (Figure 6.26), also pay attention to shorter strands, usually present in the area closest to the eye. Also look at the transition from the strands to the skin, especially observing the thickness and direction of the strands. A harder pencil will give you more precision when tracing them.

When tracing each strand, make sure it starts and ends thin to mimic the look of a normal strand. Keep your strokes light but firm at the same time.

TIP: *Practice drawing the strands on a separate sheet of paper before drawing them in a portrait.*

It's common for eyebrows to have empty spaces between the strands, so make sure that this is the case for the reference you're working with. When tracing the eyebrow, therefore, remember to leave some empty spaces between the strands.

As you finish each of these layers, run a brush with firm bristles in the direction of the strands to reduce their porosity. This will also cause the graphite to spread and darken the skin behind the strands, which is convenient as the strands cast a shadow on the skin.

For the second layer (Figure 6.27), use a 2B pencil. After you outline most—if not all—of the strands, you can try to achieve the shade of the hairs according to the reference. The idea is to darken the strands, but not all of them; this will give the eyebrow more depth and greater variation throughout.

Add a third layer (Figure 6.28) with a 4B pencil or mechanical pencil. The mechanical pencil is a good choice, because softer graphite leads are not very precise and wear out quickly, requiring you to sharpen the pencil more often.

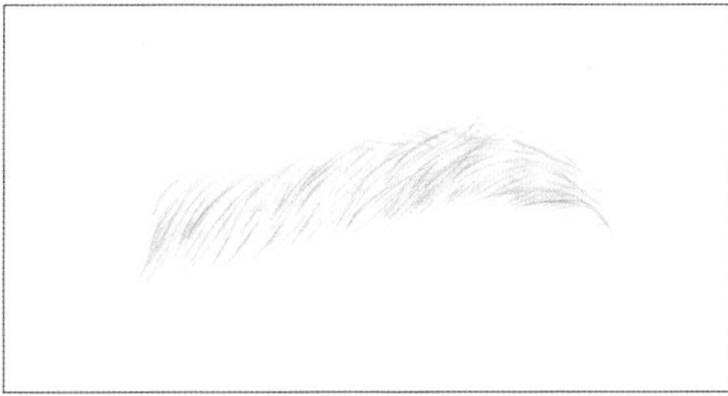

6.26 First layer

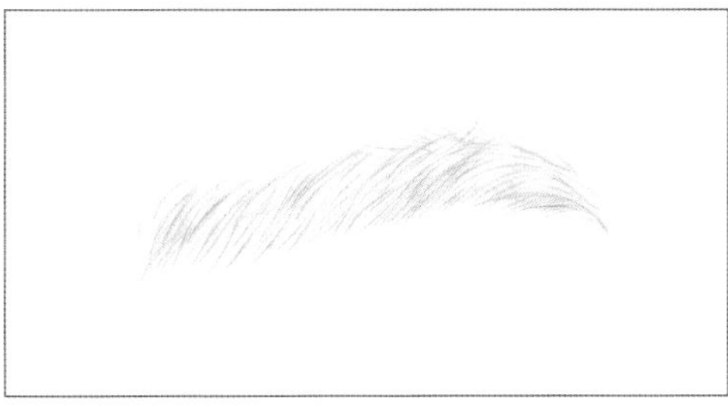

6.27 Second layer

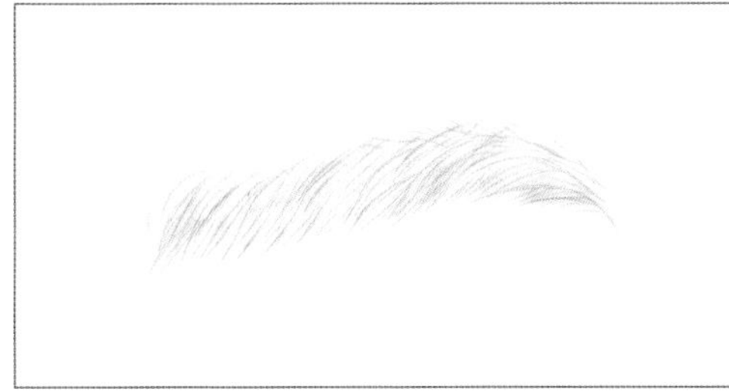

6.28 Third layer

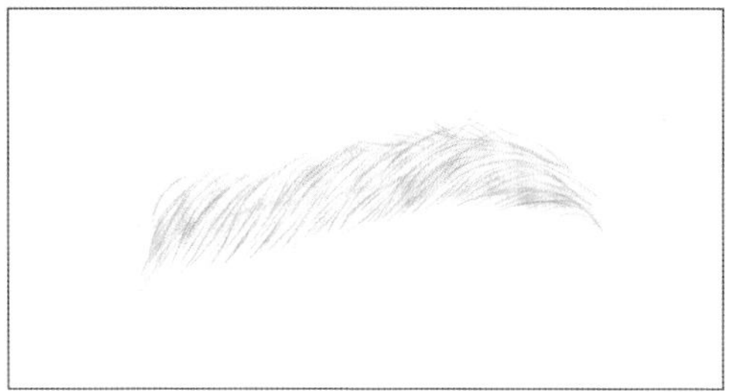

6.29 Adding highlights

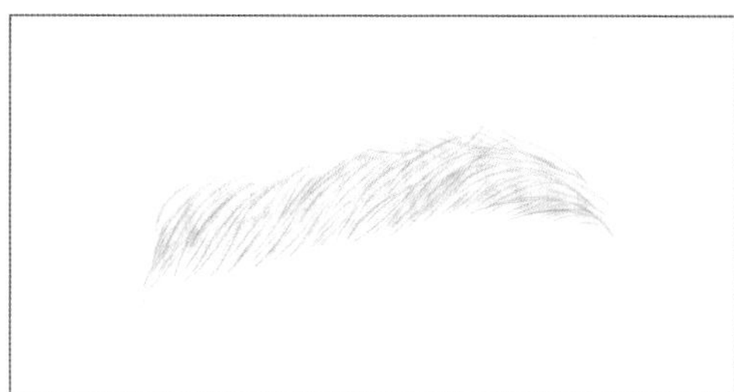

6.30 Thin strands and last touches

If necessary, use a thin eraser, such as the Pentel Clic Eraser, to add highlights (Figure 6.29) here and there. If the strands are too dark, you can also use an eraser pencil, although this tool is less precise. If the details you made with the eraser are too bright, use a brush with soft bristles to reduce the intensity of the shine.

Before finishing, check your drawing. Do any adjustments need to be made? In my case, I added a few more thin strands (Figure 6.30) that I saw in the reference but were missing in my drawing.

And that's it for a basic eyebrow. Note that an eyebrow outlined with make-up would require a different approach, especially in the way the strands are drawn. They would be neat, requiring more accuracy and patience from the artist. They also might be darker and thicker, whose effect could be better conveyed by darker pencil grades. This exercise, however, is very representative of an eyebrow drawing in general.

Animal fur

Although similar to hair and eyebrows, animal fur brings some new challenges—as well as an opportunity to try a new tool. An *embossing* or *indenting tool* is another way to create white lines and highlights in a drawing, which makes it especially useful for multi-toned animal fur. With the tool you can draw grooves on your paper that remain unaffected when you apply pencil in the area, creating a white thread effect. Basically, instead of removing tone using a fine-tip eraser, the embossing tool prevents the tone from sticking to the page in the first place. Either method or a combination of both will help you to create white hairs and highlights, so don't skip this exercise because you lack the specialty tool.

Before jumping into the exercise, practice with the embossing tool on a separate sheet to get a feel for how it works. Make some strokes of various pressures, then use any pencil to fill in that area to see the effect created.

TIP: A light source coming from the side will help you distinguish where the marks were made before using the pencil.

When you're confident with the tool, take a moment to consider the finished 7.5-cm example (Figure 6.28). You can't erase grooves, so think about the white hairs that you want to create in your animal fur texture, their direction of growth, and the fur's overall pattern. Add a series of short grooves with the embossing tool (Figure 6.31), then apply your first layer of graphite with an HB pencil.

For the example, I decided on a pattern with alternation between lighter and darker hair. In Figure 6.32, therefore, I made a first layer of graphite concentrating most of the lines in those bands of darker hairs. You can already see the marks left by the embossing tool there.

TIP: If you want to maintain some gray tone from the graphite, use the embossing tool after your pencil instead.

Next, use a brush with firm bristles to blend the graphite. It will soften the lines, diminishing the grainy look, but will not undo the lines made with the pencil (Figure 6.33), which is why I chose a brush instead of tissue or a blending stump.

Add new layers of pencil, varying the direction of your strokes. The hairs of animal fur are rarely completely aligned as if combed. Varying stroke direction will help give the fur a more natural hair effect. Because I was focusing on the darker points, I also switched to a 2B pencil (Figure 6.34).

Aiming to darken the fur a little more, I added new layers of graphite, returning to an HB pencil. Observe the pattern emerging in Figure 6.35. Also note the effect of white

6.31

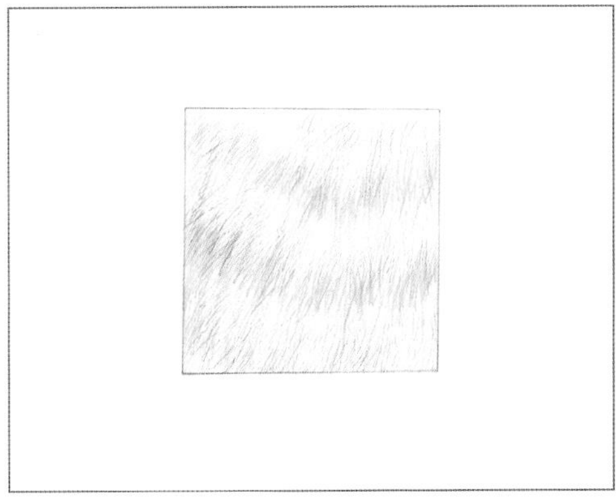

6.32

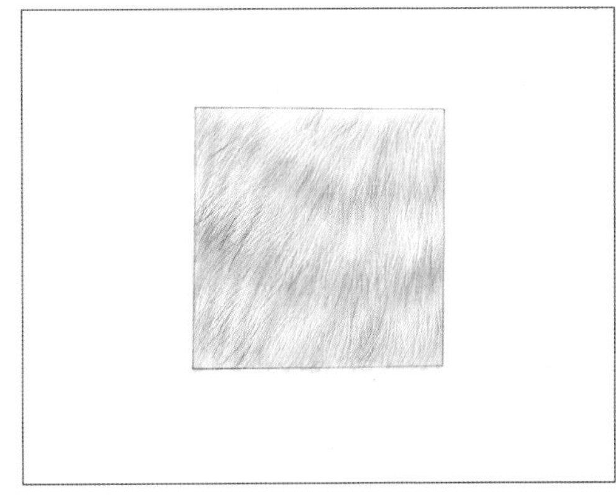

6.33

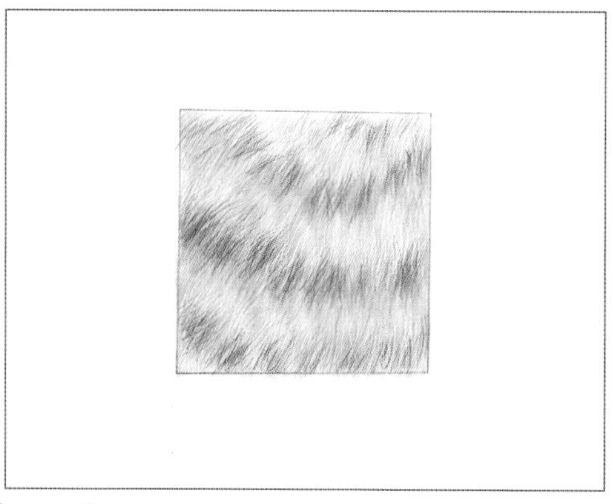

6.34

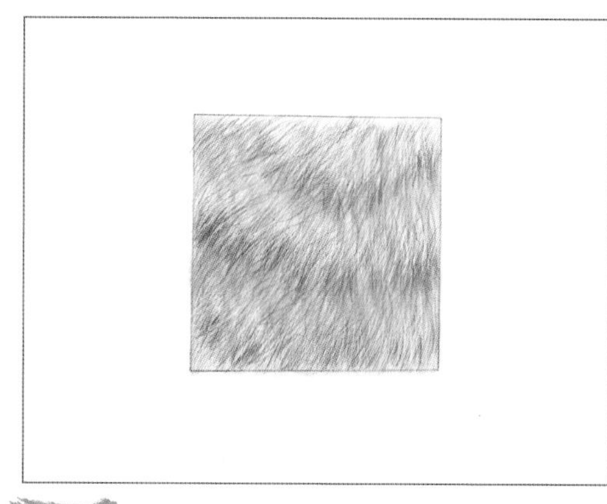

6.35

threads created by the embossing tool. Keep working on your fur shading, following your own pattern or mine.

To increase the contrast by darkening the stripes of hair that pass between the marks made with the embossing tool, I added a 4B pencil layer (**Figure 6.36**). The 4B pencil, as you already know, will leave a grainier appearance due to its softness. If you use it here as I did, give it a brush afterwards.

Pause to consider your fur for a moment. Are the lighter areas to your liking? To finish, I used a Tombow stick eraser to create the effect of light hair, combining the eraser technique with the cold edges created with the embossing tool. I used the eraser with the same logic as a pencil, drawing curved lines in different directions, as in my reference image. **Figure 6.37** shows my finished fur.

This was a looser exercise; you didn't have to worry so much about fidelity to the reference. Take advantage of this type of exercise to learn more about your drawing tools. The next exercise will follow the same line.

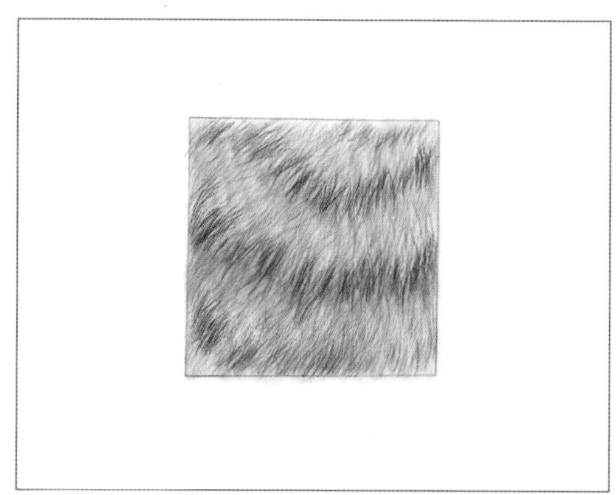

6.36

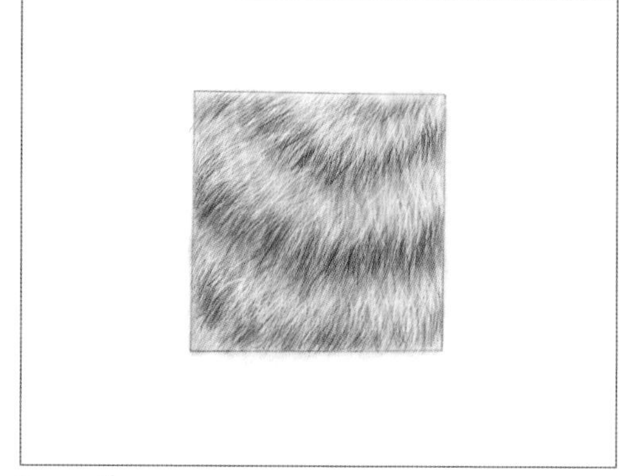

6.37

Fabric

A rumpled scrap of wool fabric offers a chance to practice two skills: creating the texture of wool and the volume of the folds. Even better, this is another exercise in which you don't need to stress over absolute fidelity to the reference as you would with a portrait. Again, plan for an outline of a 7.5-cm square, and grab two very soft graphite pencils, a 4B and 8B. The grainy marks they produce match well with the texture of the wool.

With your 4B pencil, sketch the fabric's folds, which make the composition more interesting. Use a very loose, scribbling line movement, focusing more on delimiting the shadow areas (Figure 6.38).

Next, use a blending stump and follow the same pencil stroke movement, shading by scribbling. Figure 6.39 shows the cool effect of this tool. Notice the porous appearance that still remains, even after using the stump.

Now use an even softer pencil, an 8B, to intensify the shadows. Because it is darker, use it with some moderation. In Figure 6.40, note the movement of the lines, which I brought from the reference image. If your scrap isn't a faithful copy of mine, don't worry. Mine doesn't exactly match the reference photo either, but we're both emulating the general appearance of this fabric.

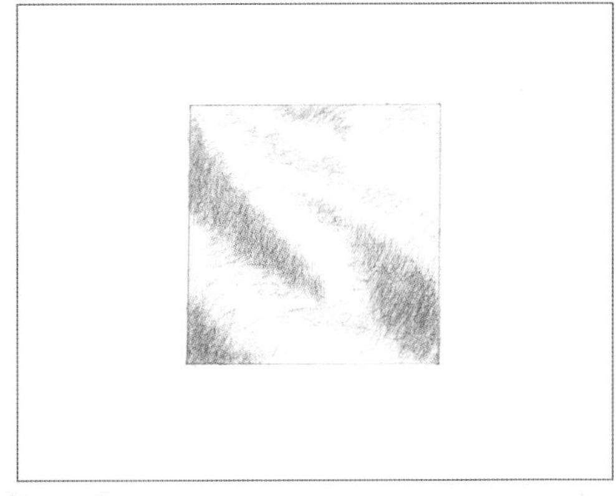

6.38

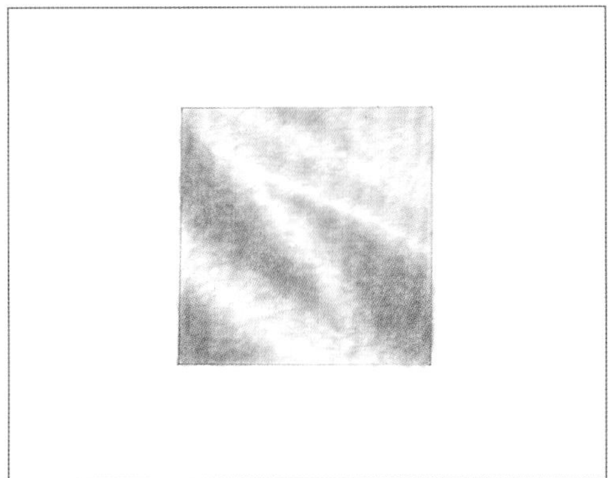

6.39

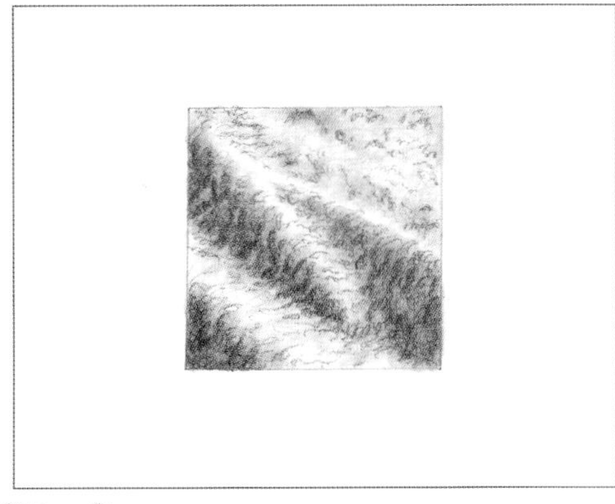

6.40

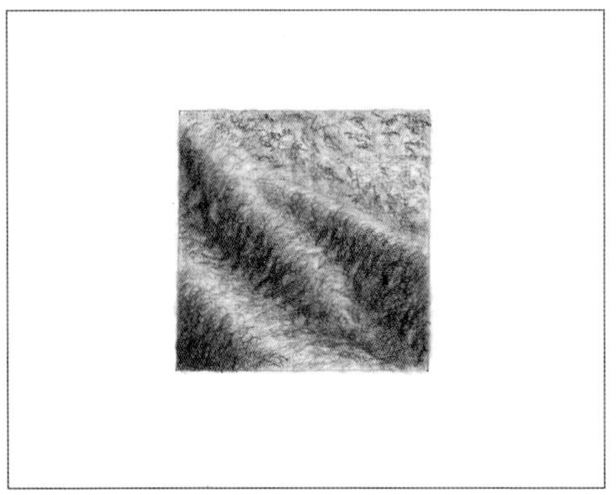

6.41

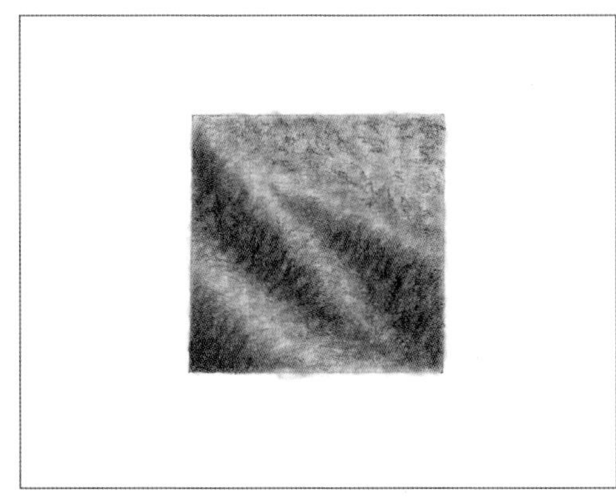

6.42

With the general values more established and an idea of where you want to go, you can easily move forward. From now on, basically alternate your 4B and 8B pencils with your blending stump to cover the drawing. By layer over layer, the drawing will become darker and closer to the expected result. Figures 6.41 through 6.43 illustrate my progress.

Once you achieve your desired tone, use an eraser to complement the effect created so far. With a Tombow stick eraser, make a movement similar to your pencil and stump scribbles while also trying to follow the flow of the folds. Figure 6.44 shows the effect my eraser and I created.

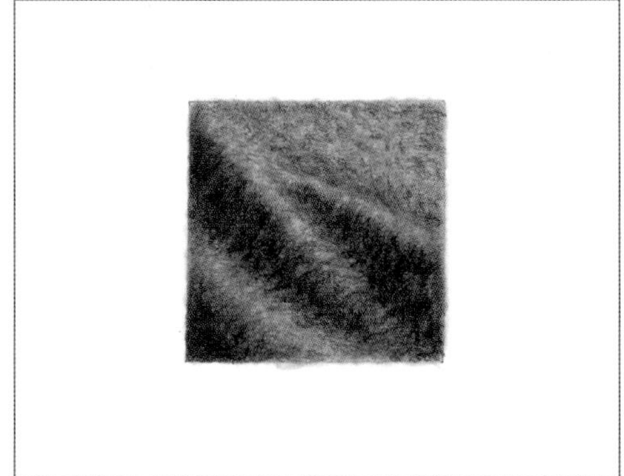

6.43

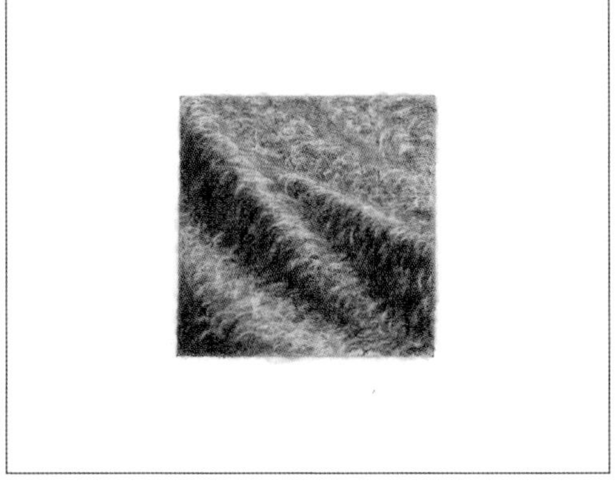

6.44

How does your finished wool compare to Figure 6.45? You might think that this drawing is too abstract, that it doesn't look very realistic, but think of the feeling of fabric that it manages to convey. Imagine, for example, a portrait of a person wearing woolen clothing. Believe me, an effect like this greatly enhances the portrait as a whole, even if it only appears peripherally.

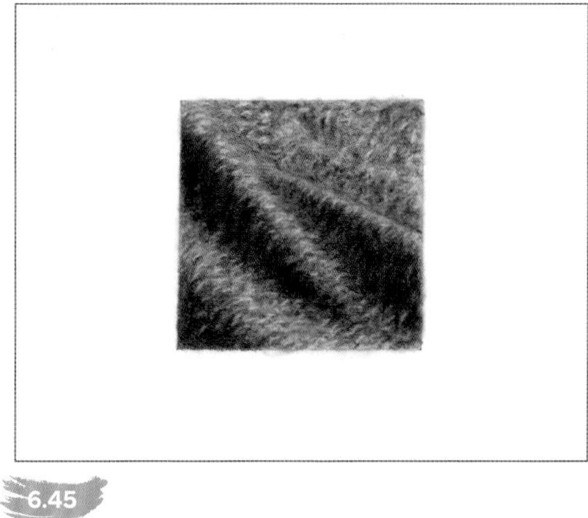

6.45

Metal

From natural fibers to industrial fasteners: The next texture exercise is about a chrome metal effect. It is interesting to observe not only how the effect is created, but also how it behaves. Again, take a look at the finished example to see how this effect presents areas of intense black, strong contrast, and distorted shapes, as well as small scratches on the surface of this screw, nut, and washer (Figure 6.51).

Given the relative complexity of the reference image I found online, I printed it, and then I sketched it (Figure 6.46) using the transfer method (Chapter 3). You can do a simplified freehand version on your drawing paper if you want or find another reference image that allows you to practice the chrome metal effect. No matter which method you choose, aim for dimensions of about 7.5 x 8.5 cm.

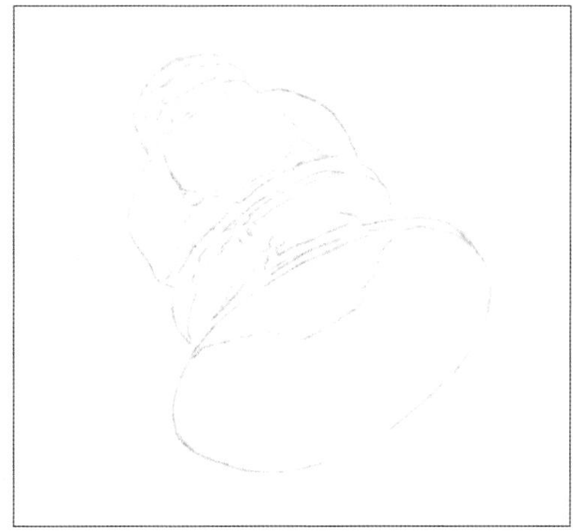

6.46

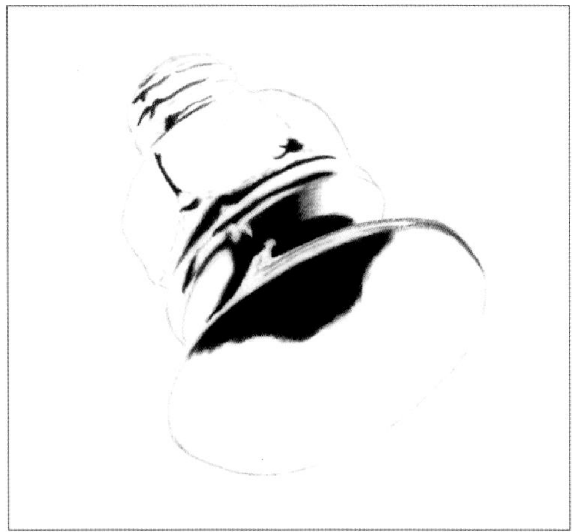

6.47

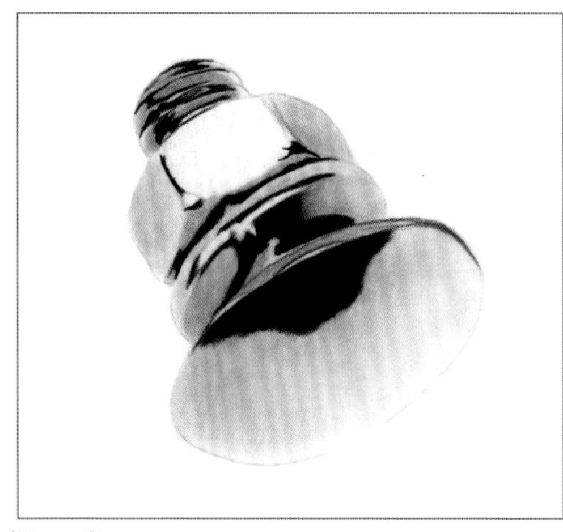

6.48

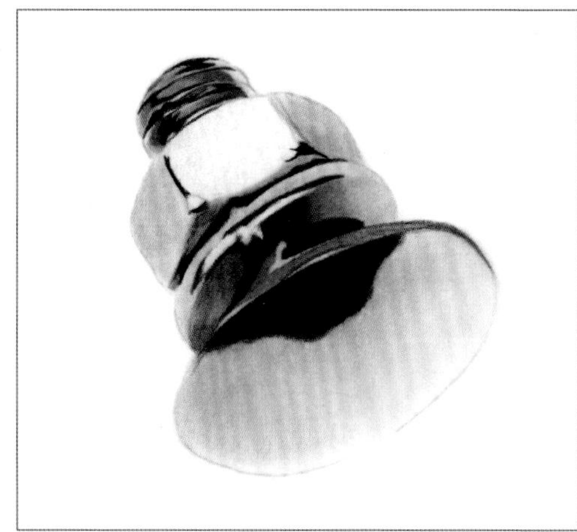

6.49

To achieve a tone close to black in my sketch, I used an 8B carbon pencil from Staedtler's Black series (Figure 6.47). If you don't have one of these or an equivalent, use the darkest graphite pencil you have to sketch, but keep in mind that you will work with a value scale narrower than mine.

When adding dark gray with the carbon pencil, be careful to leave empty spaces where the lights will be reflected in the object. This is of fundamental importance because you cannot erase the traces of these pencils as easily as you can normal graphite.

In addition to the carbon pencil, I used normal graphite pencils for the intermediate tones. With a B, establish a base layer for the entire drawing. Next, use a flat brush with firm bristles to blend the graphite and give it a smoother, less grainy appearance (Figure 6.48).

When blending the base layer out, work the graphite and carbon separately, preventing the darker area from staining the lighter one. Fortunately, carbon doesn't spread so easily and using a brush enables you to work in a relatively well-controlled manner.

With a 2B Black pencil, add some darker intermediate tones to the washer and nut. The difference, seen in Figure 6.49, is subtle. Blend the area of carbon strokes intensively using a brush with firm bristles. The brush is by far the best tool for blending carbon pencil strokes.

With the base layer practically done, you can add the details. As they are somewhat delicate, use a B pencil at first, drawing grooves and some distorted shadows, which are visible in the reference and typical to chrome (Figure 6.50). To blend the graphite, you can use the brush with firm bristles once again, especially for more delicate details, or a blending stump for slightly larger blemishes.

Finally, add a few more small blemishes with Black pencils and a regular B graphite pencil. Use a Tombow stick eraser or similar for the highlights. Notice in Figure 6.51 that the white is not so intense in this finished drawing. It is actually a light gray. What is the solution for this? Well, an alternative is to use a white gel pen or acrylic paint. You can apply the acrylic paint from a fine-tip POSCA marker, or even with a fine brush. You can also try using a white charcoal pencil, but these are typically used on toned paper.

In the end, I didn't like using any of these materials because they ended up attracting a lot of attention due to their difference in relation to graphite, charcoal, and the white of the paper itself. As much as you try to create a light effect in a single point of the drawing, you may feel like adding that white in other places, changing the nature of the drawing as a whole. I prefer, therefore, to leave the gray light and try to lighten it as much as possible with a stick eraser or even an electric eraser (Chapter 7).

Anyway, I am quite pleased with how my drawing turned out. And you, did you like yours? I hope so!

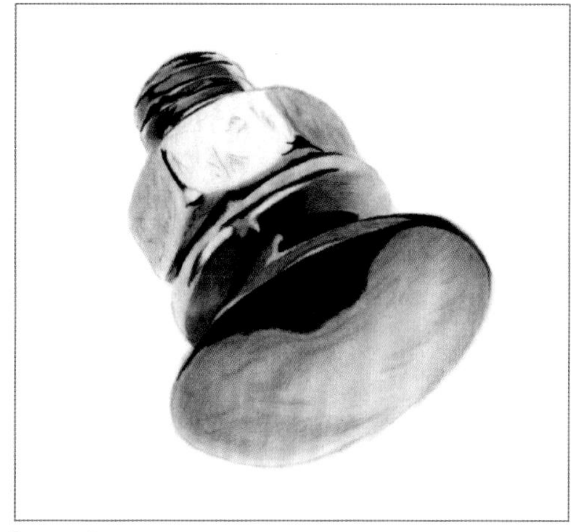

6.50

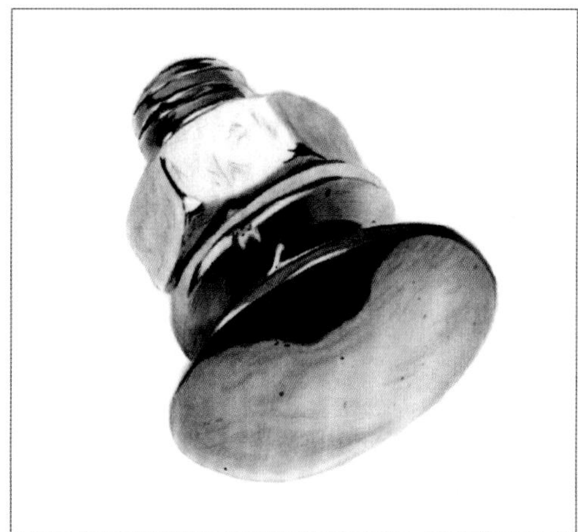

6.51

Wood

It's no coincidence that the exercises are growing in complexity! The goal is to improve your drawing skills, and that won't happen if you keep drawing the same things. Challenge yourself and keep that growth mindset!

Are you ready to take on wood? In this final texture exercise, you'll draw a mortar and pestle made of wood. The biggest difficulty this drawing may impose is the amount of details, and every detail takes time and patience to complete.

Make your sketch carefully and prepare the texture to some extent before you start shading. When tracing this drawing, I was first concerned with defining the size and contours of the subject in question (Figure 6.52), which is approximately 8 x 14 cm.

Next, define the location of the main shadow areas compared to your reference. I used a Staedtler 2B Black pencil, but you can use a 2B or 4B graphite pencil if you don't have a carbon pencil. The 2B Black is a "dry" pencil, not very dark, and not blended easily. Notice in Figure 6.53 that the stains are not drawn with sharp contour lines, because they are shadows. Make sure your transition from the shadows to the brighter areas is smooth.

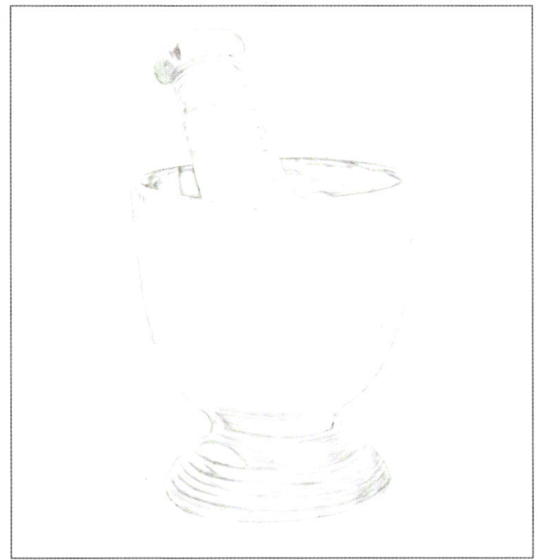

6.52

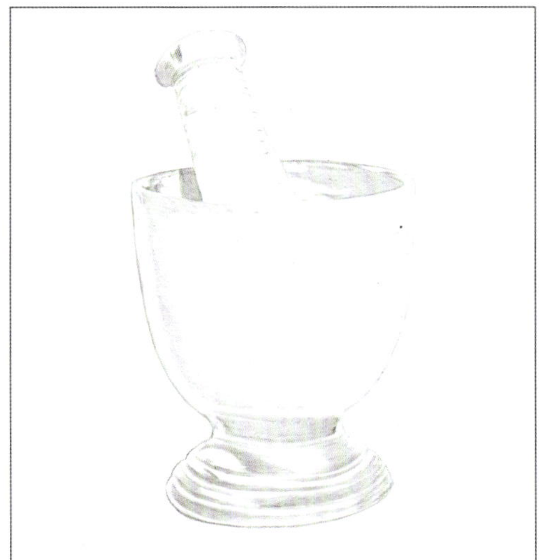

6.53

With the same 2B Black pencil, add more details to convey the idea that this is a wooden object. Do these details freehand, looking at your reference image and bringing them into the drawing (Figure 6.54). Take your time when placing these stains. That's what realistic drawing is about! It is the attention to the details that will make your drawing unique.

With this first layer of shadows and dark blemishes done, you can better establish the values of light and especially shadow. The example drawing is relatively dark in general and there are very dark shadows with values close to black. For this reason, I used Staedtler Black pencils in grades 4B, 6B, and 8B. Because they leave a very grainy appearance, I used a blending stump a little and a brush even more to give the shadows a softer, smoother look (Figure 6.55).

Having marked these shadows further, switch to more general shading using a 4B graphite pencil. Then, use tissue to blend the graphite out well to create a homogeneous gray base (Figure 6.56). When spreading the graphite, inevitably you will lose some of the details that you did previously, but this time the Black pencils' stubbornness to blend works in your favor. A good part of what you already did will be maintained.

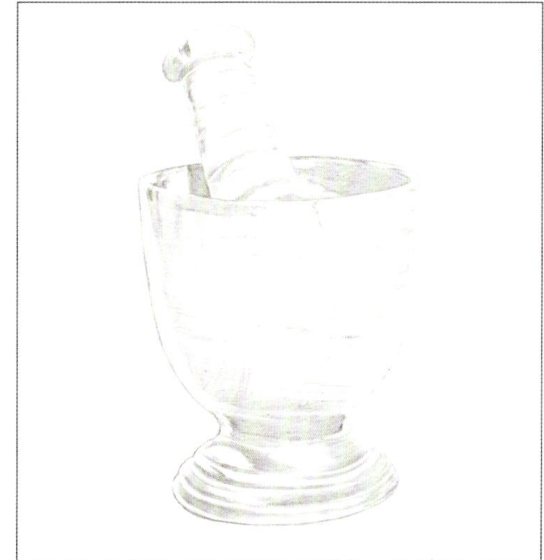

6.54

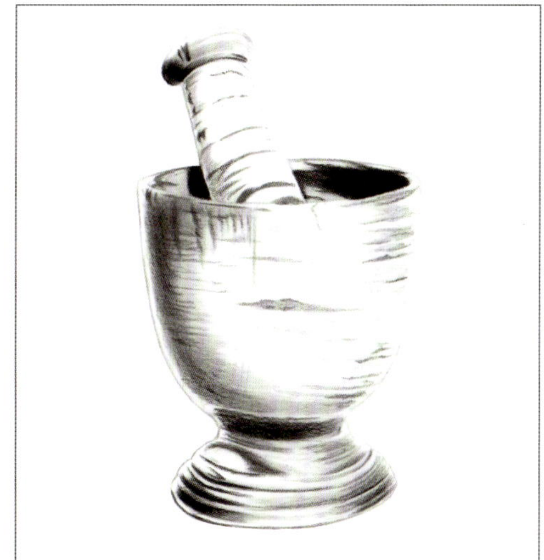

6.55

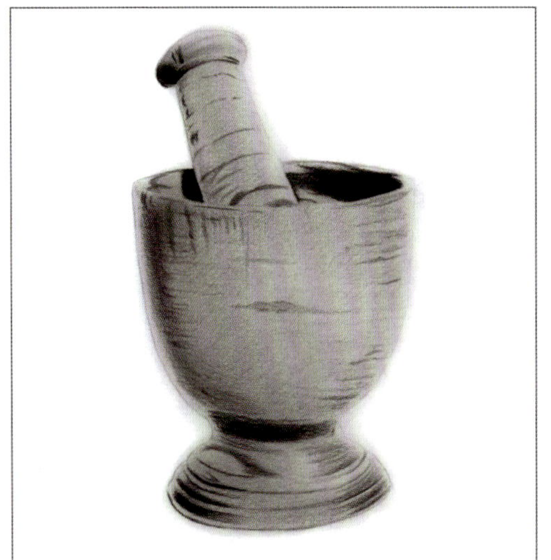

6.56

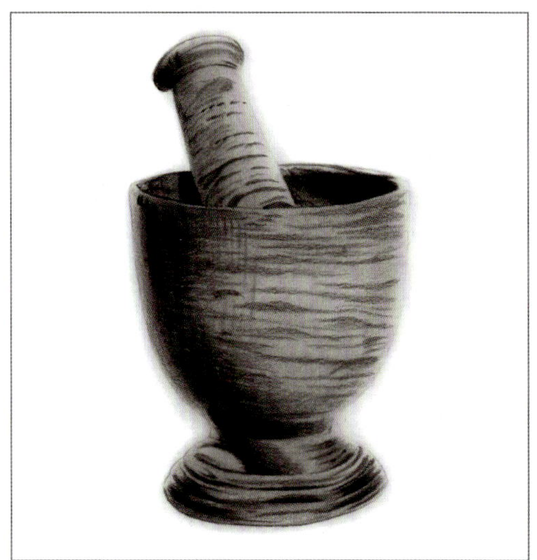

6.57

When you're happy with the overall tone of the graphite base, darken the shadows again, reinforcing and enlarging the blemishes present in the drawing (**Figure 6.57**). When you reach this point in a drawing, always double-check your reference image: Do you see any details you need to add? This step will take the most time, and the quality in which you carry it out will weigh most on the quality of the final product. So, do these details calmly, enjoying the moment. It can actually be quite fun depending on how you see this kind of activity.

Again, notice how the Black pencil leaves a porous appearance. Therefore, in a new attempt to soften these stains, use a 4B graphite pencil over them and blend them using a firm-bristle brush. With the same 4B pencil, add a few more spots that are less dark than those made with the Black pencils. Yes, use the brush over them too (**Figure 6.58**). This adds more complexity to

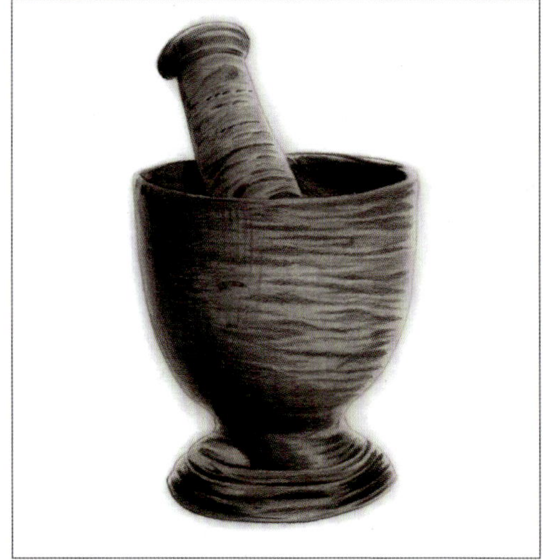

6.58

the texture work and makes the drawing much more interesting and realistic.

Look at your drawing and compare it with your reference image. Are you satisfied with the dark tones? No one knows your drawing better than you. I decided to add a few more stains with 6B and 8B Black pencils. These small tweaks may not be as easily visible as in the metal exercise (**Figures 6.49** and **6.50**), but they make a difference to the overall effect.

To finish, add the highlights you see in the reference object. When it is being illuminated by more than one light source coming from different places, you need to pay attention when carrying out this step. You can mark these lights initially with the eraser pencil and then finish with a MONO Zero Eraser. If you prefer, use the brush over them to turn them into a light gray tone and then apply the eraser once more. You can see the result of my efforts in **Figure 6.59**.

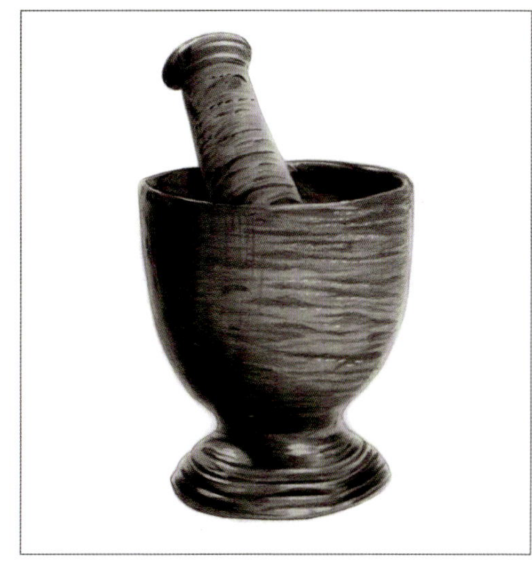

6.59

Stone

Before starting this exercise, look at the finished drawing in Figure 6.68. What do you think? Does this drawing seem too complicated? If you think so, I agree with you—at least at first glance. Don't be intimidated! Just apply the same strategy you've been using for the previous exercises: Simplify the shapes as much as possible at the beginning, and go into the details later.

To start your sketch, focus on the most general shapes only and try to understand what their parts are. Notice in **Figure 6.60** that I also added some details of the stone's grooves. These lines were clearly

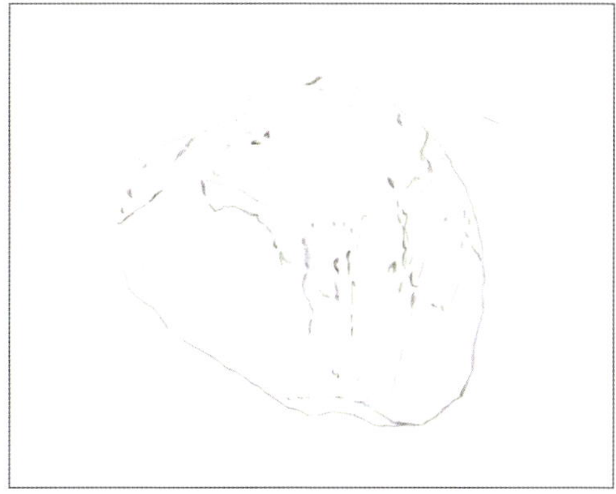

6.60

visible in the reference image I used for the example, and they will serve as a guide for the following steps (can you spot them in the finished drawing?). Look for similar guides in your reference images and add them to your sketches.

Next, add some simple shading to define the stone a bit more. I used HB and B pencils to add three shades of gray: a lighter one on the top and left, a darker one on the right and bottom, and an intermediate gray in the central area and a little to the left (Figure 6.61). With a 2B pencil, accentuate the stone's darker grooves.

Use tissue to spread the graphite and create a first layer. Don't worry that the separation between the stone faces becomes less obvious as the gray tones become quite similar to each other. You will rework the faces in the following steps. To ground the stone, add shadow cast under it with the B pencil (Figure 6.62).

Using a B pencil, continue to adjust the shading by adding the first stains of tone to spots on the stone's faces. The B pencil will keep this early work from becoming too dark and give you more peace of mind and freedom to experiment. Each stain you make darkens a little the object as a whole, so you can gradually adjust the overall tone. Figure 6.63 shows my work reinforcing the shading on the leftmost face.

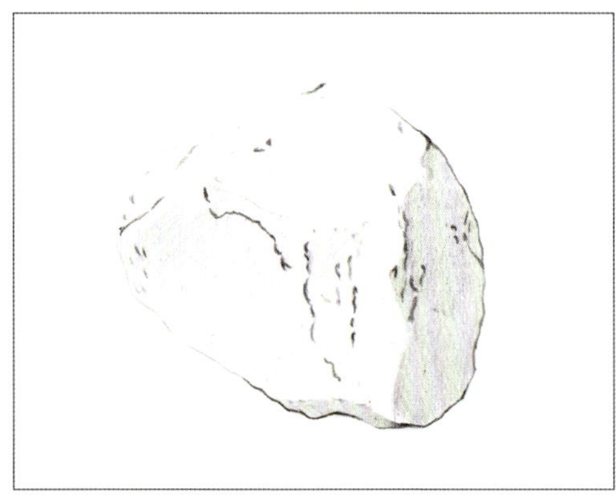

6.61

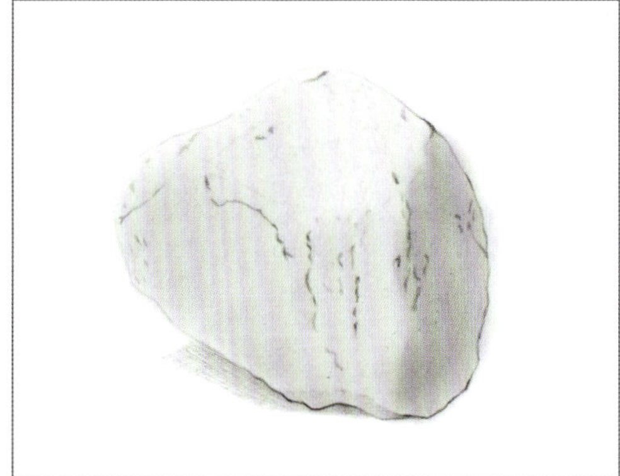

6.62

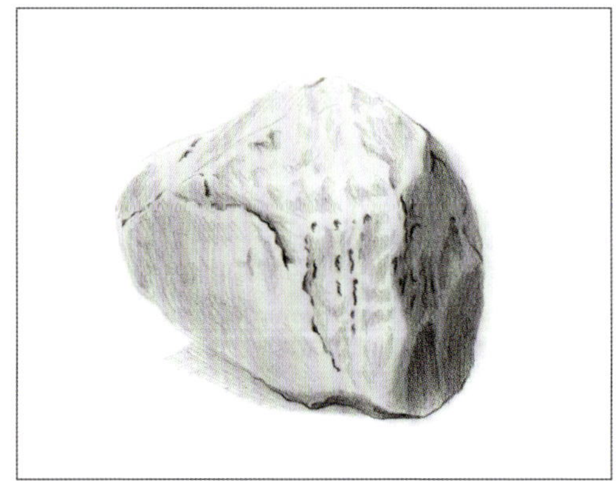

6.63

To soften these stains without undoing them, use a blending stump (Figure 6.64). I found the effect created by the stump best for mimicking what I saw in my reference image and really liked the results on the first layer. If you prefer or need a different look, it's fine to try a different tool.

For the next layer, use a 4B pencil to continue to darken the stains a little more. Creating targeted areas of tones like this is a lot more labor intensive than doing the general shading, but the resulting textures you create are worth the time and effort. Little by little this stone becomes more interesting. Remember when we talked about the flow state in Chapter 1? Here you have a great opportunity to explore it. Take advantage of drawing texture to practice and develop more patience. Allow yourself to get lost in these stains, doing them one by one, giving due importance to each one (Figure 6.65).

Use the B pencil once again, and add another layer of 4B. Together, these two pencils give you the ability to make lighter or darker stains depending on what the area of the stone you're working on. Because the darker pencil has greater porosity, use softer strokes.

Blend using a firm-bristle brush, and then blend a bit more with a blending stump. These two tools are great for softening lines without undoing the stains (Figure 6.66). The firm-bristle brush is more aggressive. It helps the graphite powder better penetrate the pores of the paper, while the stump works more on the surface.

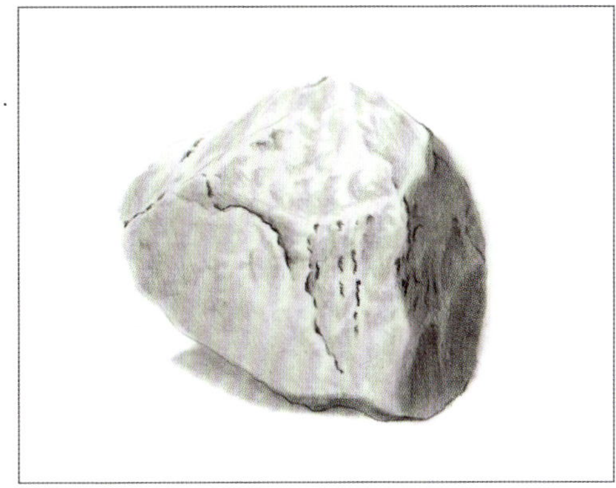

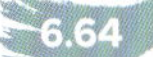
6.64

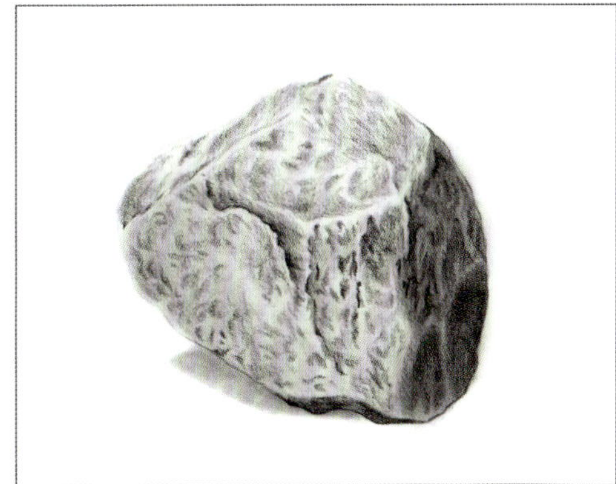

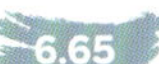
6.65

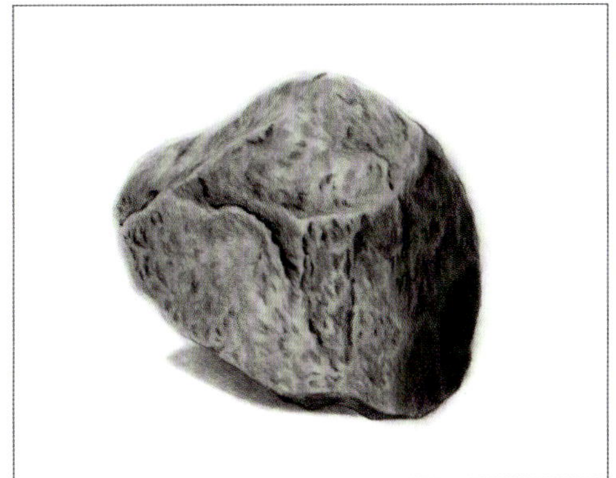

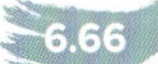
6.66

When you reach a result that you're happy with, begin work on the highlights with a Tombow MONO Zero Eraser. Use the Tombow stick eraser where you need clearer and more defined highlights, such as to highlight the edges of the stone and separate the planes from each other (Figure 6.67). Try not to make very well-defined straight lines, and instead highlight the irregularities of its surface. After all, you don't want this stone to look like an artificial object, a polygon carved by a human being.

To finish, use your eraser pencil to lightly touch the surface of the stone to highlight it very delicately. Then, to reduce the intensity of these touches, use a cat's tongue brush to spread the graphite a little over these highlights. The effect, in fact, is so subtle that it is difficult to perceive them in Figure 6.68, which shows the finished stone. Even so, it's worth the effort. No one knows your drawing better than you and you can hide some secrets in each of them.

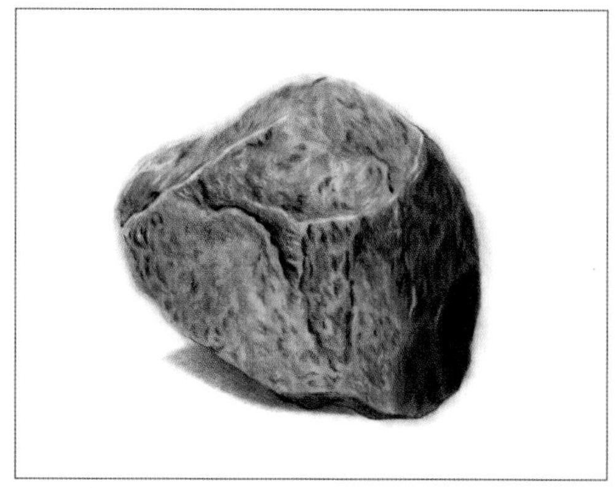

6.67

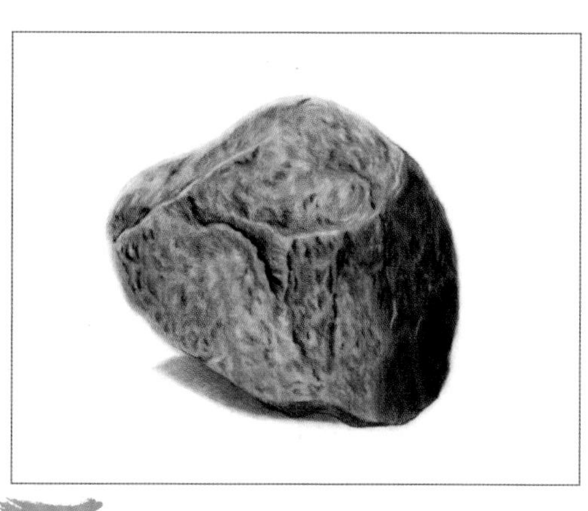

6.68

Challenge for growth

I hope, dear reader, that this chapter was of great value to you and that you enjoyed the exercises. Even if you are not totally satisfied with your results, the fact that you are challenging yourself to make drawings with this level of realism will make you improve a lot!

In the next chapter, you'll have plenty of practice opportunities. Its exercises revisit everything you have learned so far with studies that involve different textures and different shading strategies. By the time you finish, you'll be ready to make any type of drawing you want!

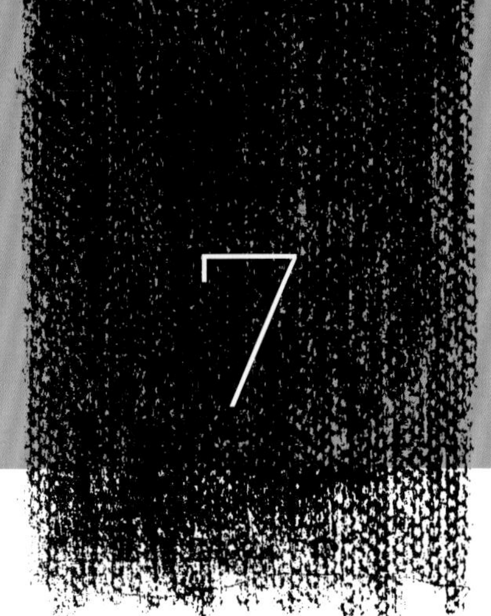

Practicing

It's time to put into practice everything you learned in the previous chapters. If you have worked your way through all those exercises, you won't have any major problems doing these last three studies. The main difference is that they are a little longer and involve multiple textures in the same drawing.

If you don't want to draw the same images I used as reference, that's okay! Choose your own images, then use one of the tracing methods or draw them freehand. Do try, however, to find references similar enough to my examples that you can follow along with the workflow.

I made all the example drawings on A5 sheets with 1-cm margins on each side. This way, the exercises are less time-consuming and do not require the advanced detailing like a larger drawing. I used smooth Strathmore 300 Series Bristol paper, Staedtler Mars Lumograph graphite pencils, Staedtler Black series pencils, brushes, blending stumps, tissue, a Tombow MONO Zero Eraser, and an eraser pencil.

Human portrait

In this first exercise, a portrait of a woman, you will have the opportunity to practice skin texture and hair, as well as draw the parts of the face, each with its own peculiarity.

Start your portrait by tracing the sketch from your reference photo. Transfer to the paper everything you think will help you when shading the portrait, including marking shaded areas (Figure 7.1).

To delimit the most intense shadows in the portrait, use a 4B Black pencil, but do not draw contour lines. Notice the smooth transition from shadow to light on most of the face. Aim for a homogeneous coverage, without sharp edges for these areas. For softer shadows, try a B graphite pencil (Figure 7.2). I included some hairs on the neck, but this is optional, as they will probably disappear when you shade the area.

Now that the darkest shadows are marked in 4B Black pencil, use the even darker

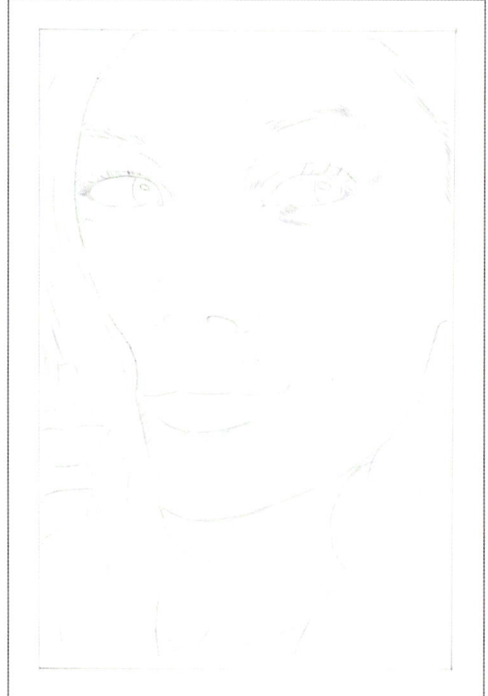

7.1

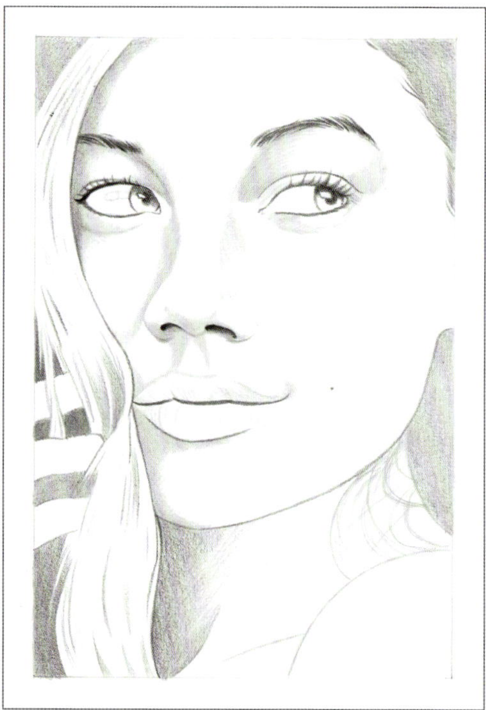

7.2

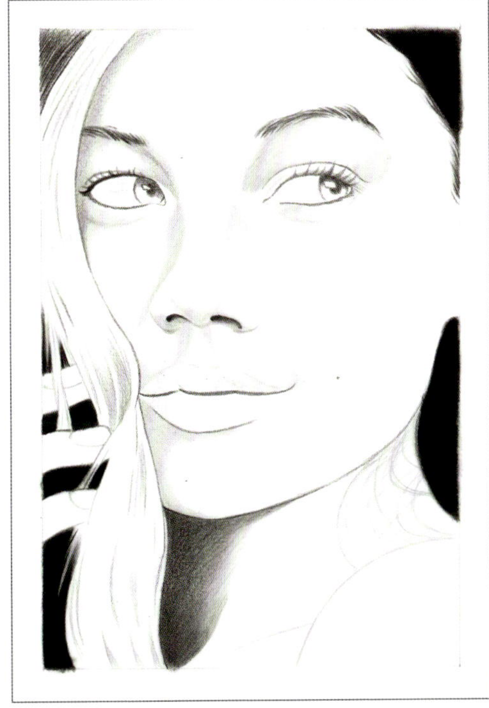

7.3

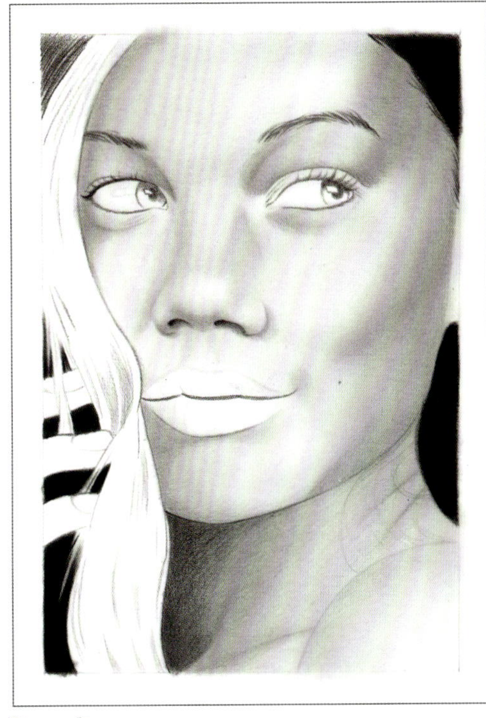

7.4

8B Black pencil to deepen them. Reduce the graininess of the coverage with a firm-bristle brush. For less intense shadows, you could use a 6B Black pencil instead (Figure 7.3). In fact, your choice of the pencil also depends on the pressure you apply when shading.

Once the base for the shadows is done, work on the first layer of the graphite base for the entire face. For this, I used HB, B, and 2B pencils. Here you must put into practice what you have already learned about homogeneous shading, using tissue frequently to blend the graphite and create a smooth base for the skin (Figure 7.4).

Notice that you already have some definition regarding the location of the most intense shadows and the brightest areas as well. This should help you feel more comfortable adding details and adjusting the tones of the entire drawing. I used 4B graphite and 4B Black pencils to do so. In Figure 7.5, the change is more visible in the leftmost shadows, both under the hair and around the neck. As an intermediate tone, 4B graphite pencil will help you smooth transitions like these. Also use a brush to soften the coverage.

Now, focus on the hair on the left side. Follow the same steps as you did for Chapter 6's hair exercise. Use graphite pencils in the lighter areas, and Black carbon pencils for the darker areas to maintain coherence of the tone with the rest of the drawing. To begin, mark the "parts" of the hair, which in this case are the locks. To shade the darkest parts, use Black pencils from 4B to 8B (Figure 7.6). Soften the lines with a firm brush.

For a more general coverage, use graphite pencils between grades 4B and 8B. These are less dark than the Black series and softer pencils, so they blend easily and are not so difficult to erase (Figure 7.7). Easy erasure is very important, because at the end you will be able to create highlights on the hair with a stick eraser.

With the hair completely covered, use a stick eraser to create a shiny effect on the locks (Figure 7.8).

Notice I already finished the fingers in Figure 7.8. You can use the same techniques to shade them as you used for the face and the neck, so I won't go into detail here. Just

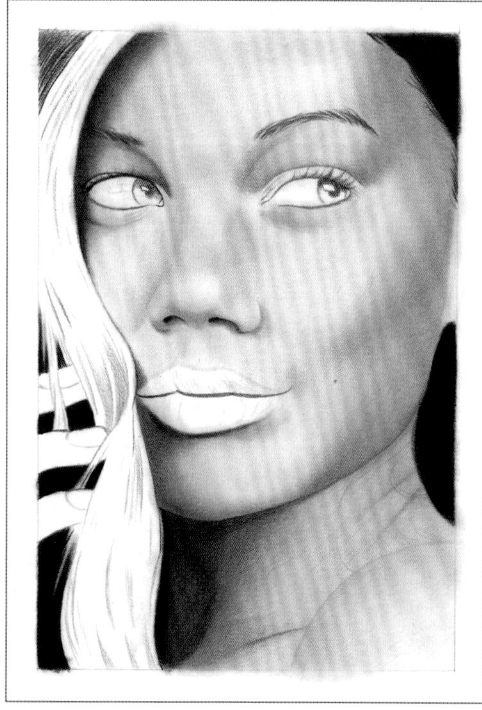

7.5

remember to add a few strands of hair over these fingers after they are finished.

TIP: Use a craft knife to sharpen the eraser's tip if it is worn so you can make better defined marks. Use a brush, preferably one with soft bristles, to reduce the brightness of these marks and give your hair a more natural appearance.

Time to focus on the eyes and eyebrows. First, add more density to the eyebrows with pencils from the Black series. Refer to the eyebrows exercise (Chapter 6) as a guide, but use pencils from the Black series. Use a 4B Black pencil to darken the strands you marked with a graphite pencil and leave

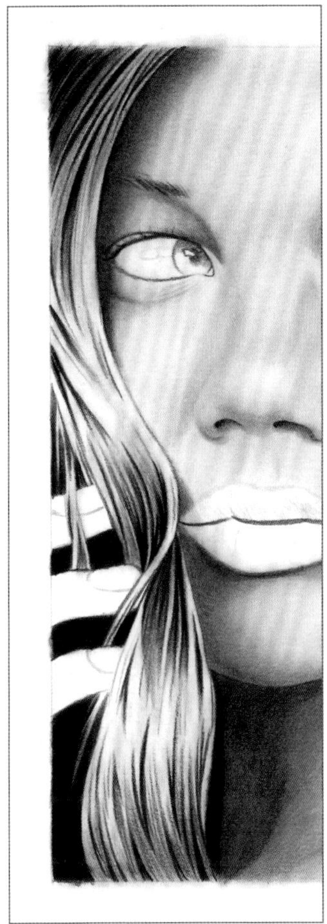

7.6

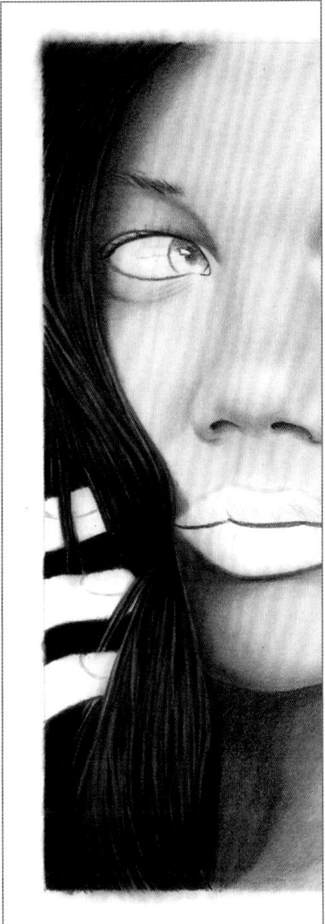

7.7

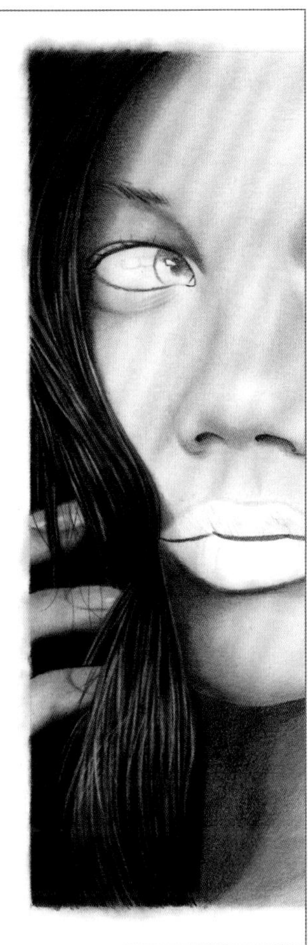

7.8

some gaps between the strands. Always keep the carbon pencil's tip very sharp; you can shape the lead more precisely using a craft knife as well. I used even an 8B Black pencil to highlight and make them darker (Figure 7.9). Use a brush with firm bristles to soften the lines.

The darkest value of the drawing will certainly be present in the pupils of the eyes, so use your darkest pencil for the pupils (I used 8B Black). Also darken the top side of the iris but preserve the space for the reflection on this area. The white of the eye, as you can see in the reference, is not white. I always choose a very light pencil, like an HB, to start the shading and add some details, and then I gradually switch to darker pencils when necessary. Blend the shading using a brush or a blending stump, but make sure they are clean before using them!

Darken the corner of the eye with a 4B Black pencil. On the iris, use only the blending stump, rather than another pencil for now. Highlight the reflection in the white of the eye with a stick eraser (Figure 7.10).

Now darken the iris to the desired tone using 4B, 6B, and 8B Black pencils. Also shade and add texture to the lower and upper eyelids of both eyes with a B graphite pencil, which is still a light pencil. You have to be careful with these textures so as not to overdo them. Therefore, start with lighter pencils so that the effect is more subtle. If necessary, you can switch to darker pencils later (Figure 7.11).

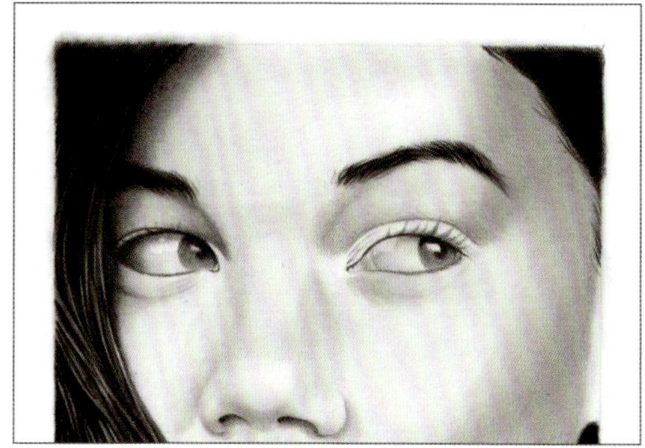

7.9

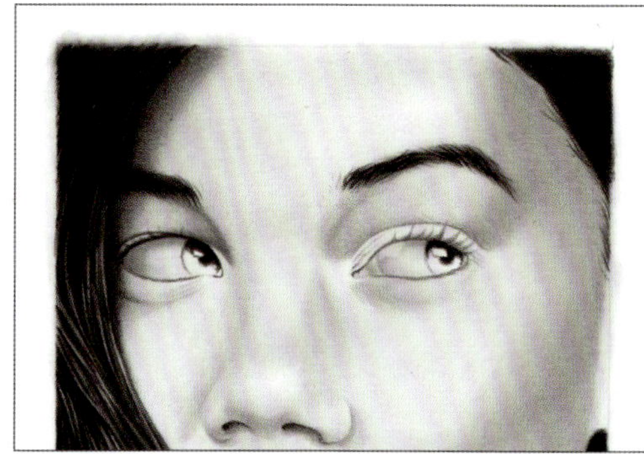

7.10

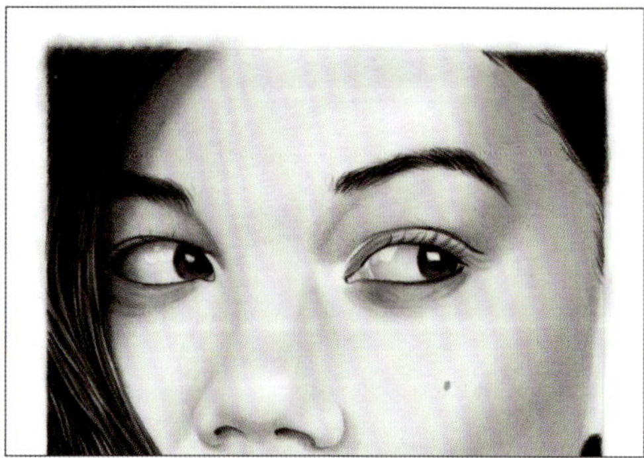

7.11

Figure 7.12 shows a continuation of this process, in which I used HB, B, and 2B graphite pencils to add more texture to the skin. Smooth out the marks made with the pencils using a brush with firm bristles; I used mine a lot. Do this step calmly, as well as the rest of the drawing. Observe where the texture is lighter or darker and change pencils accordingly.

Now, let's finish the eye area. Use an eraser pencil and stick eraser to add a little glow to the skin. So that the shine isn't too intense, use a brush with soft bristles if necessary.

On to the lashes: Note that eyelashes always start thicker and end thinner, so make them that way in your drawing. Sharpen your pencil with a craft knife to achieve the maximum degree of precision with it. Also note that the upper eyelashes are thicker and more abundant, while the lower eyelashes are thinner and sparse, which can be further adjusted by makeup (Figure 7.13).

Move on to the nose now. When drawing the skin around the eyes, I added some skin texture to the nose area (Figures 7.12 and 7.13). Continue adding texture, initially using an HB pencil, so that you don't accidentally overdo it.

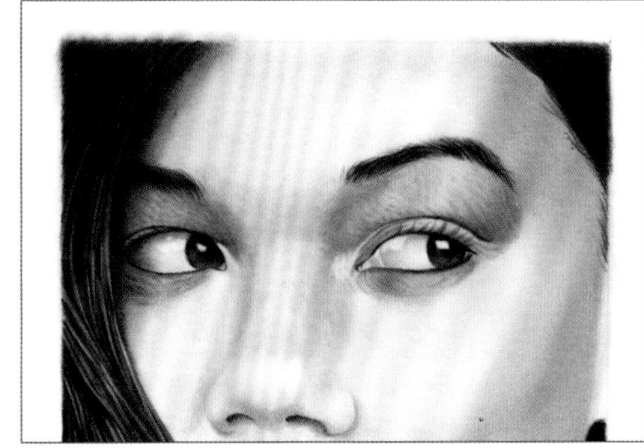

7.12

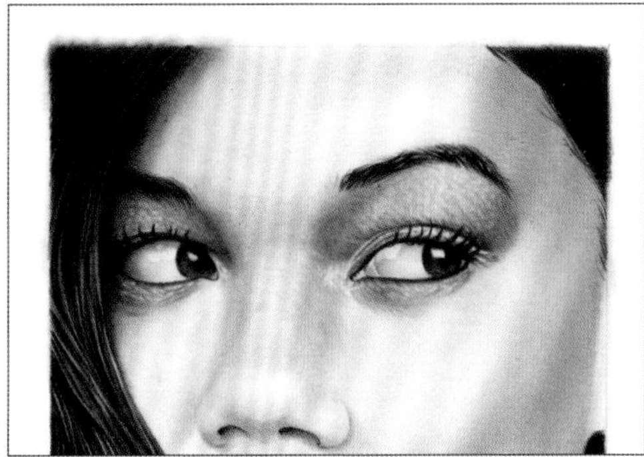

7.13

In the area below the tip of the nose, gradually intensify the shading. Here the shade should be much darker than on the sides of the nose; use darker pencils, such as graphite B, 2B, and 4B and even 4B Black. Figure 7.14 shows the beginning of the process with graphite pencils, which will become more intense soon.

Figure 7.15 shows the finished nose and the area around it. To achieve this, continue the texture mainly with an HB pencil, while using B and 2B pencils below the tip of the nose and around the nostrils. You can intensify these shadows a little more where you think necessary with a 4B Black pencil. Do the skin texture around the nose with an HB pencil as well. Wherever it is necessary to darken it a little more, just use a B pencil, albeit sparingly.

Once again, add some light touches to the tip of the nose and around it with the eraser pencil. If the eraser marks are too light, use a brush with soft bristles to soften their tone, which I do frequently.

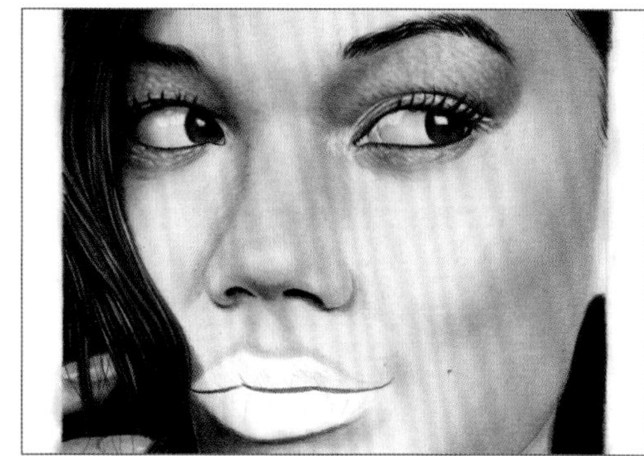

7.14

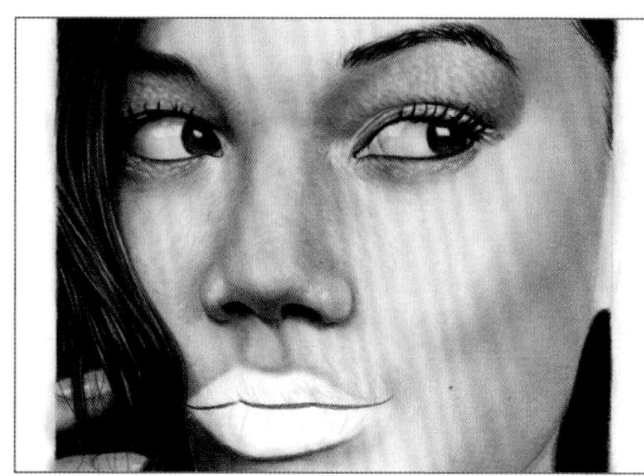

7.15

When I have to shade an area with a richer texture, full of details, I usually leave that texture highlighted first and worry about the general tone of the area later. That's what I recommend you do for the mouth: Initially, use an HB pencil to mark the texture of the upper and lower lips, then gradually darken these markings.

Before that, however, use a 4B Black pencil to mark the points where the shadow will be more intense on the mouth (Figure 7.16), especially on the upper lip and below the lower lip, on the face's skin.

You later can intensify the marks you made with a 4B Black pencil and with 6B and 8B Black pencils too, but in a very specific way, being careful not to overdo it. You can also darken the marks that you made with the HB pencil using a B graphite pencil. As you soften these marks with a firm-bristle brush, it will naturally spread the graphite powder along the lips, covering them with an intermediate shade of gray. The brush will also blend the base layer you made with the HB pencil beforehand. The mouth in Figure 7.17 has a good base to work with. Darken the right corner of the mouth a little with an HB pencil.

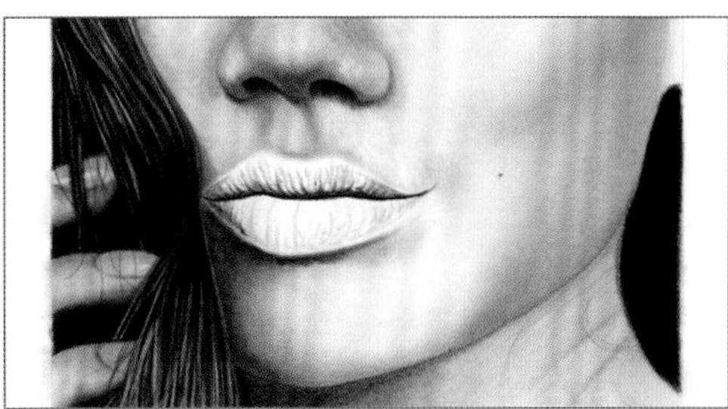

7.16

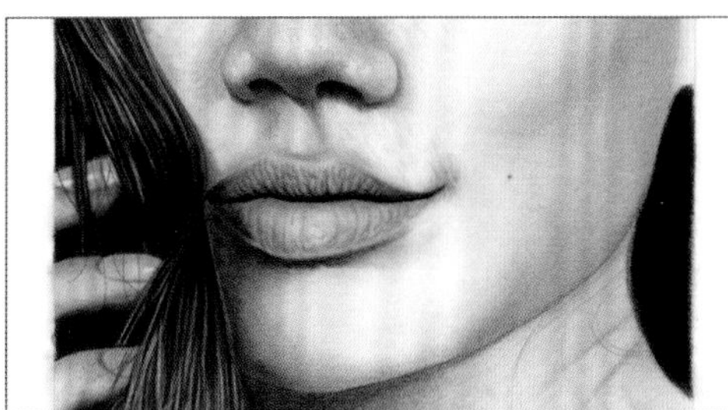

7.17

If the mouth still feels a little pale, go ahead with a 4B Black pencil, increasing the intensity and extension of the shadows, even making it play with the grooves present on the surface of the lips. Use your firm-bristle brush a lot, not only to smooth out the grooves, but also to darken the lips as a whole. I also did the same with some more discreet adjustments using B and 2B graphite pencils (Figure 7.18).

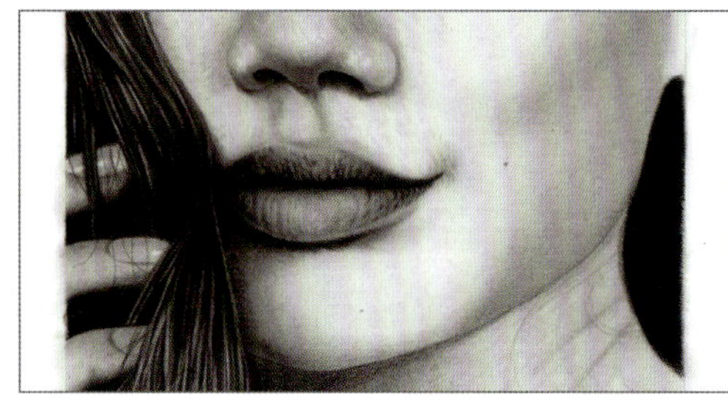
7.18

We've reached my favorite moment, which gives real vitality to the drawing: doing the highlights. Using a Tombow MONO Zero Eraser will enable you to make very delicate and precise details, following the direction of the grooves. I also erased some of the tone on the skin around the upper lip, as I noticed that this area is a little lighter in my reference image.

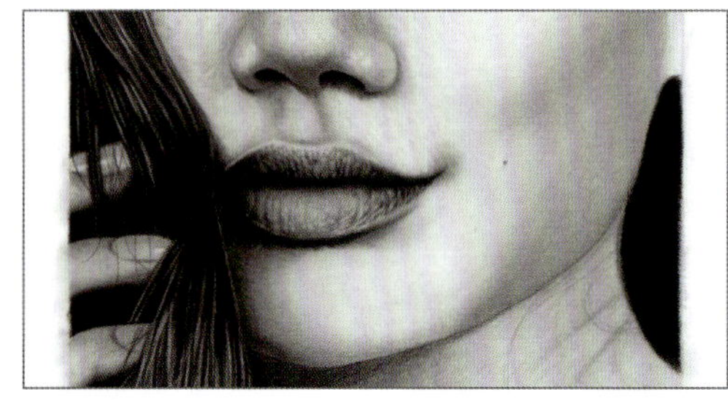
7.19

To reduce the intensity of the shine on the lips, use a soft cat's tongue brush. This adjustment is often welcome, as a very intense brightness may look a little artificial. The brush also reduces the roughness of the eraser's touch, leaving the markings a little softer, with the edges less sharp (Figure 7.19).

Before shading the neck and shoulder, finish the skin on the face. Here, I needed some time to calmly shade the rest of the face, using mainly an HB pencil as a base and using tissue to frequently blend the graphite out. Notice the changes made between Figure 7.19 and Figure 7.20.

The work on the chin is especially important, as it stands out in the portrait and has a shadow cast by the hair. Here use your Black pencils in the shadow area and graphite pencils for the base of the skin, trying to convey the ideal volume through a balanced play of light and shadow.

Figure 7.20 is not exactly the finished face (I did some small adjustments to the tone of the shadows) but already very close to it. Notice the change on the left side of the neck, where I intensified some shadows present there using the Black pencils.

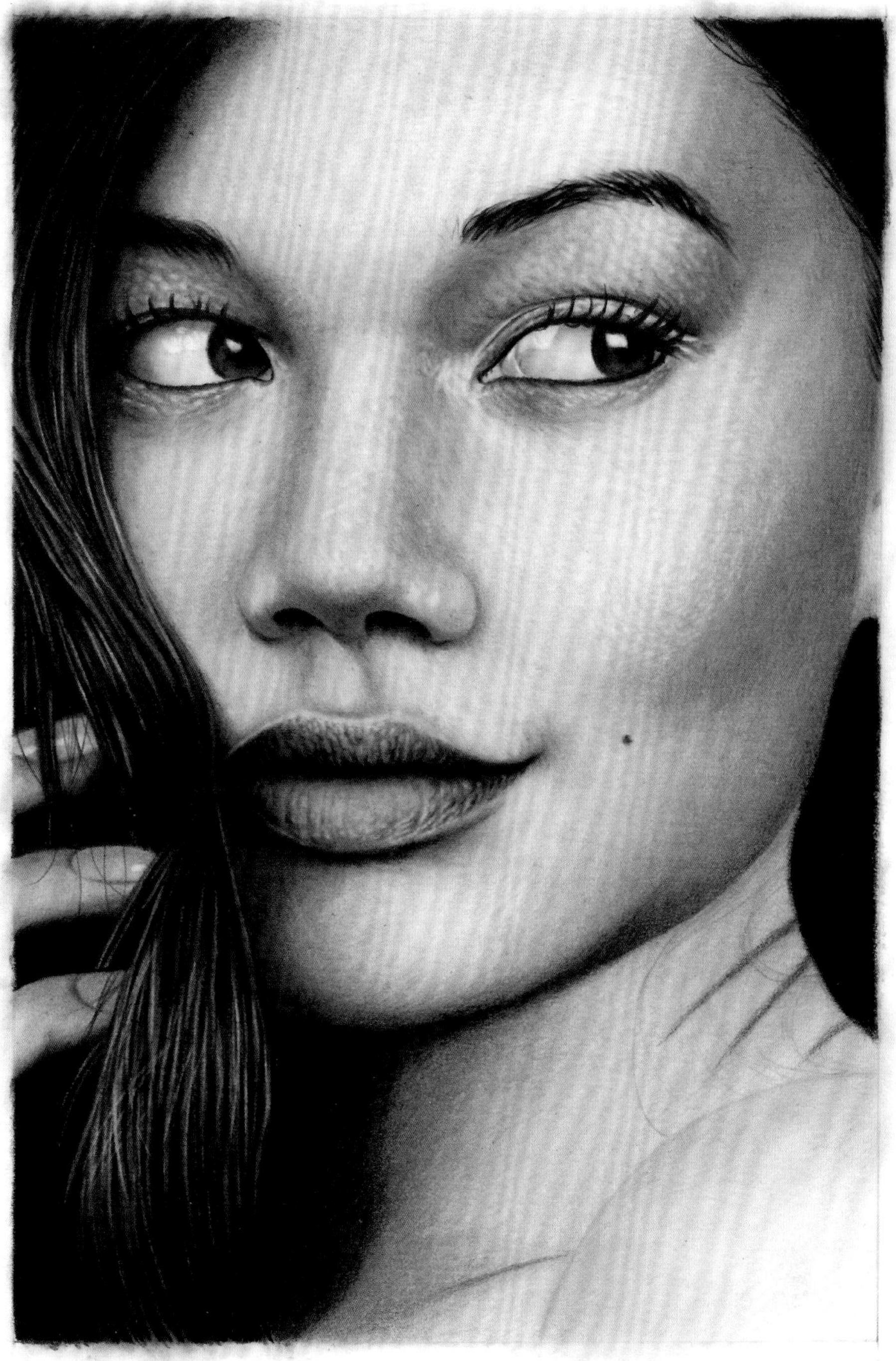

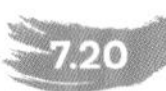
7.20

For the neck, I recommend 4B, 6B, and 8B Black pencils; I used mine a lot here. Focus on the transition from the more intense shadow to the lighter area of the neck, which is a gradient, after all. I also marked some skin folds on the right side, even knowing that they would be almost completely covered by the hair.

To advance the neck shadow, try a 4B Black, and then reinforce a darker area within it with an 8B Black pencil (Figure 7.21).

To shade the neck and shoulder more, but without making it too dark, use a variety of graphite pencils, but mainly a 4B, which will cover in an intermediate tone. Blend with tissue a lot here. It's a wide area, and you don't want the pencil strokes to be visible at all.

This is not just simple shading, but also texture work. In this case, you can also use B and 2B graphite pencils, which create stains that tend to be more resistant to the use of tissue. Thus, you can use your B, 2B, and 4B pencils widely here. Make circular movements to create spots on the skin, then partially dissolve them with tissue to create an interesting effect (Figure 7.22).

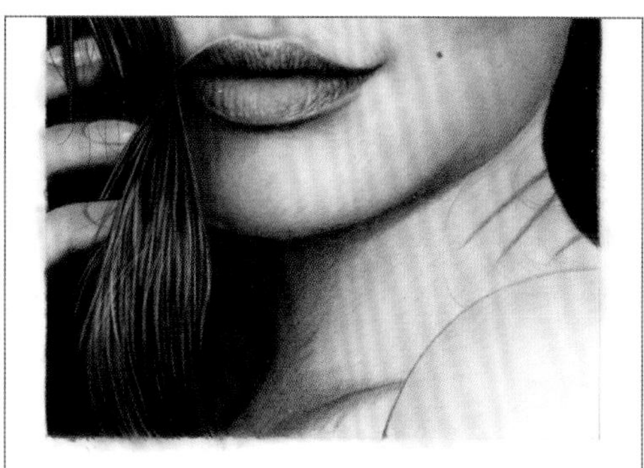

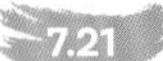

7.21

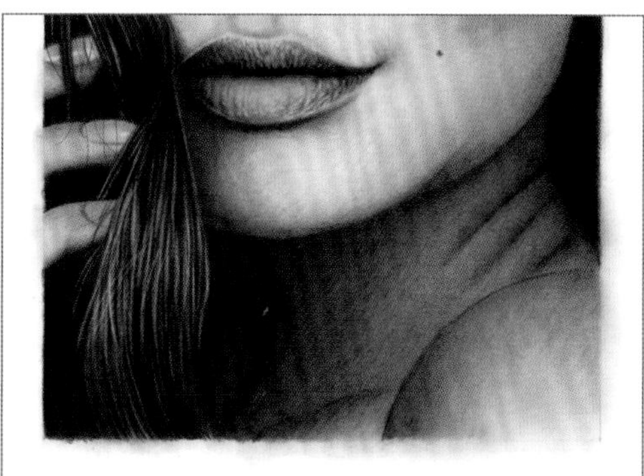

7.22

The appearance of the skin at this point, for me, was already quite satisfactory. However, I still used an eraser pencil to add some lighter spots. I confess now that I don't know if it was a good choice. We don't always get everything right, and in this case perhaps the skin would have had a more natural appearance without the use of the eraser. In any case, the result is that of Figure 7.23, which was only partially attenuated with a brush with a cat's tongue tip.

With the skin finished, all that remains is to draw the strands of hair over the neck on the right side of the drawing. To do so, make successive layers of hair strands alternating pencils of different grades. Due to its relative rigidity and dark tone, make the first layer of strands with a Staedtler 4B Black pencil. Using a lighter pencil here would amount to nothing, as the area as a whole is already quite dark (Figure 7.24).

In the first layer of strands, I made a tangle of thin strands. In the next layer, I reinforced some of these strands and also created some thicker strands and even some thin locks using the 6B and 8B Black pencils. I chose these pencils because the hair of the girl portrayed is dark, and their tone helps to highlight her face even more, drawing attention to what matters. You can see the finished portrait in Figure 7.25.

TIP: The darker a pencil is, be it graphite or carbon, the greater the chance of its tip to break, as darker pencils tend to be softer. Therefore, tracing a strand of hair is easier with a 2B pencil than with an 8B, and this applies to Staedtler Black pencils as well. Therefore, do not apply too much pressure when handling a pencil, especially darker ones.

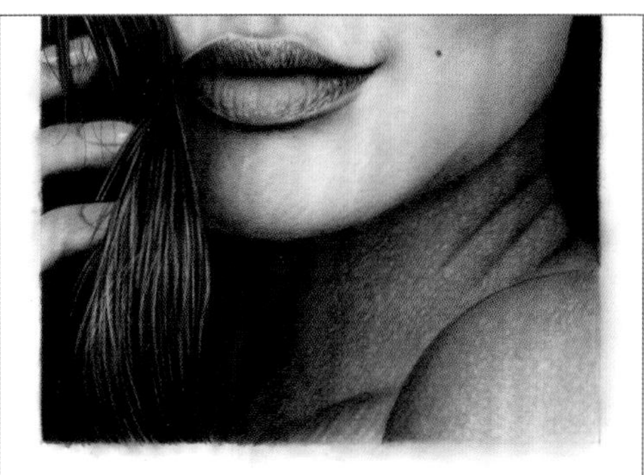

7.23

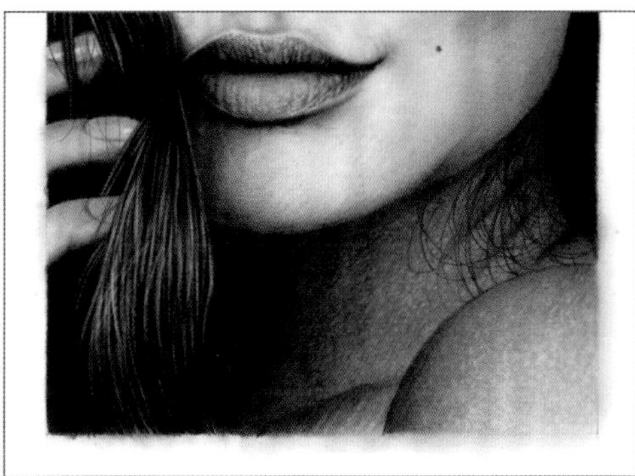

7.24

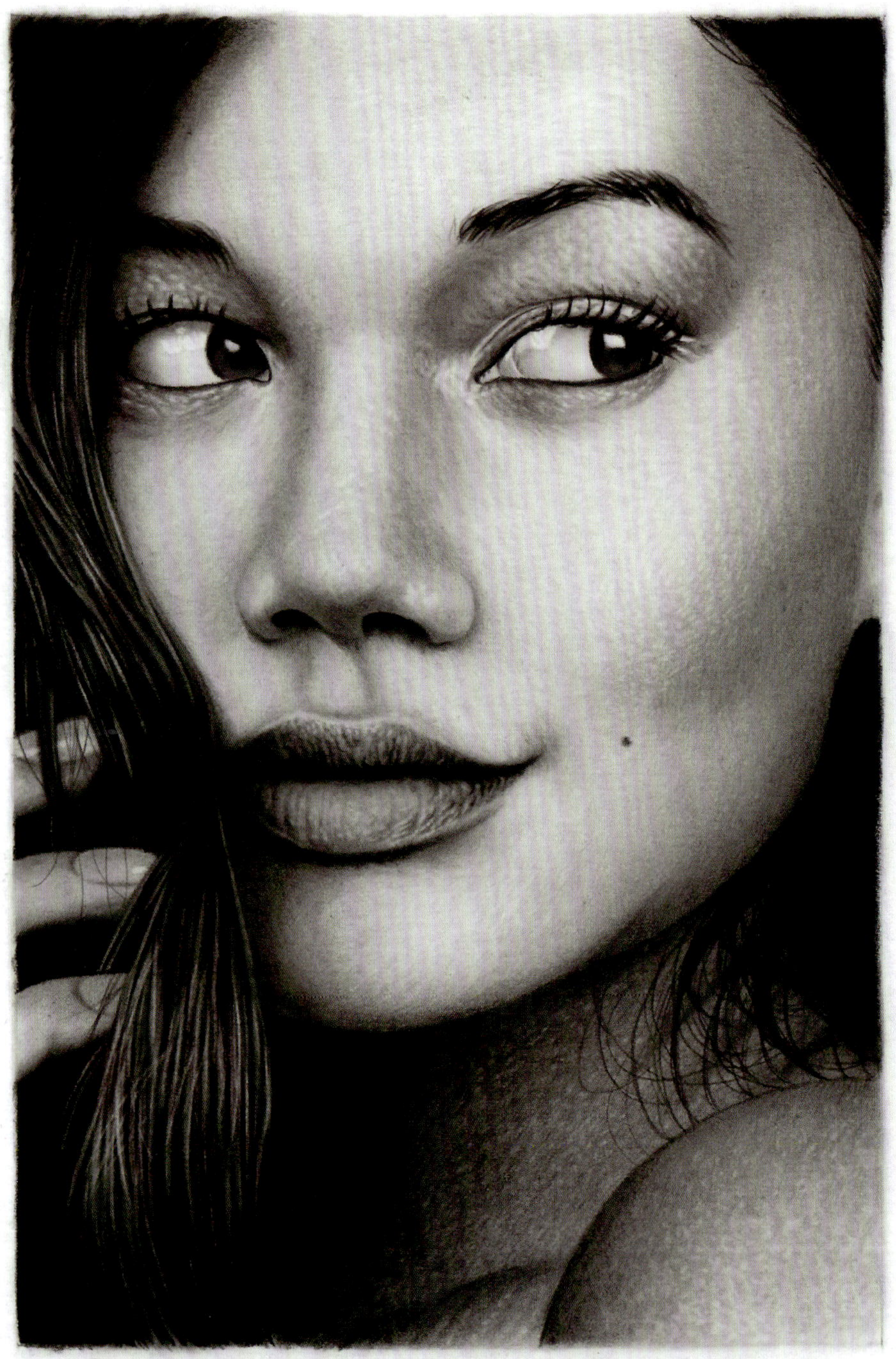

7.25

Animal portrait

As this animal portrait will demonstrate, you don't always have to follow the same steps to make any type of drawing. Don't worry, this exercise does build on the techniques you learned in the animal fur exercise (Chapter 6), and what you're going to do now is a practical application of what you saw there.

Start by drawing a sketch of a cat portrait (Figure 7.26), but avoid drawing continuous contour lines, except for the eyes and snout. Because the animal is covered with fur in all other areas, obey this logic. Draw the cat with thousands of short strokes, as if you were drawing strand by strand.

The cat has long white whiskers, and the background of the reference image is completely white. How do you represent the whiskers? Simple: Change your background to gray! To keep the background from feeling too heavy, however, create a partial coverage with a gray tone up to a certain height, like a large gradient (Figure 7.27). To do so, use HB and B graphite pencils and blend with tissue.

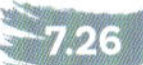
7.26

7.27

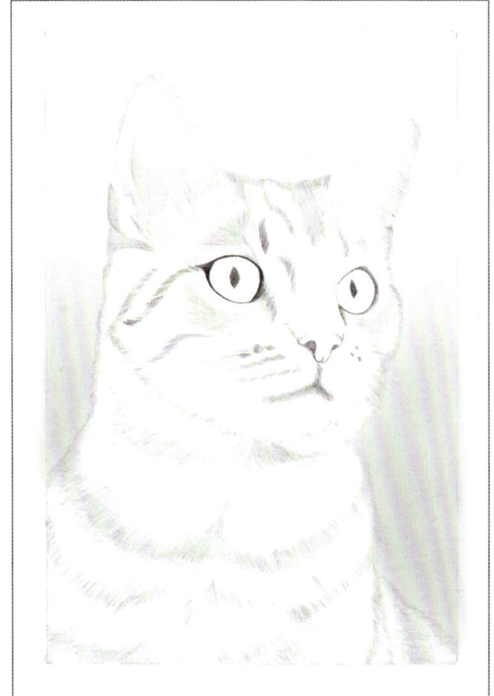

7.28

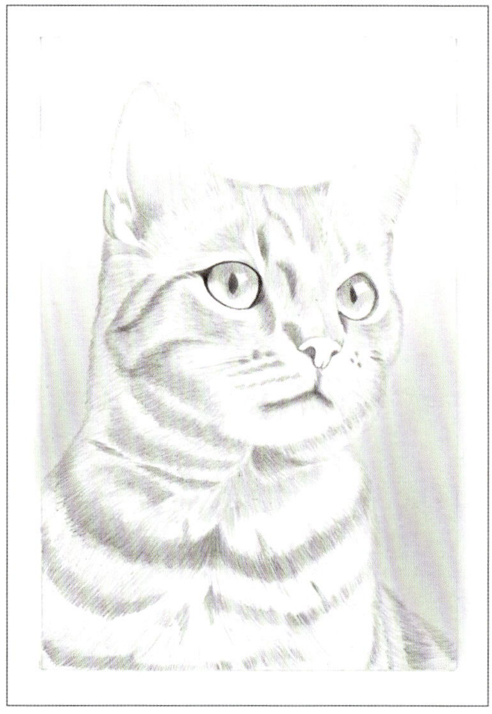

7.29

Turning your attention to the cat, start to demarcate the darker areas of the portrait using a 2B graphite pencil. After all, the overall tone of this drawing will be lighter. Always draw strokes parallel to each other, simulating fur. Remember to sharpen and shape the lead of the pencil to a chisel (Chapter 4) and try to use the sharp edge of the pencil tip at this stage. Mark the eyes with a 4B Black pencil (Figure 7.28).

Using a 2B pencil when you begin shading will help you feel more confident and avoid darkening the drawing too soon. Once you have a base with the 2B, reinforce these same marks using a 4B graphite pencil. In the other lighter areas, use the same 2B or even a B graphite pencil, always drawing fur strands. Don't use a brush to spread the graphite and soften the strokes yet. You can darken the eyes a little with an 8B Black pencil now, but lightly (Figure 7.29).

The next steps will focus on the upper part of the portrait; the body will follow the same logic and will not require such a detailed explanation. So, first mark the white strands of the cat's whiskers, making long lines with your stick eraser. It's natural for these lines to be a little thick, as the eraser wears out quickly and its precision decreases. This is not such a serious problem, because you can adjust the thickness of these lines later. Still, try to draw them as thin as possible. (See why I've advised you not to use Black pencils on the fur yet? The strokes from these pencils are very difficult to erase.)

Once the whiskers are done, including over the gray background, you can darken the fur to better match the reference. Start with a 4B Black pencil. At the end of each layer, use a firm-bristle brush to soften the coverage (Figure 7.30). Continue, as well, to darken the eyes, snout, and the mouth gradually.

The more homogeneous coverage has its function, which is to give the drawing as a whole a softer and more natural appearance. However, the fur needs more details. To add them, use a harder graphite pencil, a B, to draw a series of short strokes, which simulate shorter strands. Afterwards, use your brush—a lot. Don't worry, it will not undo these lines. Using 4B Black and 6B Black pencils, make the darker strands even darker (Figure 7.31).

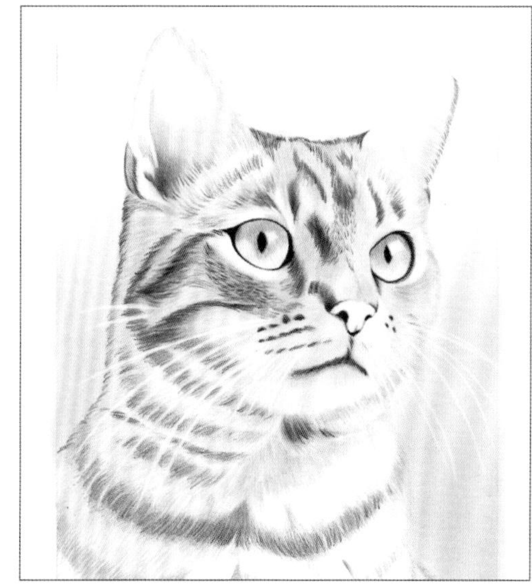

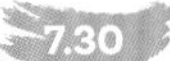
7.30

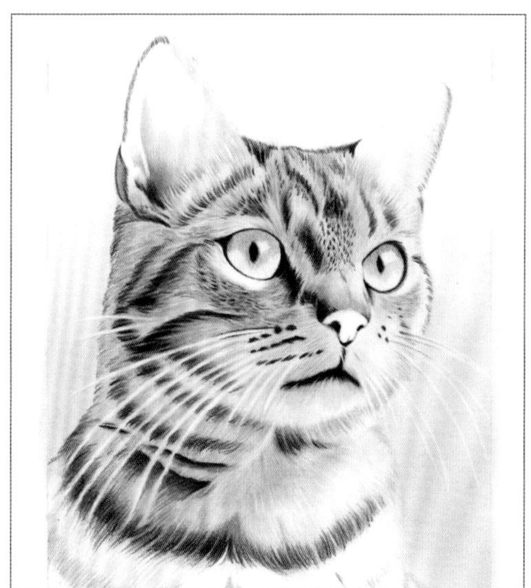

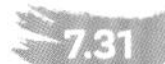
7.31

Continue the darkening process. Because I wasn't satisfied with the shades I'd achieved so far, I decided to also use a 4B graphite pencil on the lighter hair, especially on the left side, to darken the intermediate tones in some parts of the cat. At the same time, you can narrow the cat's whisker hairs a little by tracing more strands around them. With the same 4B pencil, shade the ears and snout, which have a homogeneous coverage layer base. You can cover the ears completely, because normal 4B graphite is easy to erase and you will have to do this to add the white strands later anyway. In these areas, use tissue and a blending stump after the 4B graphite pencil (Figure 7.32).

Use a 4B Black pencil to darken in the upper part of each eye, and then use the firm-bristle brush to soften the lines (Figure 7.33). Use a stick eraser afterwards to give more definition to the light reflections seen in the eyes.

As for the ears, add white strands with the same thin eraser. Based on the reference image, I added long and short strands that followed different directions. This is the type of detail that enriches the drawing, even if it is not the center of attention in a composition. At this point, you can clean the white background above the cat's head if necessary; an eraser pen would work well.

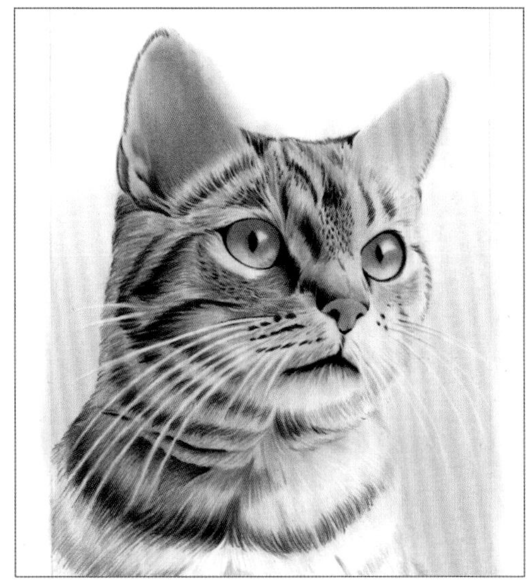

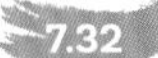
7.32

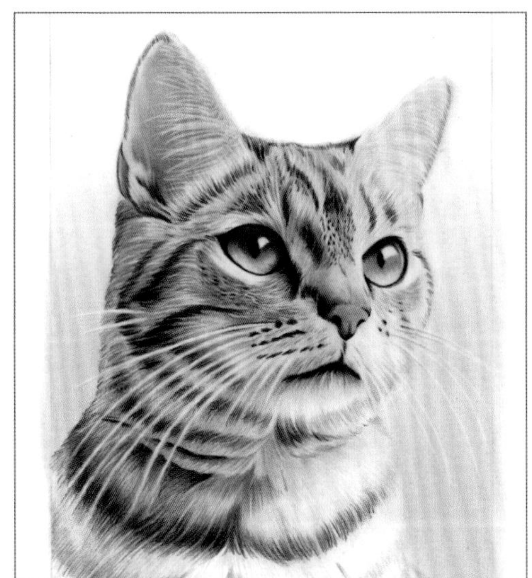
7.33

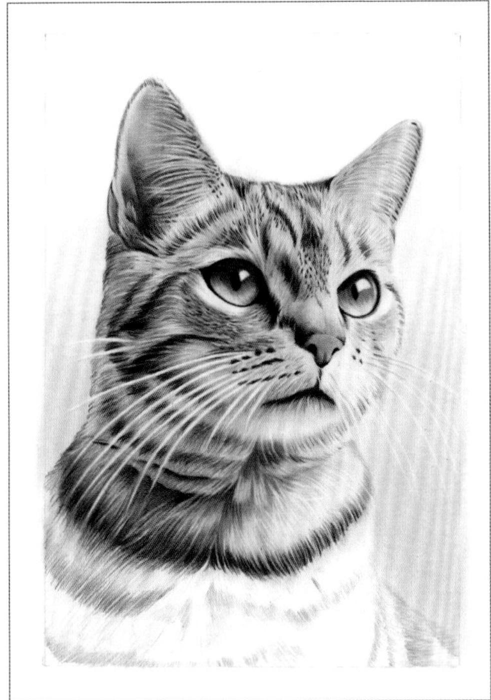

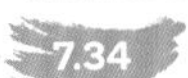
7.34

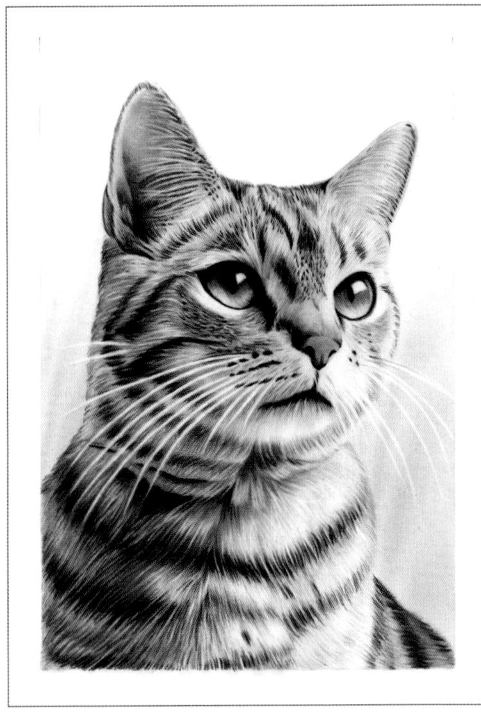

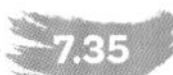
7.35

Continuing with the details of the ears, use a 4B Black pencil for the darker shadows in the area, shading around the eraser marks. Add some less dark shadows to both ears with a B graphite pencil, then brush. After you use the brush to soften these shadows, the strands may become darker, but you can use your stick eraser once more to lighten them.

With your B graphite pencil, add more details to the eyes, as well as darken the lower right area of the cat. With these pencils, the brush, and the stick eraser, you can create a weave of strands that is lighter than those in other areas (Figure 7.34).

The general values are now more or less established, in addition to most of the details. From here, adjust the tones and add details in the lower region of the portrait, carrying out the same procedure as for the upper body. I used Black pencils more to intensify the darker fur, graphite pencils to adjust the intermediate tones, including shaping the whiskers, and a thin Tombow MONO Zero Eraser to lighten the strands that are lighter, including the mustache. And now it's finished (Figure 7.35)!

Flower

In this next exercise, the flower has a very dark overall tone, which differentiates it a little from the previous exercises. For this or a similar drawing, I recommend using Staedtler's Black series of carbon pencils. You could do the exercise using only graphite pencils, but your drawing would have a more limited range of values and be quite shiny due to the graphite. A matte setting spray (Chapter 2) would calm the shine for you, though.

Take a look at Figure 7.36, my sketch of the example flower. The most complicated area of the drawing is the petals, especially those in the center. The lower area, the leaves, is very dark, and I sometimes got lost there. If you find it hard to understand what you're drawing, too, simply draw what you see. If you see stains, draw stains even if you're not sure what they represent. When making your sketch, treat this area as an abstract drawing, if you need to.

I followed this approach for the example, so you may notice some differences between the initial sketch and the shape of the final flower, because I made some adjustments while shading—and you can too.

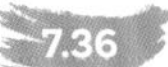
7.36

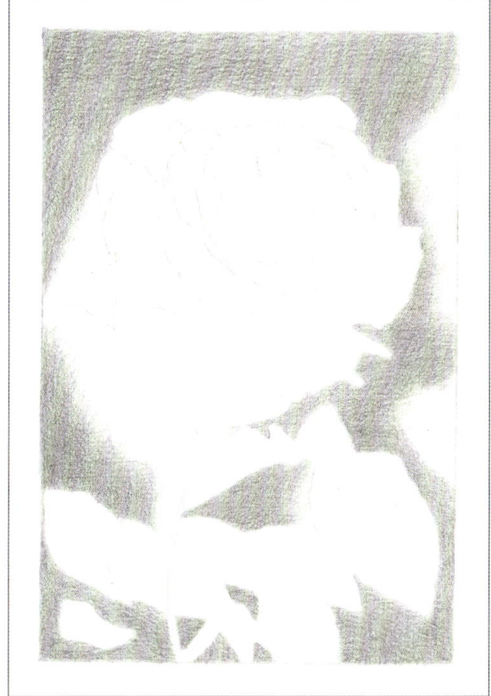

7.37

7.38

Start shading the background, as the general tonality of the drawing will be determined by the tone established in the background. To differentiate the darker areas from the less dark ones, use a 4B Black pencil to create homogeneous coverage where the background will be darker (Figure 7.37). The background will not, however, contain the darkest tone of the entire drawing. Based on the reference image, the darkest tone is in the flower, so save your darkest pencil, such as my Staedtler 8B Black, for that. (Can you spot it in Figure 7.47, the final image?)

Use a 6B graphite pencil to fill in the gaps in the background reserved for lighter tones (Figure 7.38). These lighter areas not only break the monotony of a merely black background, they also highlight some shadows of the flower itself and make it stand out a little more from the background, even though both are dark.

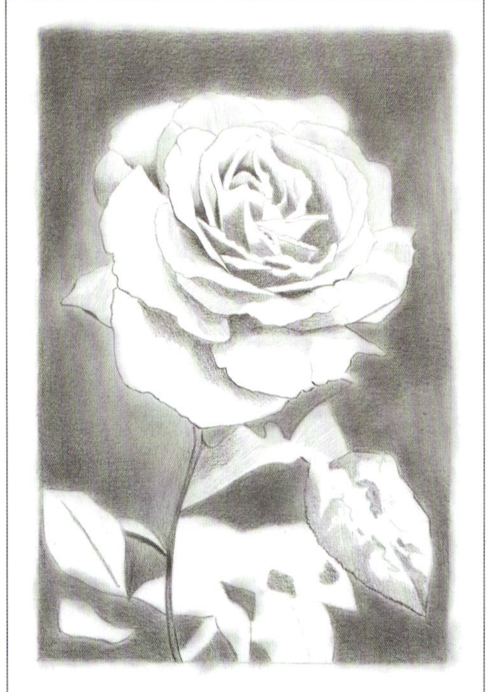

7.39

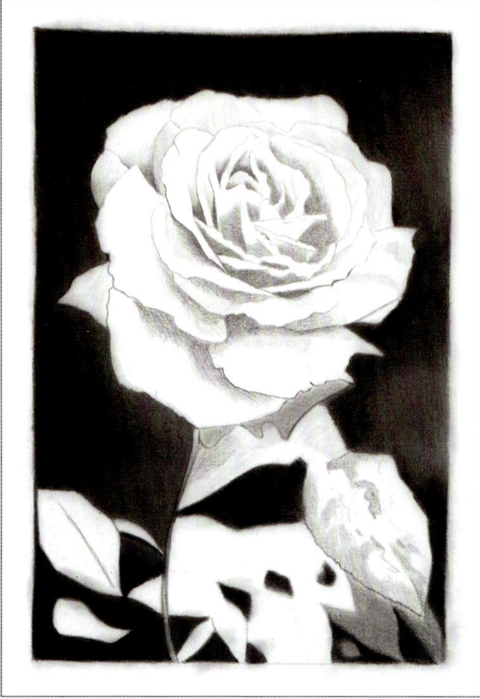

7.40

Start blending the graphite using the firm-bristle brush and tissue. The brush will give you more precision, so use it in the areas closest to the flower and use tissue further away. To give greater definition to the contours of the petals and leaves (okay, the entire flower), trace them. I used a 4B Black pencil for the darker contours and an HB graphite pencil for the other contours. You can start shading the inner areas of the flower with the same two tones, as well (**Figure 7.39**).

Return to the background and darken it to its finished tones. Make repeated layers with a 4B Black pencil and a touch of 6B Black, always crossing the lines and blending the coverage using the brush and tissue. You can reinforce the less dark areas of the background with a 6B graphite pencil (**Figure 7.40**).

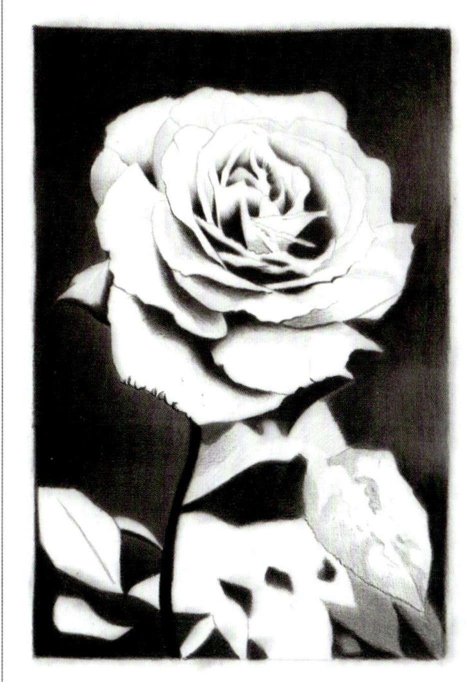

7.41

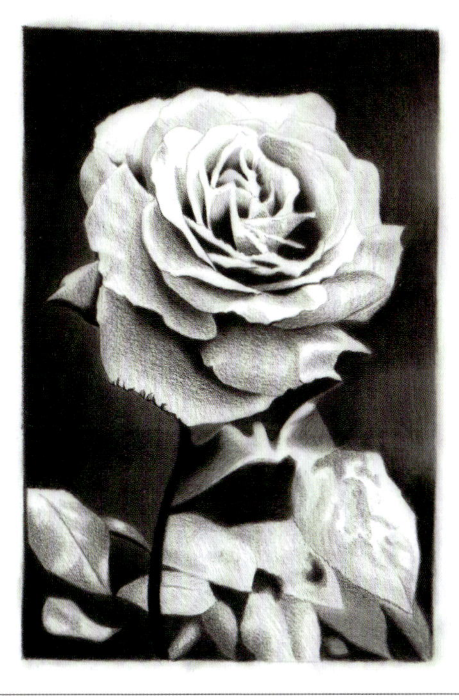

7.42

The time has come to add the darkest shadows to the entire drawing using the 8B Black pencil. These shadows will be in the stem and between the petals. After applying the 8B Black, soften the shadows with a firm-bristle brush (**Figure 7.41**). As this is, once again, an A5-size drawing with very small details, I used my smallest flat brush.

Little by little the flower is taking shape. Next, try to create a general base for the flower and the leaves in the lower area of the drawing. Carefully use a 4B Black pencil,

paying attention to details and trying to make smooth transitions from shadow to light through gradients (**Figure 7.42**).

This step is a little more laborious, as the shadow is what conveys three-dimensionality to the object. Notice that the flower area is in focus with very well-defined contours, while the leaves area is out of focus with little definition. The shading in these two areas also needs to be different. Blend out your shading immediately using tissue, a stump, or a brush depending on the location.

As you may have already noticed, the base layer provides a mapping of where the shadows and lights of the drawing will be. There is practically no way to leave the finished drawing with a single layer of coverage. So, add new layers using not only a 4B Black pencil, but 6B and 8B Blacks too. In the lighter areas, I also used a 2B Black, a pencil that I don't really like because of its stiffness, but it allowed me to make a softer coverage in the lighter areas of the petals.

You can use tissue to blend everything that has been done so far (Figure 7.43). The overall shape will not be lost, because the

material used for the Black pencils does not blend as easily as common graphite.

Staedtler's Black pencils are very good for giving a darker shade in a controlled way, but they also have a grainy appearance that sometimes bothers me a little. Therefore, on top of the coverage done so far, I used 4B and 6B graphite pencils to "mix" the carbon from the Black series with the graphite, which is easier to blend, and used tissue to obtain more smooth and consistent shading. Take a look at Figure 7.44 and give the method a try if you like the result. Either way, make the flower even darker at this stage.

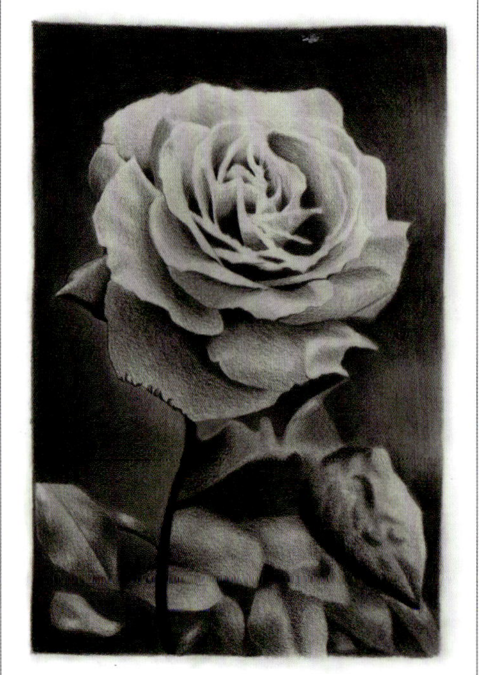

7.43

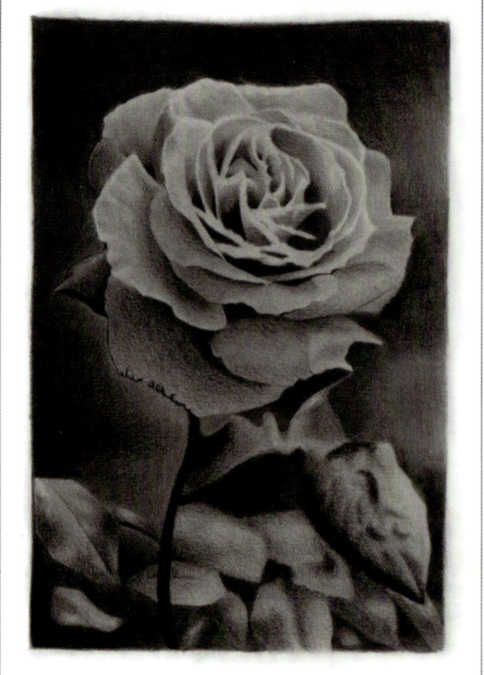

7.44

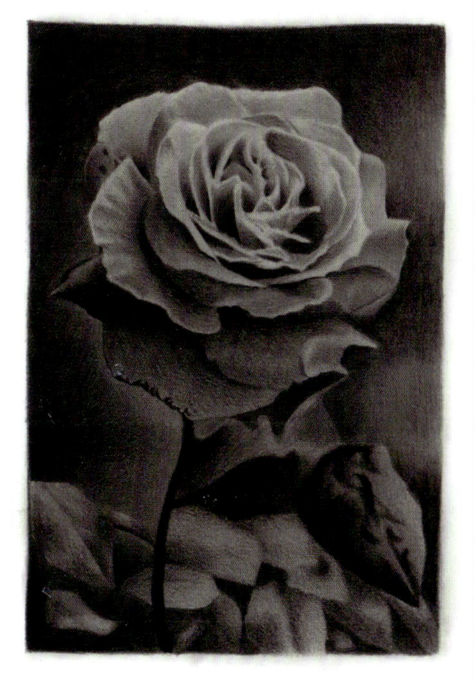

7.45

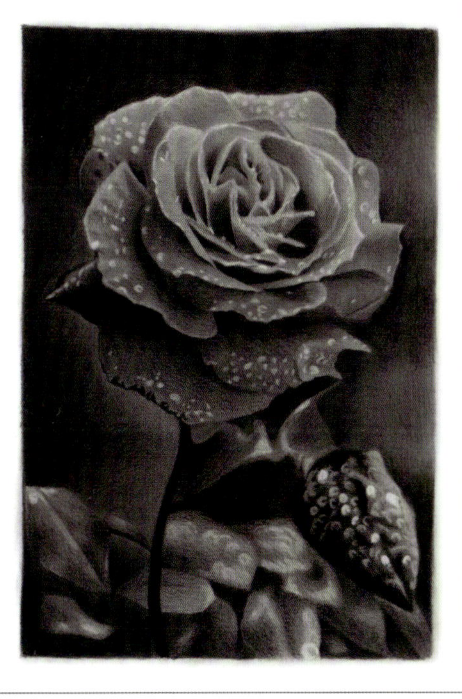

7.46

Add more layers of coverage with 6B Black and 6B graphite pencils, going deeper into the details. Blend these new layers with a firm-bristle brush (**Figure 7.45**). Focus on achieving a greater degree of definition, as we approach the final stretch of this drawing.

Up until now the drawing (mine at least) has been somewhat monotonous, lifeless. Let's take it to a new level. One of the reasons I chose the reference image was the presence of water drops, which make the flower more vibrant and full of luminous details. To make them, use an eraser pencil (a stick eraser is not as effective). Initially the drops

are just lighter spots with little definition, and the eraser pencil can create light spots even in areas shaded with carbon pencil. Yes, these are still undefined spots (**Figure 7.46**), but you practiced water drops in Chapter 5 so you know what to do. Before finishing them, however, highlight some edges of the petals with your eraser pencil, always considering the direction of the light (from right to left in the example).

I used an electric eraser to highlight some water drops, because it can create the brightest highlights and that interested me here, especially on the leaf in the lower-right corner.

To finish, you can highlight the presence of the drops by using different pencils to create the shadows they cast. I also added a few more drops using an eraser pencil, intensified some highlights discreetly with the electric eraser, reduced the intensity of the shine in others with a soft brush, and softened the shading in a few more areas with a firm-bristle brush (**Figure 7.47**).

This flower has been a different theme from the book's portraits, but I hope you found it fun! Drawing nature is a universe worth exploring.

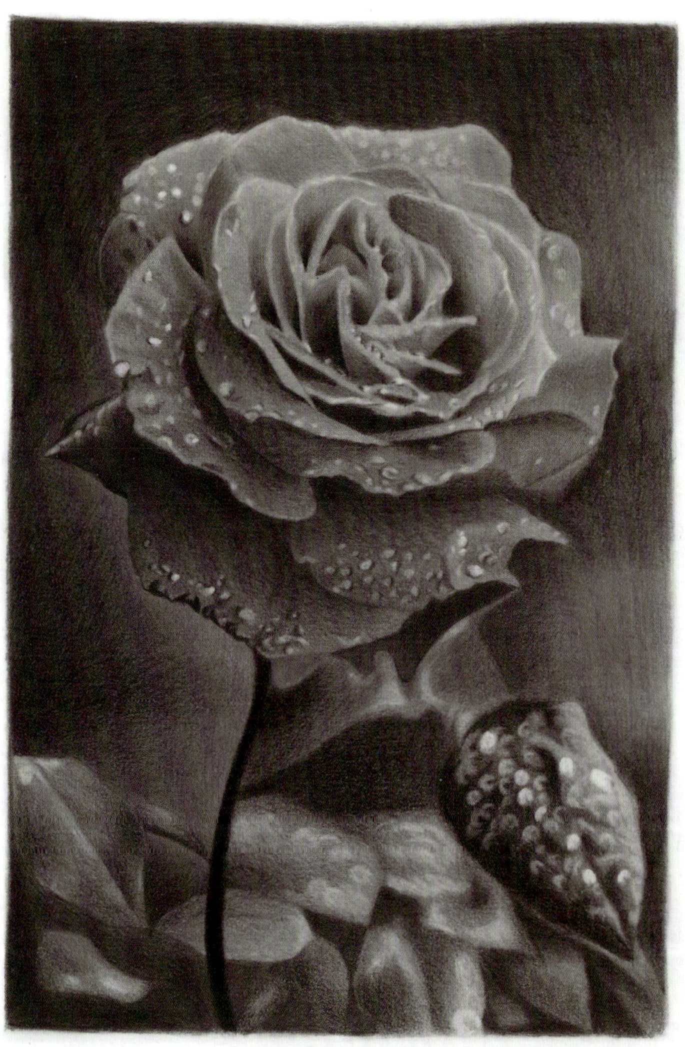

7.47

Sculpture

To wrap up this book, we'll draw a sculpture of Asclepius, the Greco-Roman god of medicine. If you like challenges, this exercise is for you. It is probably the most difficult drawing in the book, but also the most rewarding to complete successfully. You'll build on what you learned in the stone drawing exercise in Chapter 6. Although the texture of the sculpture's stone is a bit different, the techniques will be familiar. So will the paper size: A5. Again, I recommend using carbon pencils, which will enable you to work with a larger value range, achieve very dark shades of gray, and give a lot of depth to the drawing. Be sure to study the finished example in Figure 7.63 before you begin.

Trace the sketch using the transfer method once again. Note in Figure 7.48 that I avoided continuous lines and did something closer to scribbling. Finding straight or continuous lines in stone can be difficult, except in the parts carved more carefully by the artist, such as on the face. If you follow this looser, scribble-like approach, your sketch will already convey a little of the feeling of the stone.

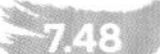
7.48

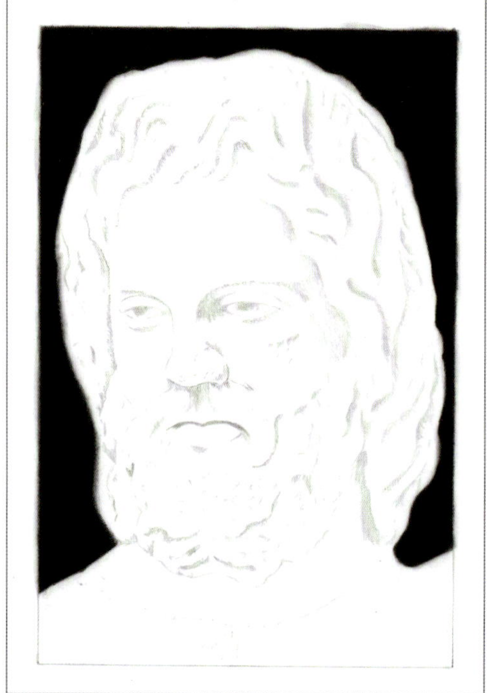

7.49

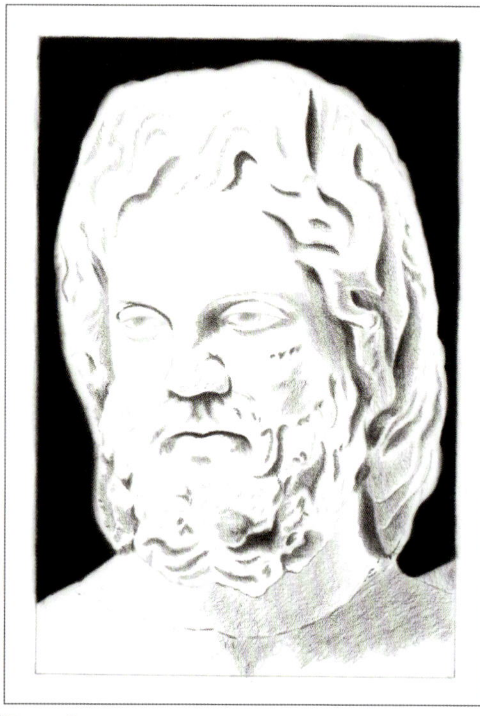

7.50

Next, start the background. Use your darkest pencil (for me, an 8B Black), and darken the background as much as possible. Overlay layers of dark gray, and then use a firm-bristle brush to spread the powder and achieve a coverage in which the pencil marks are not obvious (**Figure 7.49**).

With the background done, you can focus on shading the sculpture. Begin by mapping the most intense shadows in the drawing. I used a 4B Black pencil for this. Why not use the 8B Black? Gradually darkening the drawing with a 4B gave me (and will give you) greater control of the process. In the end, it will be easier to identify the shadows whose tone is closest to black. Because the sculpture has so many details, it may be difficult to make all the darker shadows right away, but **Figure 7.50** includes most of them.

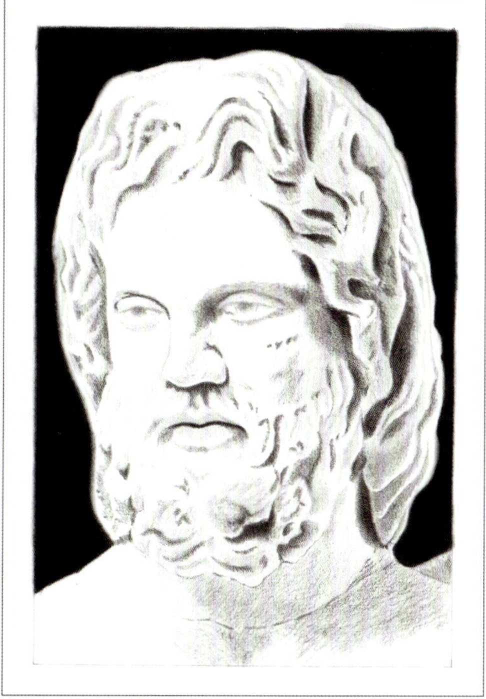

7.51

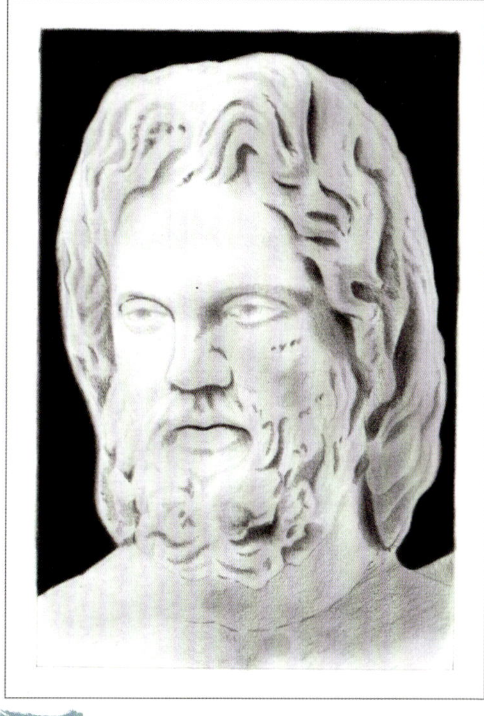

7.52

Now, go in the opposite direction and map the points of light. How do we draw light? By darkening what is around it. With your lightest pencil (for me, an HB graphite pencil), make a general shadow base for the drawing. Although you should add this shading with some attention to detail (Figure 7.51), this is far from necessary. Your next step is to spread the graphite with tissue, which, in a way, will mess everything up.

Note in Figure 7.52, however, that all is not lost: Most of the 4B Black pencil work remains visible, and even the lighter areas are partially preserved. Use these two reference values to guide you from now on.

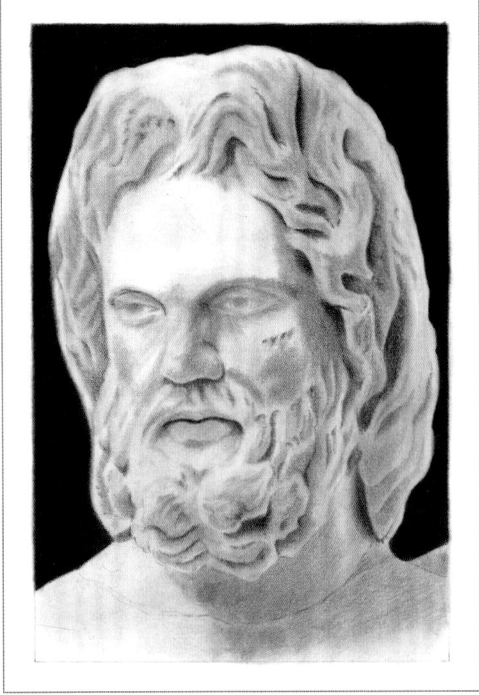

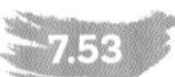
7.53

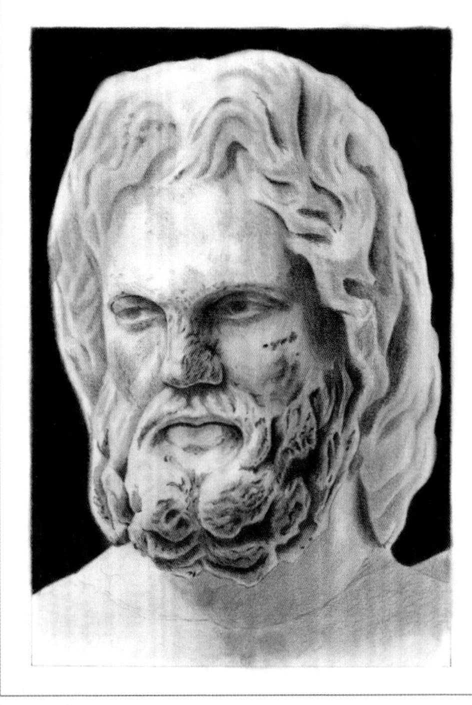

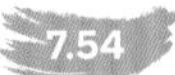
7.54

The drawing is still very opaque and without depth. Use the 4B graphite pencil to go deeper into the shading. Focus on being more detailed and enhancing the volume of each part. To soften the shadows, use a blending stump for a little more precision (**Figure 7.53**). There's no way to do this phase quickly. Take your time, look at your reference (or the finished example in Figure 7.63) carefully, and draw each piece at your pace.

Now let's focus for a while on the face of the sculpture. Building on the detailed shading base you created, use a 4B Black pencil to intensify the shadows where necessary. Be even more detailed than in the previous step, and try to imitate the texture of the stone with even more care. Remember what I said about the advantages of the chisel point? Put them to work now. For example, you can add some dark gray dots using the thinnest portion of the pencil tip. For more general shading, use the flat part of the tip. When you want to add a slightly lighter detail, use the 2B Black pencil. Be sure to use a firm-bristle brush a lot to soften the lines. Consider the level of detail on the nose in **Figure 7.54**. You will need to give this same level of attention to the beard and hair.

Continue to deepen and refine the work with the shadow little by little, using the 4B and 6B Black pencils to create even more intense shadows. As I worked on my shading, I took the opportunity to adjust some things, especially the sculpture's eyes. In Figure 7.55 the eyes and the shadows around them are better outlined, and the shadows' tone is darker.

To advance the shading in the lighter areas and increase the range of midtones in the drawing, use HB, B, 2B, and 4B graphite pencils, as well. The graphite also blends into the darker lines of the carbon pencils, softening them. The combination of graphite and carbon works very well, and I recommend you work with both materials.

To highlight the lightest values of the sculpture's face, use an eraser pencil. Try tapping the eraser pencil on the paper so that the highlights are not exaggeratedly intense. This is more consistent with the way light reflects on the stone. Figure 7.56 illustrates where I applied the eraser pencil. At this point, I felt the face and beard were practically finished.

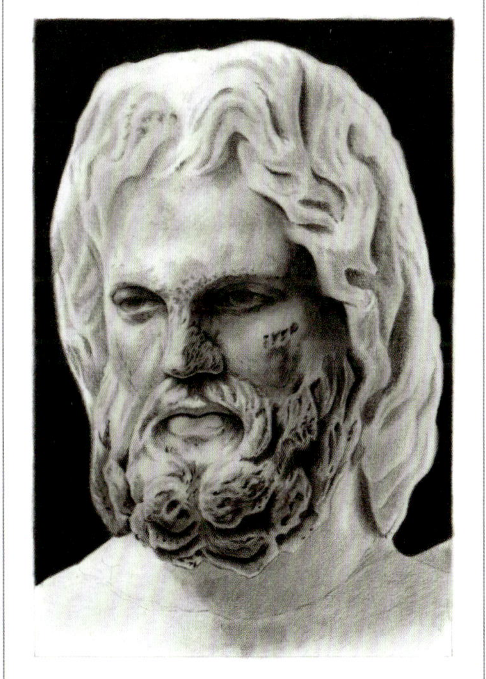

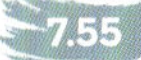
7.55

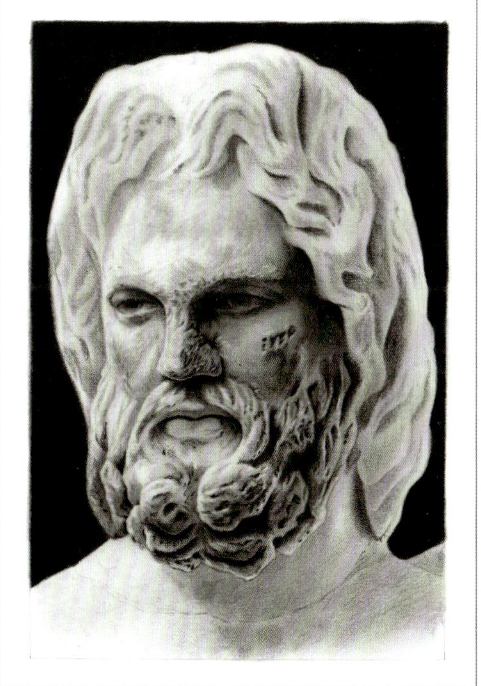

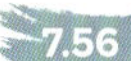
7.56

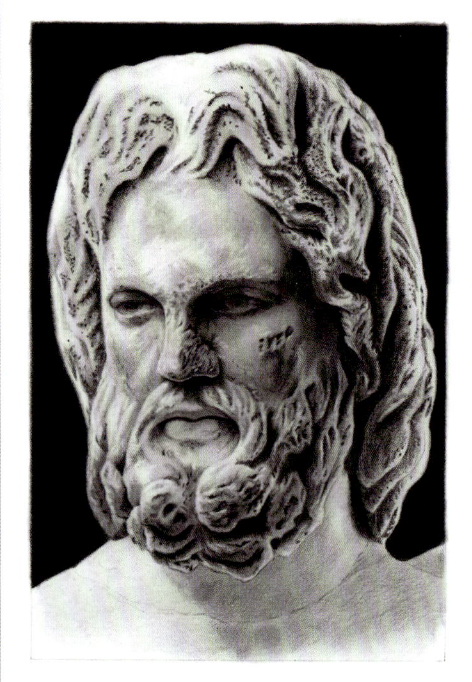

7.57

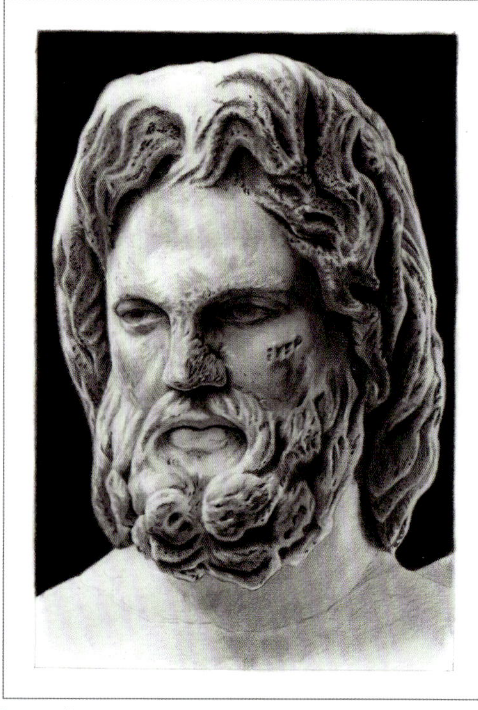

7.58

When you're satisfied with the face and beard in your drawing, move on to the hair. You can approach it in the same way, because it is made of the same material and has the same texture, only the shape of the shadows and lights change. Once again, begin with the 4B, 6B, and even 8B Black pencils to establish the darkest shadow values. As you can see in in **Figure 7.57**, this again produces intense shadows, but almost no midtones and highlights.

After carbon pencils, use graphite pencils to bring out the midtones. In **Figure 7.58**, for example, I used only a 4B pencil, but with great intensity, to cover a large part of the hair. I also used a firm brush to greatly reduce the dryness of the Black pencils and achieve a satisfying smoothness. As you can see, the look is more fluid, because the 4B graphite is quite soft and covers areas relatively quickly.

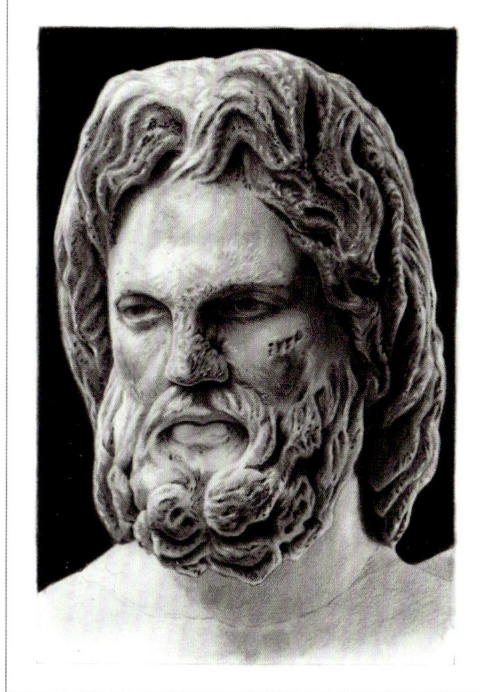

7.59

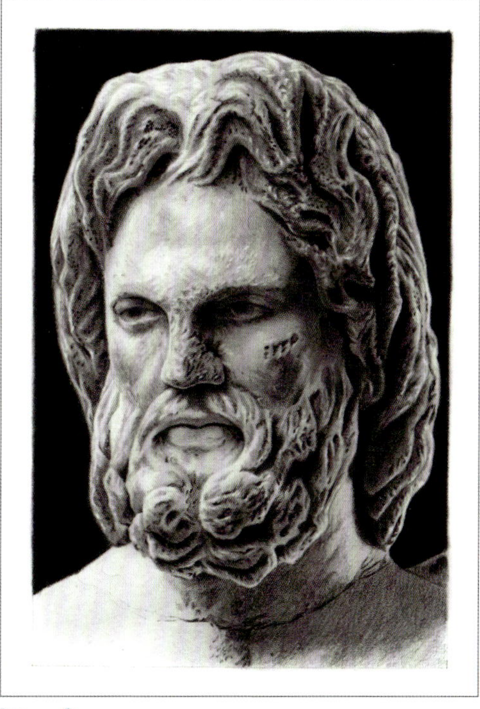

7.60

Next, add the hair highlights with an eraser pencil and a Tombow stick eraser. (I took the opportunity to add more highlights to some points on the face and beard, as well.) If the white is too intense, you can use the cat's tongue brush to turn it into a light shade of gray (Figure 7.59).

Make no mistake: This shading phase is quite laborious. If you can't finish it in one sitting, that's completely normal. I dedicated myself to this hair one Sunday and watched an entire five-set tennis match while drawing. It's hard work, but not necessarily difficult once you get the hang of it.

Repeat the process for the bust at the bottom of the drawing. The easiest part of the drawing, it features a large dark spot of cast shadow and a light part without a super complex texture. I hope by now you can guess what you need to do: Add a big smudge using the 4B Black pencil to map the shadow, deepen it with darker pencils, add the midtones with graphite, and finish with the eraser for the highlights. Figure 7.60 shows the first shadow layer with the 4B Black pencil.

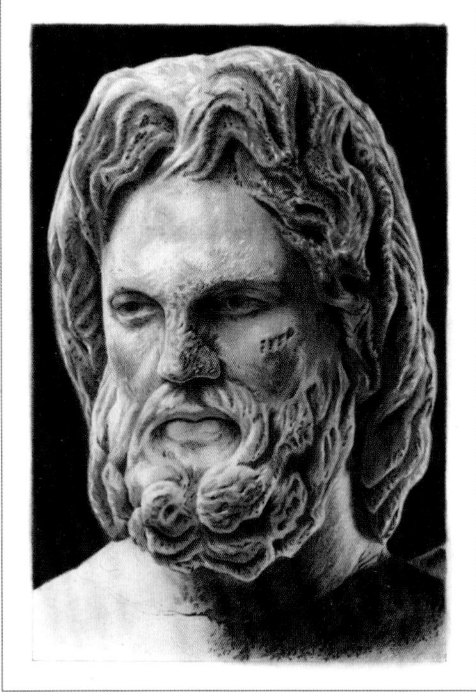

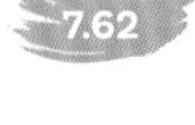
7.61

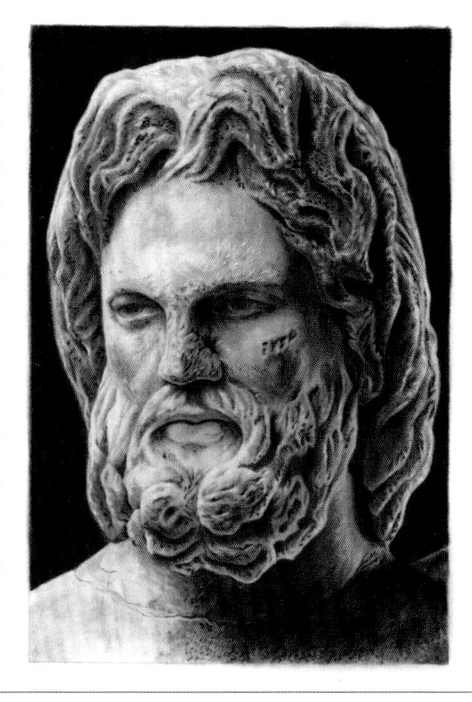

7.62

You can deepen the shadows with a 6B Black pencil and an 8B Black, in even darker areas. The difference between these two pencils is better seen on a drawing paper surface, but compare the shadow on the neck with that in the background, which was done entirely with the 8B Black pencil, to notice this variation in tone (Figure 7.61). This tone scale is not widely used by beginners, so it may be that your perception is not yet that accurate for these tones.

Figure 7.62 illustrates the addition of more intermediate grays. I suggest using a 4B pencil near the darkest shadow and an HB pencil in the lighter area on the left. With the HB pencil, you can also give more definition to the grooves present where the neck connects with the rest of the body. That crack adds an element of curiosity—perhaps this ancient sculpture had to be repaired over the ages.

To finish, use the eraser pencil to add the lights that fall on the sculpture. Note in the finished drawing (Figure 7.63) that the sculpture is illuminated mainly by a light source coming from the left, but a secondary light coming from the right illuminates it laterally, as well. Photographers and filmmakers use this lighting technique to separate a subject from the background. Be sure to replicate it by adding highlights to both the left and right sides. Study your drawing. Do any fine details need adjusting? These can be easier to spot when you look at a drawing carefully in its more advanced stages, than when you're in the midst of working. For example, I made a small correction with my eraser pencil on the right upper eyelid, as well as a few other refinements.

I encourage you to challenge yourself by drawing a sculpture, even if you don't want to draw your own version of Asclepius. As I said at the beginning of this exercise, when you successfully draw something at this difficulty level, you realize how rewarding realistic drawing can be. I hope this book helps you get closer to your self-realization in this art.

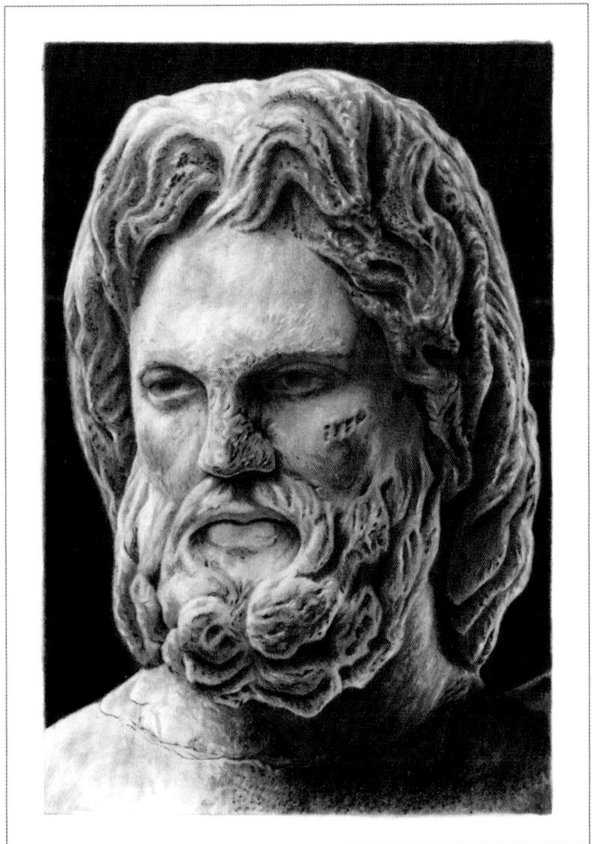

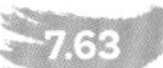
7.63

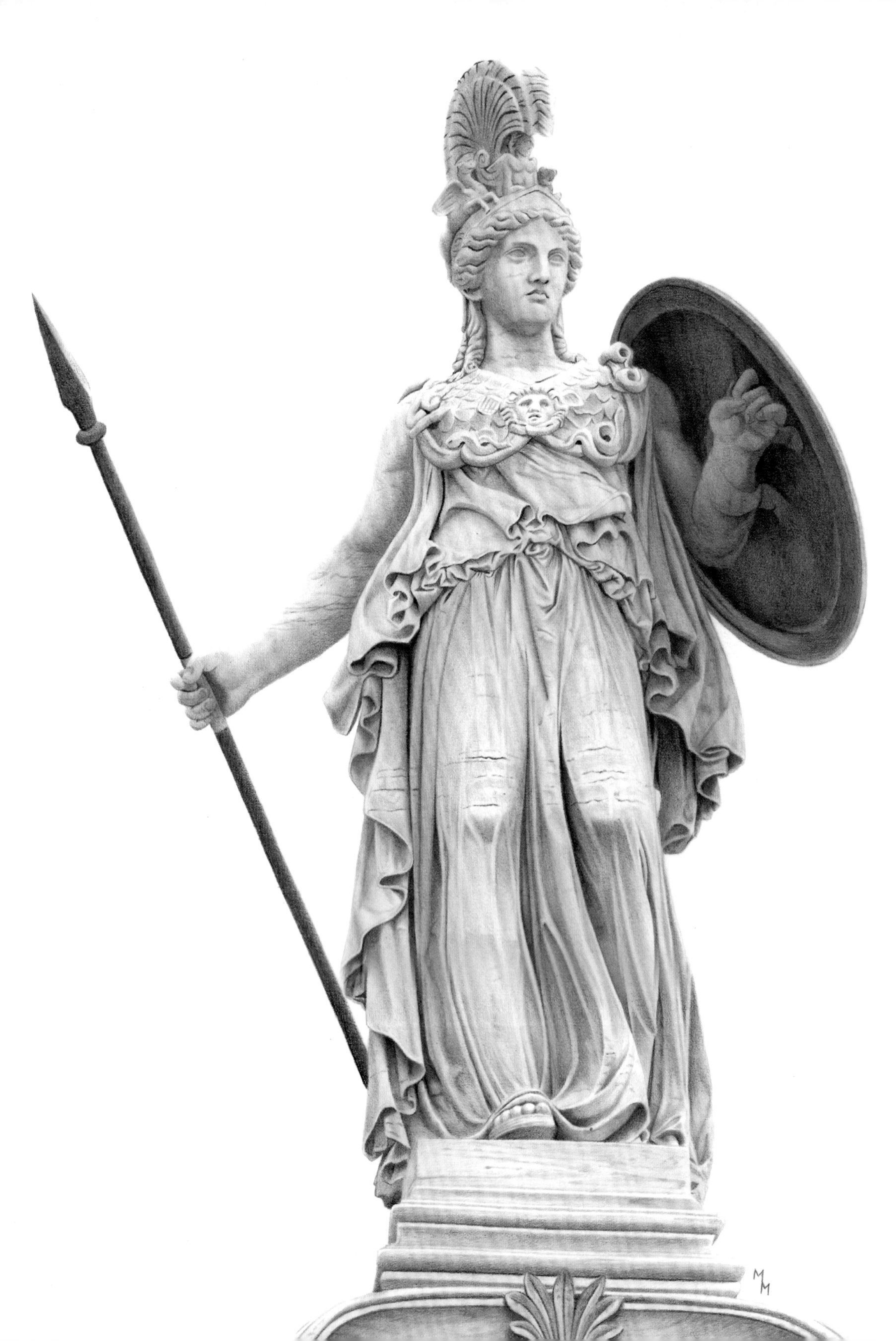

Conclusion

I hope that the tips presented in this book serve as support and give you confidence to continue practicing the art of drawing. If you did well with the exercises, congratulations! Keep challenging yourself with more and more varied topics to build on this foundation. If your drawings didn't turn out as well as you hoped, my advice is the same: Keep challenging yourself. Identify your drawings' weaknesses and work on them. No artist ever likes everything they create, but every drawing is another chance to refine your technique, grow comfortable with your tools and materials, and simply practice.

For that is the most important thing to do: Keep practicing. If you are feeling unmotivated or having difficulty fitting drawing into your routine, review Chapter 1 for some insights and tips to help you refresh your mindset.

Finally, if you feel this book didn't help you as much as you had hoped, that doesn't mean that drawing isn't for you! Realistic drawing is a huge topic, and there are many different ways to achieve the same results. This book shares the ones that work for me. Perhaps other methods will work better for you. Look for other course formats (in-person group or 1-on-1 classes, video tutorials, and so on) or for different instructors who have mastered the art of teaching. You will certainly find something that meets your particular needs.

Enjoy the journey!

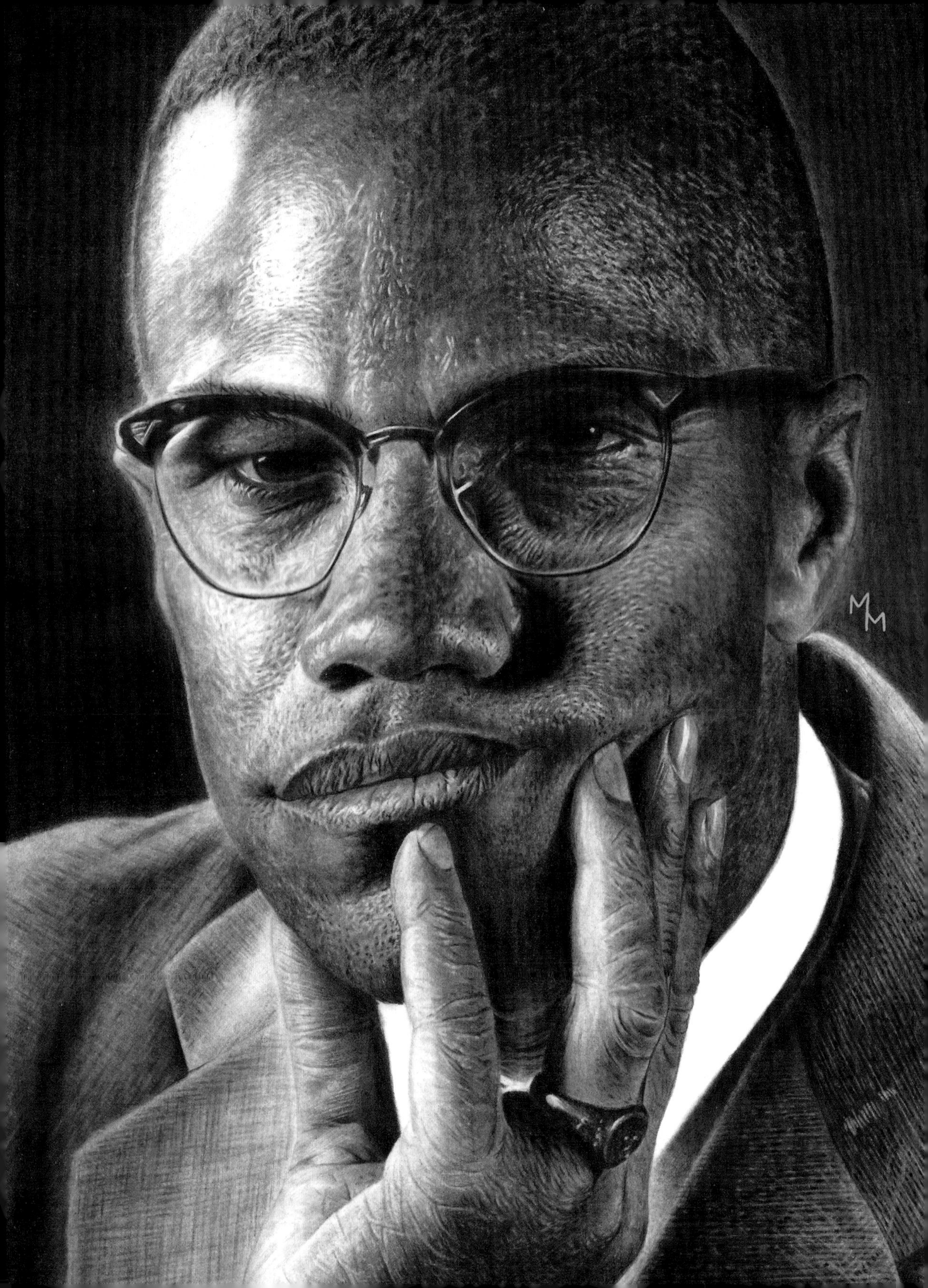

About the author

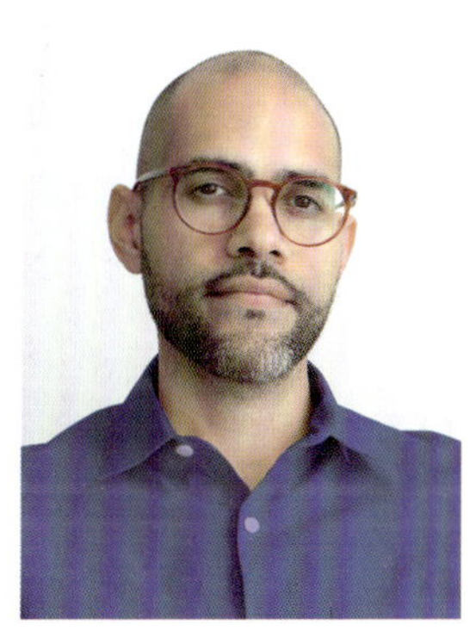

Matheus Macedo is an artist and art instructor born in Brasilia, Brazil. He started drawing as a child and never stopped. While earning a degree in Architecture and Urbanism from his hometown university and an exchange period at the Politecnico di Torino in Italy, his interest in drawing remained. He took a series of in-person and online courses and workshops with world-class artists and fell in love with realism after experimenting with different materials and styles. He began giving private drawing lessons and would soon promote his work on social media. As interest in his work grew, he was repeatedly asked about his drawing process until he decided to share his secrets by recording online courses, reaching thousands of students all over the world. Macedo was one of the winners of the international American Art Awards in 2022, and today he dedicates his time to sharing his technique for creating works in black and white and color.

You can find his classes on Skillshare and connect with Matheus at:

Website: macedodrawings.com

YouTube: @MacedoDrawings

Instagram: @macedodrawings

Facebook: www.facebook.com/macedodrawings

Resources list

The list below includes many stores that carry art supplies where you will certainly find most of the materials that I recommend in this book. Most of these stores are located in the United States. To explore shops in other parts of the world, you can look on Etsy and filter by shops in your country as well.

Art supply stores

Artist & Craftsman Supply
artistcraftsman.com

BLICK Art Materials
www.dickblick.com

Cass Art
www.cassart.co.uk

Jackson's Art Supplies
www.jacksonsart.com

Jerry's Artarama
www.jerrysartarama.com

Websites for reference images

Adobe Stock
stock.adobe.com

FreeImages
www.freeimages.com

Freepik
www.freepik.com

Getty Images
www.gettyimages.com

Google Images
www.google.com/imghp

Instagram
www.instagram.com

Pexels
www.pexels.com

Pinterest
pinterest.com

Pixabay
pixabay.com

Shutterstock
www.shutterstock.com

Unsplash
unsplash.com